THE LONDON BOROUGH
www.bromley.gov.uk

Please return/renew this item
by the last date shown.
Books may also be renewed by
phone

D1421920

ARBELLA STUART

THE UNCROWNED QUEEN

JILL E. ARMITAGE

AMBERLEY

This edition published 2019

Amberley Publishing
The Hill, Stroud
Gloucestershire, GL5 4EP

www.amberley-books.com

Copyright © Jill E. Armitage, 2017, 2019

The right of Jill E. Armitage to be identified as
the Author of this work has been asserted in
accordance with the Copyrights, Designs and
Patents Act 1988.

ISBN 978 1 4456 9346 8 (paperback)
ISBN 978 1 4456 5020 3 (ebook)

British Library Cataloguing in Publication Data.
A catalogue record for this book is available
from the British Library.

Typesetting and Origination by Amberley
Publishing.
Printed in the UK.

CONTENTS

I

COUSINS IN CONFLICT
FOR THE CROWN

On 10 October 1562, Elizabeth Tudor, Queen of England, was at Hampton Court Palace when she became unwell. She had the potentially deadly smallpox that in the 1500s could cause blindness and scarring in those lucky few who survived, but many didn't. Treatment was primitive, and smallpox was a major killer. As Elizabeth fell unconscious, things looked bleak. The childless queen had not named her successor, and with no obvious heir, anxiety over succession rose to a peak.

The Tudor dynasty, founded seventy-seven years earlier by Henry VII when he defeated Richard III at the Battle of Bosworth near Leicester on 22 August 1485, had brought peace to England and an end to the Wars of the Roses. England was richer and calmer than it had been for hundreds of years, but the English crown was never destined to sit securely on Tudor heads. Throughout the sixteenth century the direct line of succession was tenuous or non-existent. Henry VII was an only son, and of his four children, two were daughters, at a time when England was opposed to queens regnant. In 1502 his eldest son, Prince Arthur, died young, but his younger son Henry succeeded as Henry VIII in 1509.

Henry married his dead brother's wife Katherine of Aragon, who after many miscarriages produced a daughter they named Mary. She was Henry's undisputed heir but he desperately wanted a son. With his queen unable to give him a son and heir, Henry divorced Katherine to marry Anne Boleyn, turned against Rome and made England a Protestant country.

Hoping for a son with Anne Boleyn, by the 1534 Act of Succession Henry excluded his daughter Mary. He refused to be bound by the tradition of primogeniture – an exclusive right of inheritance belonging to the firstborn who claimed pre-eminence and authority. After Anne Boleyn gave birth to a daughter in 1533, under the 1536 Act of Succession Henry was given the right to nominate his heirs. When a further Act annulled the king's marriage to Anne Boleyn, making it as void as his marriage to Katherine of Aragon, the law regarded their respective daughters Mary and Elizabeth as illegitimate, with no claim to the English throne.

Henry was betrothed to Jane Seymour the day after Anne Boleyn was executed, married her on 30 May and on the feast of St Edward, 12 October 1537, she gave Henry the son he so wanted – the future Edward VI. Jane Seymour died a week after giving birth to Edward, and despite three further marriages Henry had no more children. Edward died young and without issue, so if the Tudor line was to continue, a woman had to be crowned. The question was – who? Under the third Act of Succession in 1544, Henry bequeathed the throne to his son Edward, followed by Mary, then Elizabeth, but by restoring Mary and Elizabeth in line, Henry was ignoring the laws that excluded illegitimate children from inheriting the throne of England.[1]

The absence of obvious heirs was to dominate the lives of those who were born close to the throne, whether they wished to succeed to it or not. Eager or reluctant, Catholic or Protestant, since the formation of the Church of England and the break with

Rome, England had been in religious turmoil. If the law was to be followed, next in line was eleven-year-old Mary, Queen of Scots, great-granddaughter of Henry VII and Elizabeth of York, but she was betrothed to the Dauphin of France and thus out of favour. The choice then fell on Lady Jane Grey, another great-granddaughter of Henry VII and Elizabeth of York, but the attempt to place Jane on the throne of England proved abortive: she was queen for just nine days before her first cousin once removed, Henry VIII's daughter Mary Tudor, took the throne.

Mary Tudor turned the religious wheel round by making England a Catholic country again and acquired the nickname 'Bloody Mary' for the barbaric way she attempted to do it. When she died childless in 1558, there was the same lack of male heirs, and Mary's half-sister Elizabeth, despite being labelled a bastard, succeeded without too much opposition. Elizabeth, like her half-brother Edward, had been raised as Protestant, so England was again made a Protestant nation.

It was just four years into Elizabeth's reign when anxiety over succession again rose to a peak because the childless queen had contracted smallpox. At this time, any disease accompanied by a rash on the face was always so described. Unmarried and the last of the direct issue of Henry VIII, the situation was widely regarded as disastrous because the Protestant faith, peace and the stability of England was at stake.

Each of Henry VIII's three children had reigned for a short time, but with no other direct heirs the Tudor line could only continue through Henry's two sisters, Margaret and Mary Tudor, and their descendants.

As Elizabeth's life hung in the balance, the nobles met privately in each other's houses for heated discussions, but no agreement as to who would succeed Elizabeth could be reached. The succession was the shuttlecock of politics, the tenure of power was precarious; and there was the ever-present danger that if the situation was not handled with tact, a squabble between cousins in conflict for the crown could slide into an open war.

A powerful faction headed by Thomas Howard, 4th Duke of Norfolk, was in favour of Katherine Grey, younger sister of Jane Grey who had reigned for just nine days. Katherine, like her sister, was a direct descendant of Henry VII and Elizabeth of York through their younger daughter Mary, Katherine's grandmother. (See the full story in the later chapter 'The Story of the Sisters Jane and Katherine Grey'.)

Margaret Tudor, eldest daughter of Henry VII and Elizabeth of York, had married into the Scottish Royal House of Stuart, and their representative was the Catholic Mary, Queen of Scotland. She had the strongest claim to the English throne but because of the barbaric way Mary Tudor had tried to reinstate Catholicism, it was doubtful that England was ready to return to the papal fold. However, this did not prevent the Catholic community at home and abroad from constantly plotting to put Mary on the English throne and return England to Catholicism.

One such ardent Catholic was Margaret Douglas, Countess of Lennox, always referred to as 'Meg'. Granddaughter of Henry VII, half-sister of James V of Scotland, first cousin of Queen Elizabeth and aunt of Mary, Queen of Scots, Meg should have been a strong candidate for the English throne through her mother Margaret Tudor, Dowager Queen of Scotland, but she bore the stigma of illegitimacy. It was claimed that after the death of King James IV of Scotland, the Queen Dowager Margaret Tudor had secretly married Lord Stuart of Annerdale, who was still alive when she married Archibald Douglas, 6th Earl of Angus. Furthermore, it was claimed that at the time of the marriage Archibald Douglas had another wife still living – so this was a case of double bigamy. The illegality of the marriage made their daughter Lady Margaret (Meg) Douglas illegitimate, something that was always held against her by the Scottish Parliament.[2]

Meg spent her childhood at the English court as a close friend and companion of her cousin Mary Tudor (later Bloody Mary), where she fell in love with Thomas Howard, brother of the Duke of Norfolk and uncle of Henry VIII's second wife, Anne Boleyn. While she was in favour, their courtship was viewed favourably but when Anne was in disgrace, Meg and Thomas were sent to the Tower, where Thomas died.

In 1544, Meg married Matthew Stuart, 4th Earl of Lennox, a man of ambition who as a descendant of a daughter of James II possessed a claim to the Scottish throne. He had already attempted to overthrow the Regent of Scotland during the minority of Mary, Queen of Scots, and having been pronounced guilty of treason his Scottish estates were confiscated by the Scottish Parliament. But Meg was a favourite of her uncle Henry VIII, and the Lennox fortunes thrived in England and continued to do so during the reigns of Edward VI. During Queen Mary's five-year reign, Meg had rooms in Westminster Palace to serve her cousin and lifelong friend, who, it is claimed told the ambassador Simon Renard that Meg Lennox was better suited to succeed her to the throne than her half-sister Elizabeth. Many Catholics also sought this, but fearing a repetition of the wretched fate of Jane Grey, it was considered prudent for the crown to go to Mary's half-sister Elizabeth.

Meg was the chief mourner at Queen Mary's funeral in December 1558, but because she refused to denounce her faith and remained a staunch Catholic (and did so all her life), she was not acceptable at Queen Elizabeth's court. She spent more time at her home at Temple Newsam on the outskirts of Leeds in Yorkshire. It was known to be a centre for Roman Catholic intrigue and a thorn in the flesh of her cousin Elizabeth. As a staunch Catholic, Meg Lennox was constantly persecuted, harassed and heavily fined.

Meg was an indomitable woman with royal blood coursing through her veins. She had been denied the fruits of majesty but was determined that her children would not. Despite giving birth to eight children, only two sons survived to adulthood and in 1562, as her cousin Elizabeth lay critically ill, Meg was working on an ambitious plan to marry her eldest son, Henry, Lord Darnley and Douglas, to his cousin Mary, Queen of Scots. Mary had inherited the Scottish throne when she was six days old, but had been brought up as the betrothed, then the wife of Francis II, King of France, at the French court. When Francis died she left France in 1561 to take up her Scottish throne. Mary was a Stuart (the earlier spelling was Stewarde) and the Stuarts had an uninterrupted link in the Scottish royal chain and a circuitous claim to the English throne through Margaret Tudor, daughter of Henry VII.

Mary's claim had superseded that of her aunt Meg Lennox, and many Catholics wanted Mary to replace Protestant Elizabeth on the throne of England. As Elizabeth's most direct heir, the twenty-year-old Scottish queen would unite the crowns of England and Scotland, but she needed a suitable husband by her side. In Meg's eyes there could be no one more suitable than her own seventeen-year-old son Henry, Lord Darnley and Douglas (earlier spelling Dowglas). He was in line of succession as a great-grandson of Henry VII, so Mary and Henry could rule together; her son would be a king.

Against all expectations, Queen Elizabeth recovered from smallpox, although from then on she painted her face white to cover up the unsightly scars caused by the smallpox. She avowed that 'death possessed every joint of me', but the Privy Council and the country as a whole gave a collective sigh of relief and rejoiced. The Royal Mint struck gold coins to celebrate the queen's recovery but the situation could not be allowed to continue. When Parliament assembled in January 1563, it petitioned Elizabeth to name a successor, but Elizabeth ignored the appeal. Unlike her father, Henry VIII, who had given the question of succession serious consideration, for the duration of her reign the ever-devious Elizabeth held to the position 'so long as I live, there shall be no other queen in

England'. The lack of a decision and its public announcement meant that she could play off one party against another, hold out hope in exchange for favours sought, or dash it for favours refused. It was a dangerous game that she played for over forty years.

Refusing to name her heir meant that all the nobles' plans and schemes came to nothing, and although the Countess of Lennox had slightly more success, there was a price to pay. When Queen Elizabeth discovered that Meg Lennox and her husband had been making plans to marry their eldest son, Henry Darnley, to Mary, Queen of Scots, she summoned them to London. The earl was placed in the Tower and his wife was placed in the custody of Sir Richard and Lady Sackville at Sheen. The earl fell ill, probably suffering from 'jail fever', and Meg wrote many letters to William Cecil, Lord Burghley, asking for her husband to be allowed to join her at Sheen. Eventually in 1563 they were released and, though ruined financially, they were allowed to go to their home in Yorkshire. As they were not taken back into royal favour, this made them even more determined to advance their son's marriage to Mary, Queen of Scots, so while Meg stayed at home with her younger son Charles, the earl and Henry Darnley went to Scotland to meet Mary.

Although Darnley was three years younger than the Scottish queen and an idle fop, he was good looking and extremely tall. Mary was over six feet tall (1.80 m) and he was one of the few men she had met who was taller. His appearance and his proximity to the English throne endeared him to her, and on 29 July 1565 they were married. At twenty years of age, Henry Darnley became King Consort of Scotland.

Meg must have been ecstatic, but her jubilation was short-lived. When Queen Elizabeth heard of the marriage she was furious and, unable to vent her wrath on the absent earl in Scotland and out of her jurisdiction, she summoned Meg to London. It wasn't exactly treason, but the queen viewed it in the same light. Matthew,

Earl of Lennox, was stripped of his English properties and Meg, Countess of Lennox, was imprisoned in the Lieutenant's Lodgings at the Tower. Their ten-year-old son Charles Stuart was left with a few servants to care for him but when it was found that he had developed severe behavioural problems and his education had been badly neglected, he was placed in the care of Charles Vaughan and his wife Lady Kynevet. Charles had an affectionate and gentle nature but was deficient in accomplishments befitting the son of a nobleman, a source of deep regret for his poor mother. Meg wrote to Cecil beseeching him to take Charles into his own home to educate him in a manner becoming his rank and to escape the animosity his father and brother had provoked. Instead, Cecil appointed a Protestant tutor named Mallient to balance his mother's strong Catholic ideas.[3]

Queen Mary and Henry Darnley should have been a good match – but they weren't. Darnley was a handsome degenerate with a warped mind and indulged in practices then considered unnatural. He preferred the company of other handsome young men and possessed an insolence born of his new honours. By the time Mary's eyes had been opened to his unworthiness, she was pregnant. Perhaps if her aunt and mother-in-law Meg Lennox had been present things could have been different, but Meg was being kept prisoner in the Tower. Mary had no one to turn to, no one to confide in, and in near desperation she unburdened her problems to her secretary, David Riccio. Darnley was so outraged that he murdered Riccio in the heat of passion. After that, Mary became convinced that her own life and that of her unborn child was in danger, and she was taken to the safety of Edinburgh Castle. The marriage was at an end except insofar as outward appearances had to be kept up to legitimise her son James, who was born on 19 June 1566.

The Countess of Lennox, still imprisoned in the Tower, would have been unaware of the immense friction and hostility in the

Scottish royal household. She was not around to witness the birth or baptism of her grandson, but she must have been overjoyed. Her eldest son was King Consort, and her grandson would be King of Scotland in his own right. As Mary was the nearest relative to the childless Elizabeth and theoretically her heir, the ambitious Meg saw no reason to doubt that one day her grandson, the only male in an otherwise female line, would unite the kingdoms of Scotland and England.

Queen Elizabeth must have heard of James's birth with envy. The Scottish queen had a kingdom, a husband and a son to continue the line. Elizabeth's subjects waited expectantly for news that the English queen would also marry and produce an heir to the throne, but her favourite was her childhood friend Robert Dudley, later Earl of Leicester, and he was married.

His brother Guildford Dudley had been married to Lady Jane Grey, and because Robert Dudley supported his brother and his father John Dudley in their attempt to install Lady Jane on the throne, he was imprisoned in the Tower of London. (This episode is described later in 'The Story of the Sisters Jane and Katherine Grey').

Robert Dudley was kept in the Beauchamp Tower, which is only a walkway from the Bell Tower where Elizabeth was a prisoner after the rebellion led by Thomas Wyatt; legend has it that they saw a lot of each other during that time. Then, with the accession of Elizabeth to the throne in 1558, Robert Dudley was made Master of the Horse, a prestigious position that required regular personal attendance on the queen as well as organizing her public appearances, progresses, and her personal entertainment. This position suited him perfectly. Not only was he a skilled horseman, but was a great athlete too, and he had a flair for the spectacular and shared the queen's love of drama and music.

The queen lavished titles, properties, and money on Robert Dudley, from then on known as Leicester, and spent more time with him than with anyone else. Tongues wagged at their intimacy, and it was said that they were lovers.

On 8 September 1560, when the body of Leicester's wife Amy Robsart was found at the foot of the stairs at their home at Cumnor Place with a broken neck, murder was suspected. It was generally felt to be too convenient, and many pointed the finger at Leicester, accusing him of killing his wife so that he would be free to marry the queen. Although it was never proved, understandably the subject caused a major scandal.

Throughout the 1560s their friendship continued. Leicester proposed to the queen many times, but Elizabeth was a canny operator and a doyenne of empty promises. Unmarried, she was able to negotiate many lucrative deals abroad, shrewdly yet discreetly tendering herself and the throne of England, like dangling a carrot before so many donkeys.

It seems ironic that in 1567, a few years after Amy Robsart's mysterious death, a similar situation was being played out in Scotland. Things there had taken a dramatic turn. The house where Henry Darnley was staying in Kirk o'Fields, while recovering from what was described as a great fever of the pox, was blown up. He survived the blast but his strangled body was found in the garden. His father Matthew, Earl of Lennox, attempted to obtain redress from those he believed to be his son's murderers, but the hostile Protestant lords forced him to leave the country. When news of Darnley's death reached Elizabeth, in pity she released his mother Meg from the Tower, but the Countess of Lennox was inconsolable. Her dreams were shattered.

Things changed dramatically with the death of Darnley. Although her part was never proved, Mary was implicated, imprisoned, escaped and fled to England to throw herself on the not very tender mercies of her cousin Elizabeth; but the arrival of the dispossessed Mary put Elizabeth in an unenviable position. The unmarried Queen Elizabeth sat precariously on the throne of

England, and Mary, Queen of Scots, was still her most obvious and likely heir with huge support from the Catholic community at home and abroad. What was Elizabeth to do with a fellow queen without a kingdom and in a strong position to take hers? Elizabeth was torn between protecting her own throne and wanting to be seen as a champion of the rights of a fellow queen. She refused to grant her cousin an audience, but decided that she was to be detained in England. The question was where, and who would make suitable custodians?

2

THE TWO CONSPIRATORIAL COUNTESSES

The Earl and Countess of Shrewsbury qualified as suitable custodians of the Scottish queen on several counts. He was a staunch Protestant, loyal to his queen, with a wife who was equally trustworthy. They had only married on 9 February 1568, both having been married previously and with children from those earlier marriages. For the countess, who has gone down in history as 'Bess of Hardwick', it was her fourth marriage. Bess's service of the queen went back to when she was Princess Elizabeth, being held under house arrest at Hatfield House. As the council wrote to the Archbishop of Canterbury on 29 September 1567, 'She has long served with credit in our court.'[1]

On 3 February, just a year after their marriage, the Earl and Countess of Shrewsbury became the custodians of Mary, Queen of Scots – an arduous and financially onerous task. Queen Elizabeth had informed the earl that he had been chosen as Mary's custodian in consequence of his approved loyalty and faithfulness, and the ancient state of blood from which he was descended. Queen Elizabeth was not averse to using flattery when necessary: it was cheap and effective. So the Scottish queen had become a captive under house arrest with strict instructions: 'Being a queen of our blood, treat her with the reverence and honour mete of a person of state and calling and for her degree. To be accorded all the ceremony due to her position nor by this removing have her state amended but ensuring that she does not escape or meet anyone likely to help her escape.'

Mary, Queen of Scots, and her retinue were moved around the Shrewsbury's many grand Midland homes, but no one was allowed to visit anywhere Mary was residing. In the autumn of 1574 she was at Chatsworth House in Derbyshire, often referred to as 'the gem of the Peak District'. Chatsworth had formerly been the estate of Bess's brother-in-law Francis Leche, and a Leche seat since Agincourt. Bess and her second husband, Sir William Cavendish, purchased the estate and Bess began to build a new house at Chatsworth, the first of the great houses for which she has become famous.

Although in the late autumn of 1574 Mary was in residence, Bess was not. She had set off from Chatsworth House to make the twenty-five-mile trip across Derbyshire to Rufford Abbey on the Derbyshire-Nottinghamshire border, another of the 6th Earl's palatial mansions, situated on the edge of Sherwood Forest near Ollerton. The original abbey from which Rufford takes its name was built around 1170 on behalf of the Archbishop of Lincoln, Gilbert de Gaunt, as a Cistercian monastery. It was part of the great Yorkshire Abbey of Rievaulx founded in 1146.

Rufford Abbey was a big and imposing structure, full of empty, glacial rooms and maze-like, echoing corridors that reflected its former use as a monastery. The place had been left virtually untouched since the 4th Earl of Shrewsbury acquired it after the Dissolution of the Monasteries, although Bess with her love of building had recently begun to convert the west range of monastic buildings for occasional domestic use. The abbey is only a few miles off the Great North Road that linked London with the North, so perhaps Bess, being starved of court gossip, intended to meet travellers for an update on the latest news. At least that's what she probably wanted people to think, but in hindsight it's obvious that Bess was intent upon something more than a convivial chat or a spot of home improvement.

In London a few months earlier, when Meg, Countess of Lennox, decided to return to her home at Temple Newsam in Yorkshire she found that she was required to petition her cousin Queen Elizabeth to be allowed to leave the capital and go north. Queen Elizabeth disliked her cousin and her strong Catholic connections. Her home at Temple Newsam was known to be a Catholic stronghold, and it was less than seventy miles from Chatsworth House and Buxton where the Scottish queen was allowed to take the curative waters; it was yet a shorter trip to Sheffield Castle where Mary was often held. There was a distinct possibility that Meg's journey north was a ruse to mask a potential plot to help her niece and daughter-in-law escape. But would she have wanted to? Their religious link was strong but it is doubtful that Meg would have wanted to see – let alone help – the woman who had been accused of murdering her beloved son Henry Darnley. Such a thing was hardly likely to endear the two women.

Queen Elizabeth had never ventured that far north so she could have no idea about the wild, inhospitable and difficult-to-negotiate terrain between these remote destinations. Travel was rife with obstacles: rutted highways and furrowed pack-horse routes, highwaymen, and the need to engage guides to escort them through the bleak countryside. The queen and her advisers cared nothing for that; their main worry was that Meg could be plotting a Catholic uprising.[2]

The queen and council were not the only ones who were taking an interest in Meg Lennox's proposed journey north. The Spanish and French were interested, and the French ambassador, La Mothé Fénelon, suggested that the 'Comtesse de Lenox' was proposing to continue her journey north into Scotland to kidnap her grandson, the infant King James of Scotland.[3]

Meg Lennox had made no secret of the fact that she believed her grandson would unite the thrones of Scotland and England – but by right, not rebellion. The elderly Countess of Lennox was not the person to kidnap James. The journey to Leeds would have been arduous enough for this fifty-nine year old without doubling the mileage to go to Scotland, but the queen and her ministers could not ignore any possibilities, so the request was vetoed while all risks and dangers were considered. If there was a sinister motive for Meg Lennox's journey, if something questionable was afoot, the queen and her ministers needed to know and their spies would have been primed to alert them to every possibility.

Despite the intense speculation about what might happen, there was never any thought given to the fact that Meg, Countess of Lennox, and Bess, Countess of Shrewsbury, would meet. Why should they? They had nothing in common. Bess was twelve years younger than Meg but their paths would have crossed through their various connections. Both had been key personalities at the English court but had served different monarchs. They were never friends, which made what happened next and the subsequent events totally unforeseen.

After a three-month wait, Meg Lennox's petition was granted, and on 3 October 1574 the Privy Council authorised the provision of two teams of horses or oxen for 'the removing of the Lady Lennox's stuff from Hackney into her manor of Temple Newsam in Yorkshire'. There was however a proviso that she was not to go within thirty miles of either Sheffield Castle or Chatsworth House or attempt to visit her daughter-in-law, Mary, Queen of Scots, at any other place that she might be held. A later dispatch dated 15 October reported that the countess was planning to leave London in five or six days, and as October turned to November the Lennox party made its slow, laborious progress north. The countess's rank required a large retinue of servants and quantities of baggage, with frequent overnight stops at inns and country houses near to the route.

At Alconbury, sixty-five miles from London, the Great North Road joins the Old North Road, which follows the Roman Ermine Street north through Stilton and Stamford as far as Colsterworth. Inns on this section include The George at Stamford and the Bell Inn at Stilton, famous for its extremely smelly but delicious cheese. At Colsterworth the Great North Road diverges west of the Roman road and continues through Grantham, Newark, Retford and Bawtry to Doncaster.

Moving away from the direct route, Countess Meg accepted the invitation of her old friend Katherine Bertie, 12th Baroness Willoughby de Eresby, to rest at their home in Northampton. As girls Meg and Katherine had both lived in the household of Henry VII's daughter Mary, Duchess of Suffolk and former Dowager Queen of France. Meg was her niece, Katherine her ward, and they were the same age as the duchess's two daughters, Frances (mother of the ill-fated Lady Jane Grey) and Eleanor. Later they both served various members of the royal household, so there was nothing suspicious about Meg breaking her journey at the home of her old friend. The queen had said nothing about deviating from the route, and this must have provided a welcome break for the weary travellers.

No doubt the two ladies had much to talk about. One of the topics of conversation would have been Katherine Bertie's visit during the summer of 1575 to Buxton to take the curative waters. There she had met one of her old friends, Bess, Countess of Shrewsbury, and Katherine had gone on to stay with Bess at Chatsworth House. When Meg left Northampton to continue her journey north, Katherine accompanied them as far as Grantham; their next overnight stop was at the picturesque, ancient borough of Newark. Here they probably stayed at the fifteenth-century, timber-framed White Hart Inn on the corner of the market place.

It was while she was resting at Newark that Meg reportedly received an unexpected message from Bess, Countess of Shrewsbury, inviting the countess and her party to break their long journey with a stay at Rufford Abbey, thirteen miles from Newark. There seems no obvious reason why Bess would make such a suggestion on impulse and no reason why Meg would accept it. With a vast retinue in attendance, it would have been no mean feat to diverge from the planned route. The distance travelled each day and the overnight stops along the route would have been planned well in advance; any changes would cause major disruptions.

Even more surprising was the fact that Bess invited Meg to break her long journey at an unfinished, and therefore unfurnished, house. It would have been necessary to transport vast amounts of provisions, servants, silver plate, feather beds and other necessary commodities to accommodate the countess and her party at Rufford Abbey, and that couldn't have been done in a day. It would have taken weeks for the wagons laden with provisions to travel across country, bringing these commodities from Chatsworth House. Why would they have bothered if there was no guarantee that the Countess of Lennox would break her journey at Rufford?

There was also the fact that Bess of Hardwick didn't do things on impulse; that would have been out of character for someone who was renowned for her shrewdness and thoughtful planning. She was neither impulsive nor impetuous. Many of Bess's actions exhibited a determination to carve circumstances to her own ends: so if there was a purpose to the invitation, why did it have to appear to be made on the spur of the moment? Later, under interrogation, Meg Lennox was asked why she stayed at Rufford Abbey. She retorted, 'The place was not one myle dystante owte of my weaye and a muche farer way as well to be perceived.'[4]

There can have been nothing that was fortuitous in the presence of Bess and her daughter Elizabeth at Rufford Abbey that autumn. As they made Rufford Abbey habitable, there were all the signs that something was about to take place that had needed considerable and clandestine planning. Bess was contemplating the execution of a plan that she had conceived and managed, and all the pieces of the jigsaw were about to fall into place.

To see the whole picture more clearly, it's necessary to look back to the time of Bess's marriage to George Talbot, 6th Earl of Shrewsbury, premier earl in command of the armies of the north, Lord Lieutenant of Yorkshire, Derbyshire and Nottinghamshire, Chamberlain of the Exchequer and one of the richest men in England. His wealth was securely founded on ancestral estates and on the profitable mines and industries of Sheffield, whose castle was his principal seat. Bess and Talbot were married in 1567 in an effective triple ceremony. Bess married the earl and officially became the Countess of Shrewsbury; her eldest son and heir Henry Cavendish, then aged seventeen, married the earl's eight-year-old daughter Grace Talbot; and the earl's second son, sixteen-year-old Gilbert Talbot, married Bess's youngest daughter, twelve-year-old Mary Cavendish. This was not unusual in influential families. It was an effective way to ensure a powerful dynasty – and Bess was determined to form one of the strongest in the land; her eldest daughter was already married to Sir Henry Pierrepont of Nottingham.

As a three-times widow, Bess had her own considerable wealth, land and property, but as a married woman this was all taken by her husband. Ordinarily a married woman had to give up all her financial independence, but Bess had a clause written into their marriage settlement that in exchange for giving all her land, property and wealth to Shrewsbury, one third of his unsettled income would go to Bess on his death. That seemed no problem.

As the Cavendish heir, Bess's eldest son, Henry Cavendish, would automatically inherit Chatsworth House. That again was settled. Bess's other two sons, William and Charles Cavendish, would each receive £20,000 when they reached the age of twenty-one. William, born in 1551, qualified for his inheritance in 1572; Charles, born in 1553, qualified in 1574. But Shrewsbury had refused to honour the agreement. This presented the first problem.

Then there was the question of a dowry for Bess's only unmarried daughter, Elizabeth. She was eighteen years old yet still unwed, which was rather unusual for someone of her station. Marriage in the upper society of sixteenth-century England was very much a business arrangement. Custom dictated that the bride's family would provide a dowry, and it goes without saying that the wealthier the family, the larger the dowry. The Cavendish and Shrewsbury families had enormous wealth from land holdings, mineral rights and farming. Their portfolio of properties was extensive, but everything was administered by the Earl of Shrewsbury, who had assured Bess that he would provide a marriage settlement for Elizabeth when a suitable husband had been selected. This was another clause written into the marriage agreement that should have passed without issue ...

As was the custom of the time, Bess would have considered a marriage for Elizabeth amongst many eligible bachelors in their class. In her four advantageous marriages and the marriages she had arranged for her children, she had shown incessant and insatiable ambition to provide brilliant matches; but there was now a major problem. Bess had asked Shrewsbury to settle £1,000 on Elizabeth, but he had refused. This must have infuriated Bess, particularly when Shrewsbury wrote to Sir William Cecil, 1st Lord Burghley, Lord Treasurer: 'There are few nobleman's sons in England that she [Bess] hath not prayed me to deal for at one time or another.' What he didn't disclose was that the reason why these proposals had not transpired was his refusal to provide the promised dowry, but breaking such an agreement didn't seem to bother Shrewsbury. Despite being one of the wealthiest men in England, he was known to say of his vast wealth, 'The riches they talk of are in other men's purses.'[5]

Bess must have been furious. She was forty-eight and had been married to George Talbot, 6th Earl of Shrewsbury, for almost nine years, but the cracks were definitely starting to show. She had brought her own great wealth to the marriage and now had no say over how it was spent; but Bess wasn't a woman to let things get the better of her. Shrewsbury's refusals had just made her more determined.

Bess had contacts and friends in high places. A letter to Bess from London on 3 February 1574 outlined secret negotiations taking place between Anthony Wingfield, husband of Bess's half-sister Elizabeth Leche, and Richard and Katherine Bertie, 12th Baroness Willoughby de Eresby. As already stated, Katherine Bertie, who Meg Lennox visited on her journey north, was a very well connected noblewoman having lived at the royal courts of Henry VIII, Edward VI and Queen Elizabeth. After Bess and Katherine met at Buxton while taking the medicinal waters in May 1574, the following month Katherine visited Chatsworth. It was rumoured that the ladies were planning a marriage between their offspring Elizabeth Cavendish and Peregrine Bertie, who would inherit the title 13th Baron Willoughby de Eresby on the death of his mother. Perequin was born in 1555, seven months after Elizabeth, so the ages were right – but evidently something else wasn't, and nothing came of the proposal.

Shrewsbury broadcast the fact that the two ladies amicably changed their minds on this alliance, and made the comment that although Elizabeth was intended for young Bertie, she had been disappointed in him. Was this to cover up the fact the promised dowry was not forthcoming, or was Shrewsbury being hoodwinked, knowing that he would tell his usual tale and lull any further suspicions?[6] In fact, Shrewsbury had reacted exactly as Bess had expected. He was no match for this remarkable woman who had secretly embarked on one of the boldest of all assignments. It can't be coincidence what happened next.

Charles Stuart, Earl of Lennox, had attended Gray's Inn at the same time as William Cavendish, Bess's favourite son. Although Charles was three years younger than William, there is all likelihood that they were acquaintances, if not friends. Charles Stuart was travelling with his mother, the Countess of Lennox, when they deviated from their planned route and arrived at Rufford Abbey. The journey must have thoroughly fatigued the countess because once she arrived there she became sick and didn't leave her chamber for four or five days. With Bess, Countess of Shrewsbury, in attendance, this left nineteen-year-old Elizabeth to entertain twenty-year-old Charles. This was a chance for the young people to get to know each other and an opportunity for the two countesses to take their plans further. These were two very strong, ambitious women and both had a reason for wanting a Cavendish-Lennox union. Such an alliance could have considerable advantages for both parties.

Meg Lennox belonged firmly to the highest order of society and could claim the genealogy of sovereigns. She was great-granddaughter, granddaughter, niece, cousin, half-sister, mother and grandmother to kings of Scotland, England and France. On the distaff side, she had equally close relationships to seven queens.

The Cavendish and Shrewsbury families may have had wealth and connections but they had come from humble beginnings. The hierarchical structure of the Middle Ages, with the sovereign, the nobility, the gentlemen, the squires and serfs, was beginning to crumble by the end of the sixteenth century as a new class forced itself into the order. There is no doubt that Henry VIII had relied upon the new 'middle men' such as Cavendish and Shrewsbury who were eager to do what he wished for the rewards he offered – and after the Dissolution of the Monasteries, the rewards were immense. For men and women with ambition, the prospects were boundless.

The old nobility could either stand aloof or accept the situation by marrying into this brash new ascendancy. That way they could hope to civilise it while they enriched themselves; but was Meg, Countess of Lennox, willing to forget that Elizabeth Cavendish's grandfather had been a clerk in the Exchequer when Charles Stuart's grandmother had been Queen of Scotland?

It was no secret that the Countess of Lennox was in severe financial difficulties. Most of the Lennox estates in Scotland and England had been confiscated over the years, and she had borrowed heavily as a result and interest was eating into what small income she was allowed. By allying her son Charles with a family that had such enormous wealth, she felt assured of a future free from fiscal difficulties.

There's every reason to believe that her friend Katherine Bertie had acted on her behalf as go-between with Bess – thus the meetings that summer and the correspondence. No doubt Katherine had convinced Meg that pressing financial reasons outweighed her pride. The promise of a financially stress-free future was a huge incentive for Meg Lennox to agree to Bess of Hardwick's proposal. The silver spoon could now be bought.

It was obvious that Meg was hoping to solve her financial problems; she would have made no secret of it, but at the same time, she was hedging her bets. Her son Charles Stuart, Earl of Lennox, could potentially be Queen Elizabeth's heir: his royal lineage was just as credible as that of her grandson James. Like his older brother Henry Darnley, he had been born at Temple Newsam, Leeds, which made him a British citizen and gave him an edge over James who, having been born in Scotland, was classed as a foreigner. What Charles needed was a suitable wife or one whose family held sway with the queen. The Shrewsburys certainly qualified on that score. At the time of Bess's marriage to Shrewsbury in 1568, Queen Elizabeth said, 'I have been glad to see my Lady St Loe, but now more desirous to see my Lady Shrewsbury. I hope my lady hath known my good opinion of her, and thus much I assure you, there is no lady in this land that I better love and like.'[7]

Having her daughter married to such a man as Charles Stuart was a prize Bess could previously never have dreamt of and she had the foresight to see that as a long-standing, loyal servant of the queen, she could promote him further. She had proved her loyalty to the queen, and had gone above and beyond what had been asked of her in the sensitive situation with regards to the 'protection' of Mary, Queen of Scots. With so much in her favour, Bess must have felt confident that she could persuade her majesty to name Charles Stuart as her successor when the time was right.

By keeping Countess Meg in the dark about her own financial problems, could Bess be accused of duplicity? She was known to have an implacable will and cool head, so she no doubt confronted this marriage like any other business merger. She knew from past experience that Shrewsbury would refuse to provide a dowry for his stepdaughter, but she probably thought that when faced with a marriage rather than a proposal, he would honour his side of the bargain. In the meantime she could make Meg Lennox a substantial personal loan to cement the agreement.[8]

It was an added bonus that the young couple became fond of each other, so the two conspiratorial countesses saw no reason why the marriage should not go ahead immediately, to the satisfaction of all concerned. The speed at which this momentous decision was reached definitely suggested pre-consideration and, needless to say, Shrewsbury was not informed until after the marriage ceremony had taken place. Bess would not have wanted his opinion or opposition.

Shrewsbury must have been furious when he heard the news. Always looking for a way out of his commitments, he stated that because he had not been consulted about the marriage, he did not see why he should provide a dowry.[9] He wrote to Queen Elizabeth on 5 November 1574 informing her of the hasty, unsanctioned marriage that had taken place at Rufford Abbey, while excusing himself of any involvement. He wrote: 'The young man, fell into liking with my wife's daughter, and hath so tied themselves upon their liking as cannot be apart. Such liking was between them as my wife tells me she makes no doubt of a match. The young man is so far in love, that belike he is sicke without her ... this comes unlooked for without thanks to me.'[10]

The missive must have caused the queen to work herself up into into a thunderous rage. The royal rage was notorious. For anyone of royal blood to marry, it was necessary to get the Royal Assent; without it, disobedient nobles could be thrown into prison under the 1536 Act of Attainder. Sadly, because the royal go-ahead was usually not forthcoming, couples were often tempted to marry without it, aware they would obtain neither permission nor approval. Informing the queen after the event meant that the couple and anyone who had helped them orchestrate the wedding faced being thrown into the Tower, but if the wife was no longer a virgin, the marriage could not be annulled. That would explain the need for utmost secrecy and discretion by the two countesses in the planning of the wedding, and the speed with which it was executed. But now they had to face the queen's wrath.

3

THE BIRTH OF ARBELLA

By 17 November the queen had already made her judgement that Meg, Countess of Lennox, was the culprit and had ordered her and the newlywed couple of Charles and Elizabeth Lennox to return to London, despite the rigours of the harsh winter weather that made travel difficult and dangerous. Bess was spared the journey to London and the possibility of being sent to the Tower because her credit with the queen stood her in such good stead that her part in the affair could be overlooked; she also had the responsibility of guarding the Scottish queen, which prevented her from being away for any length of time. After all, how long could the wife of the keeper of the Scot's queen be kept prisoner? For his part, Shrewsbury was so worried about being incriminated and having to face the royal fulminations of the queen that his excuses poured into the court, to Burghley, to Leicester and to the queen herself.

The Countess of Lennox, on her way back to London in the worst December weather, wrote to Leicester and Burghley on 3 December from the town of Huntingdon. She asked Burghley in the name of their friendship to help her. She excused her delay by the fact that her mules were 'over laboured ... bothe croked and lame with ther extreme labor', and that floods had forced her to leave the road and hindered her progress. She also underlined the feelings of the young couple: 'Nowe my lorde, for the haystie marryage of my sonne. After that he had entangled hymselfe so that he coulde have nowe other.'

Still on her slow journey to London, Meg wrote another letter to Lord Burghley on 10 December. In her defence, she pointed out that she had not disobeyed the queen: she had kept her promise and not been within thirty miles of Chatsworth or Sheffield. She added, 'The marriage was a chance result of the couple's affection which there had been no stopping.'

It was now obvious that the queen felt duped. She had taken every precaution and means to discover whether the countess's journey was linked to treachery, treason, abduction or undercover activities and had been assured it was not. She had been given no reason to suspect that the countess's journey north had been for an arranged marriage – and now she was outraged at their conduct.

Their journey into London would have been along what was originally part of the Roman Ermine Street connecting London to York, and one of the straightest roads in the capital. Unlike the central London streets that were narrow, noisy and extremely smelly, with a backdrop of petty crime, the cries of street vendors and the constant rumble of carriage wheels, an application of money and energy had stimulated the development of an entire new district called Hackney, away from the crowds and frantic atmosphere of the City. In the sixteenth century, Hackney was a cluster of small villages and gleaming palaces set in a sea of meadows and hunting grounds, just far enough removed from central London to keep the air clean and unpolluted. For this reason, the Tudor royalty, courtiers, aristocrats and wealthy bourgeoisie were drawn to Hackney for holidays, hunting and sometimes to conduct matters of high state. The nobility built elegant houses surrounded by gardens, orchards and fields, which became a feature of the new neighbourhood. There was plenty of money to spend on embellishing one's house and garden, where all manner of hot house fruits were grown. Some of the estates had small model farms where cows and chickens provided distraction as well as healthy food.

The destination of the Lennox party was King's Place, Hackney, not far from the bustle of the wide, tree-lined Ermine Street and its North–South thoroughfare. The earliest recorded house on the site of King's Place dates back to 1409. It had been home to Henry Percy, who could have changed the whole course of English history if he had been allowed to marry the woman he had first proposed to, Anne Boleyn. In the 1530s the Earl of Northumberland gave the house to Henry VIII to try to get back into royal favour – thus its name. In July 1536 King's Place was the scene of reconciliation between Henry VIII and his daughter Mary after a frosty five years. He had, after all, divorced her mother and cut Mary out of the succession.

The king then passed the mansion on to his chief minister, Thomas Cromwell, who proceeded to spend vast sums of money on bringing it up to date. Ralph Sadler oversaw some of the work at the same time that his own Bryk Place was being built nearby. King's Place and Bryk Place were the biggest and most important houses in Hackney. King's Place was practically rebuilt in 1560, and there are records of fifty oak trees from Enfield Chase being felled by order of the king to be used towards building work in Hackney, almost certainly for this work.

When King's Place was given back to the king, it had been expensively refurbished. A masterpiece of elegance and comfort, it provided a leisured way of life for a series of wealthy tenants including Henry's favourite niece, Meg, Countess of Lennox. The garden was famous for its rare shrubs, the library for its rare books.[1]

The countess's party arrived at King's Place on 12 December and the council wasted no time in summoning Meg to court the following day, but it was soon apparent that Henry Hastings, 3rd Earl of Huntingdon, who was entrusted with the enquiry into the affair, was not interested in the hasty marriage. He was looking for dark, international plots.

Sir Francis Walsingham, recently appointed the queen's Principle Secretary of State, wrote to Huntingdon on 22 December telling him how to approach the enquiry and instructing him to start with the servants; they were the weakest point as their loyalty was doubtful. Huntingdon started his enquiry with one of Charles Stuart's servants named Wenslowe, and for four or five days before his examination he was committed to 'some close and straight custody'. He was warned that punishment would follow if he did not tell all he knew, for 'some kind of persuasion cunningly used may, perhaps, breed such fear and deep conceit in him to utter such truth as otherwise may hardly be drawn out of him'.[2]

Walsingham questioned Countess Meg's steward, Thomas Fowler, asking him how often and how many visits he had made to Bess at either Rufford or Chatsworth during the past year. He could answer honestly that there had been no visits and no direct contact between the two countesses. Whether he knew of the involvement of a third party was never revealed as the question was never asked. Fowler made a plea to Burghley on Meg Lennox's behalf exonerating her of any charge of dealing with Mary while in the area.

The answers were inconclusive but no connection between the Countess of Lennox, her daughter-in-law Mary, Queen of Scots, and Countess Bess was found. There was nothing sinister and the council were satisfied that there was no plot that involved the Queen of Scots. Likewise, no evidence emerged the marriage was anything but an innocent affair that had occurred quite spontaneously.[3]

Because of Charles Stuart's royal blood, the couple should have obtained the Royal Assent to marry and risked being thrown into prison, but the queen showed leniency and they were allowed to remain under house arrest in Hackney. Perhaps if Bess and Katherine Bertie had been interrogated there might have been a case to answer, but they were never questioned. The earlier correspondence between Bess's half-sister and Katherine Bertie, the meeting of the two ladies at Buxton and Chatsworth, was never mentioned. Perhaps the queen secretly approved of the marriage. Elizabeth Stuart was now expecting a baby, and if she had a son born in England, he would have all the necessary credentials to be her successor and the next King of England.

Bess may have been a favourite of the queen but Meg definitely wasn't. The two women really rubbed each other the wrong way. Queen Elizabeth considered Meg to be a troublemaker, while Countess Meg never stopped reminding her cousin that, unlike her, she was the daughter of a true queen (or at least a Dowager Queen); on the contrary, Anne Boleyn, Elizabeth's mother, was never considered to be a true queen. Needless to say, this line of talk infuriated Elizabeth, who with characteristic high-handedness did all she could to discredit her aged cousin, and imposed more fines.

When it came to dealing with Meg, the queen was not averse to using the Act of Attainder – it was a convenient way to remove nobles who were deemed to be getting above themselves. Not only could they be imprisoned for an unspecified length of time, such a move suspended a person's civil rights as he/she had no right to make a will. All titles held would go to the Crown and the guilty person's property would be confiscated by the Crown estate. This is what had happened when the countess and her husband got involved in the marriage plans of their other son

Henry Darnley and Mary, Queen of Scots. Only a portion of the Lennox lands had been returned to their rightful owners, which was one of the reasons why Meg was experiencing such financial difficulties.

The possibility that what little she had could easily be taken obviously alarmed Shrewsbury, who made a plea to Burghley on Meg Lennox's behalf exonerating her of any charge of dealing with Mary while in the area:

> I must be plain with your lordship. It is not the marriage matter, nor the hatred some bear to my Lady Lennox, my wife, or to me that makes this great ado and occupies heads with so many devices; it is a greater matter, which I leave to conjecture, not doubting your Lordship's wisdom hath foreseen it.

Meg stood alone to face her punishment for provoking the queen's rage and showing blatant disregard for royal convention over the marriage of her son Charles Stuart and Elizabeth Cavendish. Once again, as she did when arranging the marriage of her eldest son Henry Darnley and Mary, Queen of Scots, she had challenged the State and lost. Now she was required to pay the price. As Meg Lennox was sent to the Tower for the third and final time, she said, 'Thrice I have been cast into prison, not for matters of treason but for love matters.'[4]

The marriage between Elizabeth Cavendish and Charles Stuart, Earl of Lennox, should have solved the family's problems, but it just magnified them. Being out of favour, Elizabeth and Charles Stuart were kept under house arrest at King's Place. They did not attend Court, which meant a limited social life, but their lives were otherwise comfortable. King's Place was impressive, but by the standards of their class they were poor. After a lot of brawling, Bess managed to persuade the earl to give them a dowry of £3,000, but it's highly unlikely that Shrewsbury ever handed over the money. Certainly Elizabeth Lennox never saw any of it.[5]

It was at King's Place that the family received a letter from Elizabeth's brother-in-law Gilbert Talbot informing them that his wife, Elizabeth's younger sister Mary, had given birth on 10 February 1575 to a son they called George. The baby had been born at Chatsworth House, and because Mary, Queen of Scots, was also in residence and Queen Elizabeth had banned strangers, Shrewsbury lost no time in informing the queen that only the midwife had been present, and he with two of his children christened the child at the nearby church at Edensor. In response to Gilbert's letter, a reply was sent on 14 March 1575 reporting that all the Lennox family were at Hackney and well. That could imply that Meg had been reprieved and was no longer in the Tower of London.

The news of the birth of Elizabeth's baby daughter must have been announced by letter in the same way, but the first written reference to the birth of Arbella is in a letter from Meg, Countess of Lennox, dated 17 November 1575, sent from King's Place to Mary, Queen of Scots, in response to earlier correspondence: 'I yield your majesty my most humble thanks for your good remembrance and bounty towards our little daughter.'[6]

It's surprising that Meg wrote the letter, not the parents, Elizabeth or Charles. Had it also been left to Meg to record the birth? Is that why there is confusion and no record of where or when 'the little daughter' was born? She was certainly born into a tight and exclusive circle, one of grandeur threaded with a network of relatives in high places, but this simple act of recording her birth seems to have been missed. The only indication we have is the letter from Meg Lennox to Mary, Queen of Scots, that would indicate Arbella was born at Hackney and was at the Lennox house at Hackney for the earliest months of her life.[7]

Thomas Cromwell had issued an injunction in 1538 requiring that local parishes register all baptisms, marriages and funerals, but 'the little daughter' seems to have slipped through that net too as there is no accurate record of her baptism, either. At the time, the Anglican Church ordered parents to baptise soon after birth. In the 1549 and 1552 Prayer Book, it was written, 'The pastors and curates shall oft admonish the people that they defer not the Baptisme of Infants any longer than the Sunday, or other Holy day next after the child be borne, unless upon a great and reasonable cause declared to the Curate'.

Superstition played its part, too. It was considered prudent to first make the sign of the cross over an unbaptised baby before taking it in your arms. New babies were taken upstairs before being taken down, symbolically so that they would go up in the world rather than down. It was also strongly believed that babies should not be taken out of the house before baptism because taking an unbaptised baby into someone's house took bad luck in with them.

The early baptism of a baby was considered essential to its future health. People believed that a child wouldn't thrive well until it was named. If a child was sick it was even supposed to promote the cure. The baptismal custom was to dip the baby into the holy water in the font three times – first on the right side, then the left, then with the face in the font, the three immersions representing the Trinity. There's another superstition that says that a child who does not cry at this stage will not live long. This arose from the custom of exorcism that was retained by the Anglican Church; the belief held that when the devil was being driven out of the possessed person, he was supposed to do so with reluctance, so the cries and struggles of the infant at baptism were convincing proof that the holy water was driving him out. Sometimes a nurse was known to pinch the child to make it cry. During the Elizabethan period, the practice of immersion changed to sprinkling with holy water and being anointed with oil. It was traditional for a baby to be covered with a fine, white baptismal vestment called a chrysome, and it was custom that the baby slept in the clothes he/she wore at baptism.

The custom of the time also prescribed that those of high rank be baptised not in the private chapel of the family home but publicly, with all the ceremony befitting the rank of the child. Therefore, if Arbella was born at King's Place in the autumn of 1575, it is reasonable to assume that her baptism took place very soon after at the church of St Augustine, which seemed to stand guard over the little parish of Hackney. Many members of the court used the church, including Ralph Sadler of Bryk Place and Thomas Sutton of Sutton House, plus former residents Thomas Cromwell and the Earl of Northumberland of King's Place. Meg Lennox would only attend under sufferance, preferring to be fined for non-attendance rather than take part in a Protestant ceremony.

It's been assumed by some historians that the baptism took place at Chatsworth, but it would have been folly for a woman who had recently given birth and her new baby to undertake a 160-mile journey north in winter just to be baptised in the village church at Edensor on the Chatsworth estate (where her mother and more recently her cousin George had been baptised). The only evidence to support this is a Stuart pedigree – Harleian 588, ff. 1 and 23 – where the place name of Chatsworth has been added later in a different hand. This didn't bode well because if the christening date had to be changed it was considered a bad omen.[8]

The name Arbella stands out from the usual Margarets, Marys and Elizabeths that make up many English family trees. Latinized to Arabella, it may have been a scribe's mistake or a slight adaptation of the name Anabella, after Queen Anabella Drummond, a fourteenth-century distant ancestor on her father's side. Anabella Drummond (*c.* 1350–1401) was the daughter of Sir John Drummond, 11th Thane of Lennox and Chief of Clan Drummond. His sister Margaret was the second wife of King David II, and when Anabella was about seventeen the king chose her as the bride of the thirty-year-old John Stewart (later changed to Stuart) of Kyle, who was in line to inherit the throne if King David died childless. The marriage was a gesture of recognition of John Stewart as heir to the throne, and he ruled as Robert III with Anabella as Queen Consort of Scotland. Their eldest son became James I of Scotland, and several of their children married into the Douglas clan. Anabella features in the annals of Scottish royalty and had a good claim to both the Scottish and English thrones. The coincidence is conspicuous – when Arbella Stuart was born, did someone prophesy that this would also be her destiny?

The names of the sponsors and godparents, her uncle Charles Cavendish, her Aunt Mary and husband Gilbert Talbot (later 7th Earl of Shrewsbury) are given in E. T. Bradley's *Arbella Stuart* (1889), but no reference is given to substantiate this.[9] The sponsors would offer gifts of gold and silver, which were in turn blessed by the priest. The choice of godparents was more to do with social bonding than religious upbringing; it's likely that Bess would have liked Queen Elizabeth to be one of the godmothers, but having shown her displeasure at the hasty marriage of Arbella's parents, the queen could hardly give their child her blessing. Arbella's infant cousin James VI of Scotland could have been a godfather, represented by proxy, but that would have further infuriated Queen Elizabeth.

Bess was anxious to retain her friendship with the queen and show her gratitude for the leniency she had shown her daughter and son-in-law, so she went to great lengths in choosing a present that would please Elizabeth. Presents were exchanged at New Year: assiduously courting favour and knowing the queen's partiality for fine clothes, Bess presented her with many elaborately designed additions to her wardrobe. Amongst them was a skirt and doublet made of yellow satin embroidered with silver and lined with black sarcenet, and a dress of tawny satin decorated with Venetian gold lace and gold buttons. But for her 1575 New Year's gift, Bess really surpassed herself when she presented the queen with a cloak of light blue satin trimmed with velvet, a costly, original and much appreciated gift.

4

ARBELLA'S EARLY YEARS

Arbella's grandmothers were both to play large parts in her life, but she grew up without knowing either of her grandfathers, who were both high achievers and hugely successful personalities in their own fields. Her maternal grandfather, Sir William Cavendish, died in 1557, possibly from the plague. Her paternal grandfather, Mathew Stuart, 4th Earl of Lennox, ruled as the first regent for her cousin, the young King James of Scotland. After only a year in office, he was carried fatally wounded into Stirling Castle after a raid by the Queen of Scots' supporters. On his death in September 1571, the earldom would have passed to his eldest son Lord Darnley, Mary's husband, but Darnley died first, so the title Earl of Lennox went to Darnley's infant son James and became merged with the Scottish Crown.

Then on 18 April 1572 the infant King James of Scotland granted the earldom of Lennox to his uncle Charles Stuart and his heirs without condition or restriction. On 2 May 1572, Queen Elizabeth wrote a letter to the Earl of Mar, who had recently taken over as Regent of Scotland after Mathew Stuart, thanking him for proof of the king's kindness to her kinsman Charles Stuart.[1]

Charles was not blessed with good health, which limited his career opportunities and was a constant worry for his mother.

He died of consumption in April 1576 when Arbella was only a few months old. Charles and Elizabeth had only been married eighteen months. Meg called her son 'my greatest dolour'. It was never clear whether this was a term of endearment, a reference to the physical and mental pain of his sickly, puny body or the fact that his death caused unimagined distress to the little family.

Although Henry Darnley and Charles Stuart shared the same royal blood line, that's where their similarities ended. Outgoing and confident, Henry Darnley was brought up conscious of his status and inheritance. He was physically strong and athletic, which made him a good horseman with knowledge of weapons and a passion for hunting and hawking. Charles Stuart was not physically strong and hated athletics. Henry was a scholar who wrote Latin and spoke fluent English and French; he excelled at singing, dancing and playing the lute. Charles was a poor reader and slow to learn; a family legend has it that he once read Aristotle and the Book of Common Prayer and decided it was unnecessary to ever read another book. He may have had learning difficulties, but he was not unintelligent. He learnt to read, write and speak fluent French.

Charles' death occurred just four years after the death of his father Matthew, which precipitated the real crisis. The title and the Lennox Scottish estates that had been confirmed by the young King James to Charles soon after his father's death were seized by the Scottish Crown. The loss of income from these estates meant that Meg Lennox, already paying interest on debts outstanding to the English Crown, was now in dire financial difficulty.[2] As mentioned earlier, the loan she had taken from Bess in lieu of a dowry also necessitated an annual repayment of £500 over four years, and Shrewsbury was still refusing to honour his word and provide the promised dowry despite Bess's protestations. To stop the tirade, he eventually agreed to a sum of £3,000, but there is no record that he ever kept his word.

Meg refused to renounce her title, and as the 5th Earl's widow she was adamant her son's widow Elizabeth shouldn't either; but Arbella was a dilemma. She should have automatically inherited the Lennox lands and title but she didn't. Legally, the Scottish Crown had no right to seize them because they had been granted outright to Charles Stuart, 5th Earl of Lennox, and his heirs forever; but they *were* the law, so what chance did the little family have?

The month after Charles Stuart's death, Countess Bess went to court to try to get Queen Elizabeth's help to push the Lennox claim with King James of Scotland or the Regent who ruled for James during his minority. The Earl of Lennox's successor, the Earl of Mar, had developed a virulent sickness and died on 28 October 1572 at Stirling. His successor, the Regent Morton, came up with any number of excuses as to why Arbella was prevented from taking up the earldom. First he claimed it was her gender, then the fact that she had not been born in Scotland. Then the rapacious Morton decided that because the boy King James was a minor when he granted the title to his uncle, it carried no weight and could be revoked at any time. They obviously considered Charles Stuart's death to be as good a time as any.

Countess Meg was determined to fight to regain everything that was rightfully theirs. She wrote to the Scottish Council demanding that the earldom be given back. She appealed to Lord Ruthven, Lord Treasurer of Scotland, who was married to one of her kinfolk, but he wasn't moved to help. Putting their differences aside, Meg wrote to her daughter-in-law Mary, the Scottish queen. She was sympathetic to the claim and it was certainly Mary's intentions that Arbella should have the Scottish lands. She wrote telling her son James to return the title, but she was not in a position of power to enforce her orders and James blithely ignored them. She drafted a codicil to her will, dated February 1577, in which she stated that she recognised Arbella's claim and commanded

James to relinquish the title in her favour. The following year, Mary repeated her instructions to her ambassador, the Bishop of Glasgow, but in spite of reason, argument and persuasion, nothing had the slightest effect.

Notwithstanding the support of the English queen, the Scottish queen and many others whose authority was not recognised in Scotland, James was unwilling to change his view. His stubborn, uncompromising intransigence was utterly frustrating.

In 1540 during the reign of Henry VIII, the Court of Wards and Liveries was established to administer a series of feudal dues, collect revenue and sell wardships of underage children who had lost one or both parents. After Charles Stuart's death, as a minor Arbella's wardship could have been sold to the Crown, who would have appointed a guardian and been able to profit from her position, but instead they saw fit to appoint her grandmother Meg as her guardian, provided that they continued to live at King's Place, Hackney. That was no doubt to prevent Arbella being in the company of the Scottish queen at any of the Shrewsbury residences.

Then Meg Lennox came up with a new idea. Could Queen Elizabeth ignore a portrait of Arbella, the apple of her grandmother's eye, her adorable, cute little granddaughter who was being robbed of her inheritance? Anything was worth a try, so a painting to convey Arbella's rank and position in society was commissioned. On Meg's instructions it was to be inscribed 'Arbella, Comttessa Levinae' – then no one would be in any doubt that she was the rightful Countess of Lennox.

Arbella was not yet two years of age but was expected to pose for long periods, dressed in new, dazzling baby finery yet looking like a miniature adult. Their all too real penury was not allowed to diminish her dress. She was a chubby-cheeked, blue-eyed, serious little girl, wearing a small mob cap surrounded by pearls and diamonds set in gold on her Titian hair. Real pearls dripped from the centre of embroidered gold-and-crimson flowers on her white satin gown, and she wore jewelled bracelets to emphasise the frills at her wrists. Round her neck were a close-fitting necklet of fine gold and three strands of loosely hanging beads. In the centre swung a shield showing a countess's coronet and the Lennox motto, '*Pour parvenir, j'endure*'. The necklet includes a symbol of magical significance, the Star of David.

Many years later her grandmother Bess had the portrait hung at Hardwick Hall, where it remains to this day. Arbella was given a painted, wooden doll dressed in the Elizabethan style complete with ruff as a reward for her patience, which she was allowed to hold while she posed.

Whether the queen ever saw the portrait is uncertain. To have spent so much on Arbella's attire when they were practically destitute seemed extravagant in the extreme, but Meg obviously considered it a wise investment and intended to get her money's worth. If it didn't impress Queen Elizabeth, it might have been used to impress an appropriate suitor. Meg would most certainly have used it to their advantage. Many people including Queen Elizabeth considered the dowager countess to be a nuisance and a troublemaker, but she worked unceasingly to try to regain what she considered to be Arbella's birthright and a better future for Arbella and Elizabeth.

How she managed to stay out of Fleet Prison for debtors is a mystery, but she still mixed in the same exalted circles she had always mixed in, dining regularly with courtiers and high-ranking officials who might have helped her cause. On 4 March 1578 she dined with Queen Elizabeth's favourite, Robert Dudley, Earl of Leicester, and would no doubt have used the occasion to pressurise him to exert his influence on the queen in her favour. Everyone knew how tiresome her constant haranguing was. Perhaps she was just a bit *too* irritating. When Meg became ill, Elizabeth immediately suspected the countess had been poisoned; Dudley lost his temper in a fit of exasperation.

Meg, Countess of Lennox, died in excruciating pain on 7 March 1578. What few people knew at the time was that in the Middle East at approximately that time, the Arabs had developed a poison that was odourless and transparent, making it difficult to detect. They called it arsenic. Dudley could have got hold of such a substance, and there were rumours that he had poisoned Meg Lennox but nothing was ever proved. Her untimely death came just two years after the death of her son. Arbella was not yet three years old but had already lost two of the three most important people in her short life.

The unsympathetic queen immediately seized all the Lennox's English land and their revenue on the pretext of the debt the countess owed the Crown. Throughout this ordeal they seemed to have retained only a little estate called Smallwood in Cheshire – the rest undoubtedly paid for the lavish state funeral arrangements and the magnificent monument to Margaret, Countess of Lennox. She was interred in the same vault where her son Charles Stuart had been buried two years before, in the south aisle of Henry VII's chapel in Westminster Abbey. No expense was spared and the Countess of Lennox's memorial was elaborate. Around the base of her gloriously painted tomb are recited the glories of her lineage, and about her effigy kneel the children who did not survive their mother: there's the six who died in infancy, Charles who had fathered Arbella, and Henry Darnley who had fathered James VI of Scotland with a crown above his head. A few years later it was dwarfed by the tomb of Mary, Queen of Scots, which her son James rather belatedly erected to salve his conscience.

James of Scotland's minority ended officially in 1578, although he did not gain full control of his government until 1583. He started flexing his muscles by demanding the Lennox English lands and their revenues, but Queen Elizabeth used the excuse that the high cost of the countess's funeral and her debts had taken them all. She insisted there was nothing left. When she reminded the Scots that they had the Scottish land and property that rightfully belonged to the young Elizabeth, Countess of Lennox, and her daughter Arbella, James retaliated. On 3 May 1578, just two months after Meg's death, he officially revoked the earldom. The following month, in the most callous move of all, he gave it to Robert Stuart, Bishop of Caithness. Robert Stuart was the brother of the late Matthew Lennox, Arbella's grandfather.[3]

Elizabeth and Arbella lost the Lennox titles and estates, but when Meg died, she placed the casket containing her jewels into the hands of Thomas Fowler, executor of her will. She specified that the jewels were to be delivered to 'the Lady Arabella' at the age of fourteen, and itemized the jewels in her will:

1. *A jewel set with a fair table diamond, a table ruby, and an emerald with a fair great pearl.*
2. *A cross set with fair great diamonds, with a square linked chain.*
3. *A jewel set with a ballast and a fair table diamond set beneath it.*
4. *A H-shape of gold set with rock ruby.*
5. *A burrish set with a fair diamond.*
6. *A rose set with fair diamonds.*
7. *A carcenet set with table diamonds.*
8. *A girdle set with table diamonds.*
9. *A border set with table diamonds.*
10. *A fair pearl chain.*
11. *A chain set with rock rubies, pillar wise.*
12. *A chain of small turquoise set upon a three-square pillar.*
13. *A clock set in crystal with a wolf of gold upon.*
14. *Buttons of rock rubies to set on a gown.*
15. *Table diamonds to set upon a sleeve.*

16. *Two tablets of gold, the one with two agates with divers small turquoise; the other enamelled the form of a globe.*
17. *Bracelets, two pair; one of agate, and the other of plain gold with other things that be not yet in memory.*

Perhaps the jewels worn by Arbella in the portrait painted when she was eighteen months old were already in her possession, but one extra item Meg did not mention was a heart-shaped locket, said to have been made to commemorate the changing fates of Margaret and Matthew Lennox. The face is studded with precious jewels around a central sapphire. The four figures of Faith, Hope, Victory and Truth are exquisitely enamelled and set in gold, rubies and sapphires, with a crown between the figures of Faith and Hope. Around the edge is their Latin motto, which translates as 'Who hopes still constantly with patience shall at last obtain victory'. Hinged on the top edge, the inside is inlaid and enamelled with a whole anthology of emblems.

When Elizabeth Lennox heard that Fowler had gone to Scotland she became suspicious that he had absconded with the Lennox jewels. On 19 September 1579, eighteen months after Meg's death, Mary, Queen of Scots, wrote to Thomas Fowler Esq. on Arbella's behalf, issuing a warrant ordering Fowler to hand the jewels over:

> Be it known that we, Mary, by the grace of God, Queen of Scotland … do will and require Thomas Fowler, sole executor to our dearest mother-in-law and aunt … to deliver into the hands and custody of our right well-beloved cousin, Elizabeth, Countess of Shrewsbury, all and every such jewels … for the use of the Lady Arabella Stuart, her grandchild, if God send her life till fourteen years of age; if not then, for the use of our dear and only son the prince of Scotland … [4]

Fowler replied from Scotland claiming that he had been waylaid and robbed on the way, but no one was surprised to hear that the jewels were later found in the possession of James of Scotland. Queen Mary tried to put pressure on her son to return the priceless Lennox jewels that rightfully belonged to Arbella, but despite all her efforts they were never returned.

In September 1578, six months after Meg's death, Arbella's other grandmother, Bess, Countess of Shrewsbury, went to court to press their claim. Queen Elizabeth promised to do what she could, but her authority did not extend into Scotland. She did however award Arbella an annual sum of £200 and £400 for Elizabeth, which undoubtedly would have been a small portion of the revenue from the land and property that was rightfully theirs anyway.[5]

In less exalted circumstances £600 would have been sufficient to keep a mother and child, but there was no way that Elizabeth and Arbella could continue to live at King's Place. Arbella was of royal blood, descended from Henry VII, and her mother was adamant that she had to live in a style befitting her station. The only solution was for them to leave London and move back to Derbyshire. The Shrewsburys were like Derbyshire royalty, but living with the Shrewsburys was something the queen had been anxious to avoid in order that Mary, Queen of Scots, 'that frustrated, disappointed and neurotic captive' as she called her, could not have a detrimental influence on Arbella, an impressionable child. Seeing no satisfactory alternative, the queen eventually agreed that they could move back to Derbyshire on condition that Arbella and her mother were not to be under the same roof as the captive queen.

In December 1578 when they arrived in Derbyshire, Queen Mary and the Shrewsbury family were at Sheffield Castle, so Bess was forced to leave her daughter and granddaughter at Chatsworth House and continued her journey to Sheffield. She wrote to Walsingham from Sheffield Castle on 29 December 1578: 'I came hither to Sheffield of Crestoline's Eve and left my little Arbella at

Chatsworth. She endured very well with travel and yet I was forced to take long journeys to be here with my lord afore ye day.'[6]

Amongst the staff at Chatsworth was a seventeen-year-old named Anthony Babington, who had been appointed page to Mary at Sheffield Castle the year before. He was from a local farming family with interests in lead mining, and owned a manor at Dethick only a few miles from South Wingfield Manor. No matter what the weather, he would ride regularly between Chatsworth and Sheffield delivering personal messages and greetings between Bess and Elizabeth. When Queen Elizabeth heard of this she put an immediate stop to the communication, and in 1579 Anthony Babington was sent to London to study law.

The impracticality of maintaining two households at the same time sorely tested Bess and the earl, and Bess prevailed on Queen Elizabeth's close adviser William Cecil to allow them all to live in the same household. Finally it was agreed.

5

THE CHATSWORTH
HOUSEHOLD

Esmé Stuart, thirty-seven-year-old cousin to James' father, arrived in Scotland in 1579. A polished operator, he quickly gained the trust and affection of thirteen-year-old James, who regarded him as a father figure. After the execution of Regent Morton in 1581, when James was fifteen, Esmé Stuart took more power into his own hands. He began to gather rewards and preferments, and went on to join the Privy Council. During his rise it was noted that Stuart was also careful to maintain his popularity with the burgh administrators of Scotland's towns.

James bribed the old Bishop of Caithness into parting with the Lennox title and estates that had been given him in June 1578, and for doing so he was rewarded with the earldom of March. Then James gave the Lennox title and land to Esmé Stuart, who was created Earl of Lennox on 5 March 1580. His possession of the title was so assured that even though Bess appealed to the queen for help, she was unable to pursue the matter further.

In 1572, Esmé Stuart had married Catherine de Balsac, and they had five children. The law stated that on the death of Esmé, the title would go to his eldest son and heir, Ludovic Stuart, and in March 1581 Queen Elizabeth made the suggestion that seven-year-old

Ludovic would make a suitable husband for Arbella. Their marriage would neatly solve the problem of the earldom of Lennox and give Arbella back her rightful title. It was her first betrothal: she was five years old.[1]

Esmé Stuart was Catholic and a leading member of the anti-English party in Scotland, so although Meg might have approved, Elizabeth and Bess were not at all keen. Even more of an insult for Elizabeth and Arbella, on 5 August 1581 Esmé Stuart was created the first Duke of Lennox. Unfortunately for Esmé Stuart, the Kirk and the Scottish lords resented the influence he had on James, and proved that the young king was not yet master of his own kingdom when they seized James and took him by force to Ruthven Castle, home of the Earl of Gowrie. James was freed on condition that Lennox, who had resided in Scotland for four years, was sent back to France immediately.

Grieved though the boy king was to lose his first friend, he had no option but to submit, and Lennox was forced out in January 1583, leaving his family behind. He was given safe passage through England to France, but in passing had a curious and secret meeting with Queen Elizabeth. Could it have been to discuss the possibility of Arbella's marriage to his son Ludovic Stuart? Whatever agreement they may have made, it was cut short a few months later when Esmé Stuart died on 26 May 1583, shortly after his return to France.[2]

Ludovic Stuart took the title 2nd Duke of Lennox but, being only nine years old, on his return to France on 14 November he was taken into the household of James VI at Kinneil House, where he was educated under the supervision of Mr Gilbert Moncreiff. His return to France had delayed the matter of the betrothal, but in 1588, as had been his father's wish, it was proposed that Ludovic Stuart, 2nd Duke of Lennox, should be married to Arbella Stuart. Mary wrote to Fonteney, Secretary of her Council, on 28 September 1584: 'As to the young Duke of Lennox's journey out of the country and his marriage with Arbella, these are things that do not require haste, and therefore I will refrain for this time for making a reply thereunto.'[3]

She was wrong to believe that she had time to delay in writing. The English council were about to prevent all unauthorised communication between Mary and her friends, and the young Duke of Lennox was about to marry Sophia Ruthven, daughter of William Ruthven, 1st Earl of Gowrie.

From the age of three, Arbella was considered old enough to start her education. A young lady of her standing would be required to know Latin, Italian and French; she would have to write with a firm and elegant hand in the elegant Chancery script which was then becoming fashionable; she studied her globes, embroidered, stitched, danced and played musical instruments like the lute and virginal. Her formative years were spent without a father figure but were dominated by her mother and grandmother Bess, who appeared to be invincible. The child Arbella would have liked a pet such as a dog or a monkey for company, but Bess was not keen on small, noisy, dirty animals with no profit in them. A hawk was a different matter. Arbella was encouraged to hunt and hawk – pursuits befitting a noble.

Also in the household was Arbella's fifteen-year-old cousin Elizabeth Pierrepoint, better known as 'Bessie', daughter of Arbella's aunt Frances who was married to Sir Henry Pierrepoint. Bessie had been in Mary's service since she was four years old, and Mary called her '*mignonne*' and 'bedfellow'. She gave her great love and affection, treating her as she would her own daughter. She made her dresses in the fashion of the French court with decoration in appliqué work, embroidered flowers in mossoul stitch, flat stitch, chain stitch, stem stitch, and raised satin stitch embroidery with openwork centres. Arbella would have had daily contact with the Scottish queen and her cousin Bessie.

Mary had led a fascinating life and was an incomparable story teller. Arbella and Bessie would sit listening to her experiences as they sewed together. She would tell them about her happy years at the French court, the campaigns in Scotland, the escapes, the flattery and the festivals, with all the tragedy omitted or played diminuendo for the girls' benefit.

The Scottish queen had infinite patience where the girls were concerned and loved joining in their games and pastimes. Often she would sing in French and teach them the words so that they could sing with her. She was extremely musical but the arthritis in her hands frequently made it difficult for her to play her instruments.

No doubt the girls were enthralled by Mary, Queen of Scots, but were also aware of the true situation: she was not a guest in the Shrewsbury household, she was a prisoner. Mary was allowed a household of thirty, but the number had risen slowly to forty-one and Shrewsbury was constantly moaning about not receiving an adequate amount for her upkeep. Sometimes the Scottish queen would be very kind and thoughtful; sometimes she would be angry, hostile and tearful. Her moods changed on a regular basis. (See note on Porphyria, page 254).

Arbella's mother Elizabeth Lennox became ill. She must have known she was dying, for in those last days she dictated a letter, sent to Queen Elizabeth, asking the queen to permit Arbella's grandmother Bess to be her legal guardian. She also asked that the land allowed to her that paid £400 annually should be transferred to Arbella. She amended her will, leaving her best jewel, a ring set with a great diamond, to Queen Elizabeth in the expectation that she would provide for her infant daughter and in the hope that this would sway her. Sadly it did not. Queen Elizabeth took the diamond but gave nothing in return, not even one of her vague responses.

Elizabeth also dictated letters to Leicester, Walsingham, Hatton the Lord Chancellor, and Burghley the Lord Treasurer, requesting them to continue their goodwill towards her 'small orphant [sic]'. And finally she asked Bess to look after her money until Arbella was either married or of age, at sixteen, when she was to receive the residue. Elizabeth Lennox died at Sheffield Manor on 21 January 1582. She was twenty-six years old. She was interred in the Shrewsbury vault at Sheffield Cathedral.[4]

Shrewsbury wrote immediately to Burghley and Walsingham, asking them to inform the queen. He mentioned that Bess was 'so mournth and lamenteth that she cannot think of anything but tears', indulging in the uncontrollable weeping that he found so tiresome and unattractive. Fearing that the £400 allowance for Elizabeth Lennox would now be stopped, the point of the letters was to say that Arbella was left destitute. Bess's argument highlighted the obligation to suitably educate 'my dear sweet joull [jewel] Arbella'. (Jewel was a common form of endearment during the period.)

Normally their letters would have been written to the queen's favourite, Robert Dudley, Earl of Leicester, but he was then out of favour over his secret marriage to the queen's cousin Lettice Knollys, Countess of Essex, in 1578. She already had children from her previous marriage and they now had a son, young Robert, Lord Denbigh. The marriage had taken place shortly after he had dined with Meg Lennox and everyone in the Lennox household had been more concerned with her death than Leicester's marriage.[5]

Arbella was an orphan, and despite the letters, her mother's last plea and pressure from Bess and other members of the family, Queen Elizabeth was unmoved. Bess wrote reminding the queen that Arbella was related to her by blood and needed a suitable upbringing. She urged that closeness to the throne was one of the reasons why the queen might 'well conceive six hundred pounds to be little enough'.

It was to no effect. Queen Elizabeth took back the £400 annual payment. She did, however, agree that Arbella could become the ward of her grandmother Bess, rather than William Cecil, Lord Burghley, 1st Baron Burghley and Master of the Court of Wards, as might have been expected. In a long letter to Burghley dated 6 May 1582, Bess reminded him that Arbella was related in blood to Her Majesty and needed a suitable upbringing – something that could not be achieved on her allowance of £200 a year.[6]

For the most part, after the death of her mother Arbella continued to live with her grandmother at Sheffield Castle or the other Shrewsbury homes. Shrewsbury's son and heir Francis Talbot also died in 1582 and the brother Gilbert became Shrewsbury's heir. Previously he and his wife Mary, Bess's youngest daughter, had spent most of their time at the family house near Charing Cross where he could represent his father's interests in court while Shrewsbury guarded his prisoner in Derbyshire. When not in London, they lived at Goodrich Castle in Herefordshire, another of the Talbot properties, but when Gilbert became Shrewsbury's heir they moved back to Sheffield Castle and became part of the extended family.

Even living in the same household as her Aunt Mary and family, Arbella was still very much an only child. She was seven, Mary was two and Elizabeth was a newborn. Their eldest son George, born about eight months before Arbella in February 1575, had died in August 1577 aged two and a half. John was born in 1583 but soon died, and in 1585 a daughter, Alethea, was born.

Bess's own education had not been generous but she possessed a shrewd intelligence and common sense. She made sure that all her children received a sound education, although Charles had more skill with the sword and horsemanship than with the pen and Henry had more inclination to play dice and seek ease and dalliance. After the Dissolution of the Monasteries there were no more monks to teach, so new schools were needed. Formal schooling was mostly reserved for boys – the standard of girl's education was minimal – and, as a lot of the time was devoted to the learning of Latin grammar, these institutions were known as 'grammar schools'.

Many of the new schools were named after the Tudors, others after the rich merchants who founded them. Mary Talbot contributed to the building of the second court of St John's College, Cambridge. William Cavendish's children were later tutored by the great Thomas Hobbes, but Arbella belonged to an in-between generation. Her love of learning was fostered by her solitude and she became a studious young woman. Her books were her counsellors and friends, and remained so all her life.

Bess taught Arbella how to keep accounts although she was not attracted to figures; she much preferred to spend her time reading or writing. She saw the wisdom of keeping accounts first-hand when Bess's brother James Hardwick was declared bankrupt and thrown into debtor's prison. As the only son, James had inherited the Hardwick estate that had been Bess's childhood home. She was convinced that if the estate was managed well, it could produce a good return on the minerals alone. She tried to explain this to Shrewsbury but he overreacted to Bess's imagined provocations with uncalled-for hostility.

Bess asked Shrewsbury to help her brother, to bail him out by paying off his debtors, but he refused. No doubt he believed that if he was to hand out money to every stupid man who got himself embroiled in a situation that he had no hope of getting out of, he'd be a laughing stock – and a bankrupt one to boot. Bess tried to reason with him. She urged it would show he had compassion and a caring nature, but he would not be swayed. She asked him to make her a loan so that she could help her brother. He refused. She begged him to name his terms: she was willing to accept whatever stipulations he imposed. Still he refused.

He claimed he was being reduced to penury acting as gaoler for the captive queen and her retinue. He estimated that he was £10,000 a year out of pocket over her expenses. Bess reminded him that he could hardly claim poverty when he had at least eight properties and still managed to find the money to be building a new, magnificent manor house at Worksop, estimated to have around four hundred rooms. He retaliated by saying he needed a house fit to entertain the queen on her royal progress as none of his other properties was grand enough. The fact that the queen had never been that far north and never would seemed of little relevance to Shrewsbury.

Bess immediately said Chatsworth House was grand enough to entertain the queen if she journeyed to Derbyshire. Bess was particularly proud of the mansion she had built with her second husband, but at this the earl burst into a violent temper, shouting that it was her house, not his. Bess remained calm and reminded him that it was their house and if the queen so wished to visit they could entertain her there in style; there was no reason to build Worksop Manor. The earl refused to listen.[7]

In April 1581, James Hardwick died in Fleet Prison. Shrewsbury could have saved him He could have paid off the debtors, and it's unlikely that Bess ever forgave the earl for not helping her brother. Shrewsbury always managed to wriggle out of parting with his money where Bess was concerned. He never did provide a dowry for her daughter Elizabeth and had still not honoured the agreements to give £20,000 to each of her sons when they reached the age of twenty-one. Bess never wronged Shrewsbury nor wished to be parted from him, but Shrewsbury was guilty of both and would explode into quarrels and abuse of his wife with little or no provocation.

Reports of the Shrewsburys' discontent had reached court in 1579, but Queen Elizabeth asked them to patch up their differences. That was asking a lot, and despite Bess's best efforts, it proved just too much. As the years dragged on Shrewsbury became meaner and Bess became more pragmatic. After long and heated discussions, they eventually came to an agreement that Shrewsbury would be excused from paying what had been agreed in the 1567 marriage settlement if he returned to Bess all the land and property she had inherited from her third husband, William St Loe, which was mainly in Somerset and Gloucester.

This at last gave Bess her financial independence, and although at the time it was necessary for her to stay in the background, she controlled events through her protégés William and Charles. She raised enough capital to purchase the Hardwick estate of the deceased James for £9,500. Shrewd businesswoman that she was, she had interests in land and mineral rights, and provided a much used money-lending service to members of the nobility, dipping into the coffers stacked under her bed for loans at competitive rates. For Bess, the process of acquisition became compulsive, not just as a matter of security but of power.

She was superbly competent, but Shrewsbury was not a man of intellect and argued that Bess had siphoned away his fortune into her own coffers. Nothing would convince him otherwise even though he couldn't pinpoint exactly how and where she had exercised her power. He wasn't prepared to admit that her prosperity was due to her own astuteness and he started a vendetta against Bess and her sons. Consequently, with this unbalanced outlook, his relationship with Bess deteriorated even further. There were many quarrels, and although he had agreed to return her property, Shrewsbury seized rents from the estates that he had returned to her and harried her tenants.

Arbella was the ward of her grandmother Countess Bess but as the Shrewsburys were in the middle of a matrimonial dispute, she was moved around to live with whichever relatives would house her. She spent time at Chatsworth House, Sheffield Castle and Manor, and South Wingfield Manor, usually in the wake of the Scottish queen and her entourage, who moved around on a regular basis so that the buildings could be cleaned and refreshed. Being so often alone, Arbella frequently found herself seeking out the company of the Scottish queen. Perhaps the captive queen could trust a child? She certainly couldn't trust many adults. She was a captive, a lonely, confused woman aware that even her own people were capable of plotting both for and against her. Maitland, who has been her secretary for years, could forge her handwriting and had been known to do so.

Robert Beale, Clerk of the Council, was sent to Sheffield Castle to investigate various matters relating to the Scottish queen, and in a letter to the Earl of Rutland he spoke of the situation. He found Shrewsbury to be perverse and difficult, and, despite Bess wanting to provide a stable home life for Arbella, this was proving impossible due to the constant harassment.[8]

The trouble within the Shrewsbury household in general was causing complications and concern, but amongst the disarray were the cobwebs of intrigue and counter-intrigue that surrounded the Scottish queen. They had become somehow enmeshed in more worldly matters. It was no longer a problem of Scottish internal politics, there was a rival consideration: Anglo-Spanish enmity. Spanish ships were being built in readiness to attack Britain. The Spanish referred to them as the *Grande y Felicísima Armada* – the 'Great and Most Fortunate Navy'.

Philip of Spain was co-monarch of England until the death of his wife Queen Mary. Without children, he had no claim on the English throne and was forced to return to Spain when Elizabeth took the throne. Being a devout Catholic, he deemed Elizabeth, his Protestant sister-in-law and successor, a heretic and thus an illegitimate ruler of England.

Philip was in support of overthrowing Elizabeth in favour of Mary, Queen of Scots. He had the backing of the Pope, and there were plans afoot to put this plan into operation. Mary had given up her Scottish throne to her son, but she was still Queen of Scotland, Queen Dowager of France and Elizabeth's heir presumptive. She was entitled to inherit the English crown but there was always the threat that she or Elizabeth would be assassinated. There were many who had been plotting just such things for years, and Walsingham, as the queen's spymaster, was looking for proof that the Scottish queen was planning her escape and the overthrow of Queen Elizabeth.

Walsingham also had other matters to attend to at the time. He had heard Arbella's name linked with James of Scotland. Because it could have suggested a plot to dethrone Elizabeth he had to investigate, particularly as it was rumoured that the suggestion had been made by Mary, Queen of Scots. She had written to Elizabeth hinting that it was Bess's intention for her granddaughter to marry James.[9]

If Arbella and James's names were being linked, Walsingham had to give some serious consideration to the idea. They were both of royal blood descended from Henry VII, and both were in line for succession to the English throne. One would inherit, one would not; but why should they not rule jointly to ensure a continuation and rightful succession when Queen Elizabeth died? Indeed, they could be King and Queen of England and Scotland. If Arbella was to marry James, his claim would be indisputably strengthened and her claim would be merged in his. They would no longer see each other as competing forces. Their marriage would be a perfect match and their children would continue the royal line.

With this in mind, in the spring of 1585 Walsingham sent his cousin Sir Edward Wotton on a special mission to Scotland with instructions to speak to nineteen-year-old James on the subject of marriage, and to remind him of the substantial advantages that would accrue. Wotton was to suggest that James took Arbella as a bride, but James had already been approached by a Danish contingent. He had the choice of Arbella or a Danish princess.[10]

Wotton reported back that James had so little interest in marriage that he willingly gave a promise he would take the counsel of Walsingham and Leicester when he came to make a choice.[11]

Arbella for her part was never consulted. But how different things would have been if she had married James, however distasteful he might have been as a husband! She would have been Queen of Scotland while still young and probably have produced heirs who would have gone on to change the course of history; but it was not to be. The problem was that neither Walsingham nor Wotton had any real interest in pushing Arbella's claim, and the Danish ambassadors were a lot more competent and did a much more thorough job. They pressed harder and were more persuasive, leaving James contemplating with reluctance the subject of his marriage to Anne of Denmark.

6

THE YEARS OF DISCONTENT

The idyllic early years of the Shrewsbury marriage were over. Shrewsbury's gout and finances were troubling him, making him short-tempered, and as Shrewsbury's nervous disposition became more pronounced, he reacted to his wife's imagined provocations with renewed hostility.

The marital situation was so fractious that one of Bess's manservants wrote seeking employment at Woollerton Hall in Nottingham, stating, 'This house is a hell.'[1]

Shrewsbury resented the demands made on his patience and pocket by the custody of Mary, Queen of Scots. The strain of keeping the royal captive and the constant plotting and scheming was playing on his nerves, and his frustration was taken out on Bess. The task was thankless and expensive. Although she was a prisoner, Mary insisted that she was treated as a queen, dining beneath a cloth of state, surrounded by all the ceremony of a court. When she injured her back getting onto a horse to go to Buxton, she was allowed a coach and six horses, which from then on she used to ride through Sheffield Park. Shrewsbury was expected to support the cost of her, her entourage and the guards on the £50 a week Queen Elizabeth allowed, and which was often not paid. Bess resented it, too; she was as much a prisoner as Mary. She was weary of being a gaoler's wife. She had no freedom. She could not entertain or attend court as she had once done, and they lived in constant fear that Mary would escape or be assassinated.

It was easy for Shrewsbury to blame his behaviour on the strain of keeping Mary, but everyone knew that he only pretended to despise his position as her gaoler. He was, in fact, besotted by the woman. Even the queen was suspicious that the earl was over-friendly with Mary, Queen of Scots. Burghley had confirmed this on his visit to Buxton where they were taking the curative waters. 1584 was to be Mary's last summer at Buxton, where in melancholy premonition she etched on a window a Latin couplet: 'Buxton whose fame thy milk-warm waters tell, whom perhaps I shall see no more, farewell.' She further added her signature, 'Marie R'.[2]

Robert Dudley, Earl of Leicester, had also been in Buxton in the summer of 1584 to take the medicinal waters, and he called on the beleaguered Bess at Chatsworth. Bess always liked to entertain her London friends. She relished the fact that they could tell her all the latest news. One of the reasons Bess insisted that her son Charles spent time in London at their Coldharbour house was to keep her informed of events in the capital. He actually kept two strong geldings at Coldharbour specially to get messages sent speedily north to his mother.

Distance from the court was and still is an important factor, and most gentlemen and merchants of standing employed agents in appropriate places to keep them informed of current affairs. Gilbert Talbot employed the services of a man named Peter Proby, who also sent reports to the earls of Hertfordshire, Pembroke and Derby. Letters were a vital means of communication and some booksellers made a business of supplying written news-letters to those wealthy enough to afford a subscription.

The word 'news' came into literary use in 1551, by which time the occasional news pamphlets had started to appear, but most people relied upon rumours or bruits as their main means of knowing of events. The intelligence gatherers who supplied news were paid only on results and usually had other jobs as diplomats, merchants, servants and tutors. People like Walsingham employed accredited agents to mingle and report; their motives are not wholly reprehensible.

In the autumn of 1582, William Fowler arrived in England. William was the son of Thomas Fowler, who had been Lady Lennox's secretary, the one who absconded with the Lennox jewels. William was a poet, a scholar and a theologian. He had been expelled from France where he had been studying religious matters, then arrested and imprisoned upon arrival in England. William, like many others, secured release by promising to act as an agent for Francis Walsingham. Over the years William Fowler became Arbella's friend and tried unsuccessfully to locate the Lennox jewels.

The queen also had her spies, though the word 'spy' has subtly changed its meaning – in the Elizabethan era, spies were more like agents, correspondents or reporters. The queen sent Leicester to see Bess because the prolonged dispute between the Shrewsburys was causing consternation in the Privy Council. Bess and Leicester had been friends at court, so he had been chosen knowing that as old friends they could talk freely. Although he was at Chatsworth to mediate on behalf of the queen, Shrewsbury resented his interference in what he considered to be a domestic matter.

But there was another matter being discussed between Bess and Leicester. They were planning a secret betrothal between Arbella and Leicester's four-year-old son, Robert, Lord Denbigh, who Leicester referred to as his 'noble Imp'. Arbella was eight years old at the time and the children's portraits had been exchanged. Leicester was trading his power against Bess's wealth and Arbella's royal blood, and neither Bess nor Leicester saw any reason why Queen Elizabeth would not approve of the union. Leicester and

Bess were waiting for a favourable opportunity to announce the betrothal, but the secret had been leaked. The first rumours of the arrangement are found in a letter from Lord Paget written to the Earl of Northumberland on 4 March 1584, in which he writes, 'The queen should be informed of the practices between Leicester and the Countess for Arbella, for it comes on very lustily, insomuch as the said earl hath sent down a picture of his baby son.'[3]

When Mary, Queen of Scots, heard of the proposed betrothal between Arbella and the young Robert Dudley, she felt angry and betrayed. She had been a friend to Arbella; she had, it will be recalled, tried to instigate a marriage between Arbella and her own son James. They both had a strong claim to the English throne and their union would have ensured their joint succession, but in Mary's eyes that had now been dashed by Bess. She wrote to the French ambassador Mauvissiere: 'Nothing has alienated the Countess of Shrewsbury from me more but the vain hope which she has conceived of setting the crown on the head of her little girl Arbella and this by means of marrying her to a son of the Earl of Leicester.'[4]

Mary had reason to feel betrayed. How could her son James compete for the English throne when faced with opposition from the queen's favourites? Mary's letters to Mauvissiere and her friends display a rising tide of hatred and fury towards Bess. She claimed that it was betrayal by one she had been foolish enough to trust. She thought Bess

... bound to me and regardless of any other duty or respect, so affectionate towards me that, had I been her own queen, she could not have done more for me. I had the sure promise of the said countess that at any time if my life was in danger, or if I were to be removed from here, she would give me the means of escape and that she herself would easily elude danger and punishment in respect of this.

Mary assured Mauvissiere that at the time she had accepted these assurances without question, although perhaps Bess had felt it prudent to cheer her imprisonment while there was a chance that Mary might succeed to the English throne.

Mary said that Bess had told her intimate details about the queen and her lovers. She also informed the authorities that Bess had commissioned an astrologer who foretold that she, Queen Mary, would replace Elizabeth on the English throne and would be followed by her son James and his wife Arbella. The queen was notoriously sensitive about the succession; to write or even speak about the future of the realm was treasonable.

Needless to say, Bess and the Scottish queen became venomous towards each other. Despite living in the same household for almost sixteen years, no two women were more dissimilar than Bess and Mary, Queen of Scots, and it was Arbella's misfortune that the blood of both mingled in her veins. Both were inimical female authority figures but, by some trick of heredity, it was Arbella's bad luck that the Stuart genes were dominant in her while the qualities which made Bess what she was were not transmitted. Bess was a formidable woman and could be something of a holy terror, a staunch friend and implacable enemy with a talent for invective. Queen Mary, on the other hand, was a typical Stuart, prone to bouts of depression and with an inability to understand or assess the motives of those around her. Mary was playing a dangerous game and she couldn't win.

There were rumours that Mary was the earl's mistress, but no one seemed to know whether this was fact or fiction; yet more rumours circulated that Mary had a child fathered by Shrewsbury. The queen was angry and wanted to find out if it was fact – and if not, who had started the rumours, and why? No one was above suspicion, but Mary was adamant that they had started with Bess and it was she who was telling tales to the queen.

So, in December 1584, Bess and her sons William and Charles were called to court to deny in public that they had initiated the rumours.[5]

It was true that Shrewsbury, like most men, found Mary totally intriguing. Seigneur Brantome had declared, 'No one who had loved her in youth could see her person without admiration and love, or read her history without sorrow.'[6] She was never short of male admirers and could take her pick, so the thought of her actually choosing Shrewsbury was quite laughable. It was obviously wishful thinking on his part, or a means of covering up the fact that he kept a mistress in the form of one Eleanor Britton, a rapacious lady of his household whom he had moved into Handsworth Manor, Sheffield and was showering with gifts.

It was inevitable that the rest of the family was drawn into the incessant quarrels and disputes of the Shrewsburys. The earl's son Gilbert Talbot, now heir to the earldom, tried to act as mediator between the battling elders but without success. Gilbert Talbot and Bess's son Charles Cavendish had been brought up together and remained firm friends all their lives. When the hostilities were at their height and the feuding became physical, Gilbert sided with his stepmother (and mother-in-law) against his father. In an act of retaliation, while riding home to Stoke Hall on the edge of Grindleford one day, Charles Cavendish was attacked by Shrewsbury's men and had to take refuge in the church at Ashford-in-the-Water for twenty-four hours. He also had considerable damage done to his property, and fences torn down allowing cattle to stray.

The plans to marry Arbella to Robert Dudley were not a success. One month after Leicester's visit to Chatsworth, little Robert, the 'noble imp', died and with him the high hopes of Bess and Leicester. Queen Elizabeth was probably secretly relieved and made it quite clear to Bess that from then on any prospective grooms for Arbella would be selected by her. Bess had no choice but to agree, and although the temptation to choose a suitable husband for Arbella must have been very great, this was the only time that Bess ever concurred. Ten years previously she had arranged the marriage between her daughter Elizabeth and Charles Stuart, bringing the English crown within the grasp of the Cavendish family, but now the greatest matchmaker of the period was in the ironical position of having a most eligible granddaughter that she could not advance. The decision on Arbella's marriage was a royal prerogative. She was too valuable a pawn in Continental politics.

* * *

As the persecution continued, Bess was no longer able to live with Shrewsbury at Sheffield Castle and moved to Chatsworth, a Cavendish property willed by Bess's second husband to Bess throughout her lifetime and then to their eldest son and heir, Henry Cavendish. Educated at Eton and Gray's Inn, on 9 February 1568 the eighteen-year-old Henry married eight-year-old Grace Talbot, youngest daughter of his stepfather, George Talbot, 6th Earl of Shrewsbury. Henry was sent abroad, travelling to Padua and Venice before returning to live for a short period at Coldharbour in the City. From there he wrote to assure his mother that he was not in London to play dice, seek ease and dalliance or for any other delight, but to seek virtue and honour in arms.[7]

With a favourable recommendation from Leicester in 1573, Henry Cavendish left England to fight in the Low Countries with five hundred men. He held the ranks of captain from April 1574 and colonel from July 1574, but it was due to the years he spent in the Netherlands that he accrued debts of £3,000.[8] When he returned to England, these debts caused Cavendish problems. Henry was in so much debt that he decided that the answer was the income from the lands settled on him by his father, income which until then had gone to his mother. Henry decided that he was going to evict Bess and take early possession of Chatsworth, so Bess promptly transported all the best furniture to Hardwick. Henry was so angry that he changed his allegiance and sided with his stepfather (and father-in-law) against his mother in the ongoing family feud.

Shrewsbury's harassment of Bess and her sons grew ever more extreme. Things came to a head in July 1584 when Shrewsbury's men mounted an armed attack to forcibly take possession of Chatsworth. William Cavendish, with halberd in hand and pistol under his girdle, took to the battlements and held off the attackers. Despite the fact that Shrewsbury was behaving unreasonably, he complained to the authorities, claiming that Henry was the rightful owner and wanted to take what was rightfully his. William was subsequently thrown into the Fleet Prison and Henry took possession of Chatsworth.

Unable to continue living at Chatsworth and having already quit the Shrewsbury seat at Sheffield Castle, Bess fled to Hardwick where she took refuge in fear of her life. The building at Hardwick was no more than a large, tumbledown farmhouse and was in no fit state to accommodate Bess and her household. She must have been at her lowest ebb when in April 1584 she wrote to Walsingham, 'For myself I hope to find some friend for meat and drink and so to end my life.' But Bess was a survivor, and with her independent income she made plans to rebuild the old house.

In August Shrewsbury went down to London to ask to be relieved of the responsibility of guarding the Scottish queen and his troublesome wife. Queen Elizabeth hated this marital discord and ordered them both down to London. After an insincere reunion in court at the end of April 1587 the couple returned to Derbyshire, but Bess went to South Wingfield Manor and Shrewsbury went almost immediately to Handsworth Manor, where he consoled himself with his mistress Eleanor Britton. The queen no doubt understood the situation better than she admitted, and as a sweetener she awarded Bess Crown land in the Peak Forest as a reward for her travails over Shrewsbury. The Bishop of Coventry stated, 'If shrewdness and sharpness be a just cause of separation between husband and wife, I think few men in England would keep their wives long.'

That summer Shrewsbury moved the entire household from Sheffield Castle to Tutbury Castle, and Arbella was included in the large company. There was no sign of Bess, the estranged wife. The Scottish queen hated Tutbury Castle, and it was not hard to see why. It was a loathsome place. The ancient structure, which was built beside a marsh from which malevolent fumes arose, was falling down. The middens stank and the draughts and winds whistled through the chambers. Mary's health had become a chronic problem because of her captivity, but the extreme cold and damp accentuated her physical pain. Her hands were so stiff and swollen she could hardly hold a pen to write her letters, and her face was swollen because of her constant weeping. But Tutbury was an impregnable fortress; it offered greater security, and that was all Queen Elizabeth was interested in.

As often happened in the summer months, plague was rife and once the entire party was installed at Tutbury Castle, Shrewsbury posted guards at every access road to question those who came and went as to where they had been and how they felt. Huge bunches of herbs were strung across the doorways of every chamber, and the brisk air from the moors blew through the gardens to expel evil humours.

It was at Tutbury where they received the news that Mary, Queen of Scots was being moved away from the Shrewsbury household. Someone in authority had evidently realised at last that the Earl of Shrewsbury's health was not good and that he could not continue to guard the Scottish queen effectively on his own without Bess.

Shrewsbury wrote to the queen to thank her for setting him free of two devils, his wife and Queen Mary.

The reluctantly appointed new gaoler of Mary, Queen of Scots was the gaunt and elderly Sir Ralph Sadler, who had served four Tudor monarchs; but the responsibility of guarding the Scottish queen proved to be too much. After just one year, Mary and her retinue returned to Tutbury, in early January. The Shrewsburys had managed sixteen years with very little thanks or help, but now there was going to be another gaoler, Sir Amias Paulet.[9]

Paulet was ordered to make arrangements for Mary Stuart to remain at Tutbury Castle. Finding the accommodation utterly unacceptable, he intended to stay at Tutbury Priory. Following the Dissolution of the Monasteries Tutbury Priory was granted to Sir William Cavendish, who dismantled the priory, part of the church and the chapel of Saint Stephen in order to build a house. At the time that Amias Paulet required it, the accommodation was occupied by William's heir Henry Cavendish. Despite having forced Bess from Chatsworth House, with no money to replace the furniture and fittings that Bess had transported to Hardwick Hall, Henry and his wife Grace had been unable to live there so had moved to the nearby priory. Still deeply in debt, Henry Cavendish was unwilling to move out for Paulet and asked for £100 a year for the use of the house, or alternatively that the queen should lend him £2,000 towards the payment of his debts. The queen was not prepared to meet his demands.

Sir Amias Paulet was an odious, extremely severe man in his early fifties. He was well known for his strong anti-Catholic feelings, and it was obvious that he intended to treat Queen Mary more like a common criminal than a crowned queen. He gave orders that all private letters and messages would be stopped, the Scottish queen not allowed to leave her room without an escort, and that under no circumstances was she to be allowed outside.

Security was tightened, visitors were searched and questioned, and family members only allowed to visit her singly and for ten minutes a day. Mary Talbot, as lady of the house and female authority figure, protested but was told in no uncertain terms that the Scottish queen was a captive, not a guest. Mary Talbot resembled her mother Bess in temperament; she was famous for her grim defiance of authority. She was also an obstinate recusant Catholic and non-attendee of the Anglican Church, so her sympathies were all for Queen Mary.

As the family were pressed to give reasons every time they passed through the gates, Mary Talbot wrote to Queen Elizabeth objecting in the strongest possible terms. The queen's answer was to transfer Mary the twelve miles from Tutbury Castle to Chartley Castle on Christmas Eve 1585. Once at Chartley, it really was the beginning of the end. Since arriving in Derbyshire sixteen years earlier, Queen Mary had been moved forty-six times.

Walsingham through his many and devious agents mounted a new stage in his campaign to incriminate the Scottish queen. He had an obsession and sought verification for his case that it was too dangerous to keep her alive. He set about enmeshing Mary in two separate conspiracies that made up the bogus machinations of a dubious assassination plot, known as the 'Babington Plot' after Anthony Babington, the young squire who had been in the Earl of Shrewsbury's household at Sheffield Castle. He was the young man who had acted as a messenger carrying letters between Bess and her daughter Elizabeth when she and Arbella first arrived at Chatsworth and were not allowed to go to Sheffield Castle, where Mary, Queen of Scots was imprisoned. Since then Anthony Babington had been on the Continent and in London studying law. Now he was first in line to rescue Mary, with an ill-conceived plan. Paulet and Walsingham waited, patient as crocodiles and all-seeing as sparrowhawks, for Mary to encourage Anthony

Babington in his plans. So long as Mary lived, the bosom serpent as Walsingham called her, she would continue to be the hope of all Catholics to supersede Elizabeth.[10]

On 16 January 1586, Mary received the first secret message via the local brewer. She was told to use the same pipeline to smuggle out her own notes, but she little realised that treachery was afoot. All her mail, her most private thoughts and schemes, were going directly to her jailor Paulet and her enemy Walsingham in London. Mary had fallen into the trap that had been laid for her and those trying to free her. The plans carried the inevitable implication that Elizabeth should be deposed and Mary seated on the English throne. This was treason, to which Mary's consent would make her an accessory.

Philip of Spain was poised to devote his resources to restoring England to the Catholic fold and the English conspirators were led to believe that a Spanish invasion was certain, but amongst the conspirators were renegades and double agents secretly in the pay of the English government. By August 1586, Mary's hopes of release began to rise, but she had no idea that her conspirators were systematically being found and arrested. On 11 August when the dour Paulet suggested a ride, she had no hesitation, but it was a ruse to get her away from Chartley Castle. She was escorted to Tixall by armed guards while others thoroughly searched her rooms, seized her papers and made a complete inventory of her belongings. Her servants were interrogated and arrested.

On 18 August Anthony Babington made the first of his forced confessions. Mary was incriminated, and Babington along with thirteen fellow conspirators were hanged on 20 September. Five days later, Mary was removed to the strong castle of Fotheringay in Northamptonshire, where she was tried for treason.

Queen Elizabeth wanted desperately to be able to trust Mary, Queen of Scots. She was the one person who shared with Elizabeth the dangers and difficulties of being a queen regnant. If they had met, there is every possibility that they could have become mutually supportive, but Elizabeth's views were tainted against Mary by her ministers.

When James heard about his mother's arrest at Chartley and her move to Fortheringhay, he made the heartless comment that she should content herself with drinking the ale and meddle in nothing but prayer. He showed no concern that she was on trial for her life. A trial for high treason was a foregone conclusion as far as the result was concerned, but her plight did not stir any filial passion in him; before Mary died she disowned him and willed her English succession to Philip of Spain.

In a fit of pique, James threatened that if he was excluded from the succession, he would unite with his Danish father-in-law and make war on England. It was probably an empty threat but Cecil considered it too risky to leave the matter open. So long as James thought he would succeed Elizabeth on the English throne, good relations would be maintained between the two kingdoms – and the way to ensure this was to pay him.

James was always short of money to spend on personal projects or gifts to friends and favourites, and records show that although payments were irregular and unpredictable, he was being paid quite considerable sums by the English government. The English called the payment a 'gratuity' or pension; the Scots called it an 'annuity', claiming that James VI was entitled to an income from his grandmother's Lennox estates in England. This seems manifestly unfair when that income should rightfully have been given to Arbella.

The English crown had recently been worn by a sickly boy king and two women, viewed as second-rate rulers by reason of their gender. Some at court blamed all the political and social ills of the decade on the fact that England was ruled by a woman with the weakness of character this supposedly entailed. The fact that Elizabeth refused to name her successor, playing one candidate against another, infuriated her detractors. The Privy Council wanted a king. A male monarch offered a welcome return to what they considered to be normality.

In 1586, when a secret treaty was signed between Scotland and England, James received £4,000 sterling as his first subsidy. But the Scottish monarch had to earn his subsidy by being of value to Cecil and respecting his wishes. James preferred men, but the general populace would not be aware or suspicious of his sexual orientation if he was married with sons. That would in theory ensure a male succession and long-term dynastic stability, so James was assured of a substantial sum of money when he married; the birth of a son would ensure another tranche, and so on. James was a puppet dancing to Cecil's tune.

Mary, Queen of Scots was beheaded on 8 February 1587. To Arbella she left her Book of Hours which she had brought with her from France. In the book she had written '*Ce livre est a moy, Marie Reyne 1554*'. During the years of her captivity she had filled its unprinted pages with poems and the names of her friends written in her shaking, arthritic hand.[11]

It was predicted that the execution of Mary would have far-reaching effects. It was expected that the Scots would take some form of reprisal, but James made no move to avenge his mother's death. He was prepared to swallow the insult to his family and his nation so long as the English crown dangled within his reach; that was all he was interested in. The king was being paid to avoid any form of retaliation; he did nothing. He even ignored his mother's wish to be buried in Rheims with her mother, and after being kept for months at Fotheringay Castle, her body was eventually buried at Peterborough Cathedral, a few miles from Fotheringhay. No Scots were present.

Queen Elizabeth, unmarried and without a direct heir, had removed with one blow the head of her legal successor to the throne, but she refused to name another. There were times when it suited her to let it appear that James was her chosen successor. At other times, Arbella was regarded as her preferred successor. Elizabeth feared all potential rivals. She always felt insecure and at risk of rebellion. She had every reason to be concerned. In 1586, a rather dubious character named Michael Mooney had been instrumental in a plot to kill the queen by carrying a bag of gunpowder into her bedchamber. It was probably the discovery of this plot that made her finally sign the death warrant of Mary, Queen of Scots.[12]

Mary had been the foremost Catholic claimant but had disowned her son and heir-presumptive and willed her English succession to Philip of Spain, the husband of her late aunt Queen Mary ('Bloody Mary'). The marriage between Queen Mary and Philip of Spain had been accompanied by a firm proviso that gave neither Philip nor his heirs, except those by Mary, a right to the succession, but Philip had a perfectly legitimate claim through John of Gaunt, 1st Duke of Lancaster and third surviving son of King Edward III.

John of Gaunt's legitimate male heirs, the Lancasters, included kings Henry IV, Henry V and Henry VI, but Henry Tudor's claim to the English crown in 1485 was contentious. He was a descendant of John of Gaunt's long-term mistress Katherine Swynford. She later became John of Gaunt's third wife, but the five children of this later marriage were explicitly barred from inheriting the throne, according to the legal clause '*excepta regali dignitate*' (except royal status), that was inserted with dubious authority. This charge was levelled against Henry VII, but because he married the Plantaganet heiress it was not upheld against their children.

On the other hand, the Royal House of Spain and the Royal House of Portugal were descended from John of Gaunt's legitimate children. The Spanish line was through his second wife, Constance, and their daughter Catherine, who married King Henry III of Castile. The Portuguese line was through John of Gaunt's first wife, Blanche, and their daughter Philippa, who married John I. That gave their descendants a strong claim to the English throne and it was alleged that Philip was intent upon putting his own daughter, the Infanta Isabella, on the throne of England. She was married to her cousin, the former Cardinal Archduke Albert of Austria, son of the Emperor Maximilian II, who since 1583 had governed Portugal on Philip's behalf. To many, Infanta Isabella's descent from Edward III made her the rightful Catholic queen of England.

Philip and his ally the Pope were intent upon carrying out what they considered to be God's will – the destruction of Protestantism – and were planning an offensive against England as a direct response to Mary's death. James of Scotland was not prepared to avenge his mother's death, but Philip of Spain and the Pope were.

The possibility that a foreigner could step in and claim the throne of England after the death of Elizabeth must have really alarmed James. Where other people were concerned, he wanted to promote the law that no foreigner could succeed to the English throne. He obviously did not consider himself a foreigner, although strictly speaking James *was* of alien birth, having been born in Scotland. He preferred to ignore that.

Arbella was therefore holding the trump card because she had been born in Britain, one important qualification neither James nor Isabella had. By English law this made them foreigners and debarred them both from succeeding. Perhaps it would have been a good idea to nudge things in that direction under the circumstances, but Arbella seemed lacking in support where her claim was concerned.

James must have been pretty desperate because, not content to be Elizabeth's successor, he offered himself in marriage to the fifty-three-year-old queen. She was no longer the ever youthful 'Virgin Queen' in looks or vigour, but obviously James was not interested in the physical aspects of a union; it would be a marriage in name only, so he was not going to let a thirty-four-year age gap bother him. It was obvious that James was greedy for the queen's favour and the title of king – but just how far would he go to achieve that? The last time that James and marriage had been mentioned in the same sentence was when Walsingham had suggested that he should marry Arbella. James had contemplated the subject with reluctance. The queen no doubt gave him short shrift.

Then James's ambassador made the request that he should be proclaimed the rightful heir to Elizabeth's throne and insisted upon a formal written document ensuring his succession. The secret agreement had been kept secret for too long. James also tried to secure some sort of control over the selection of Arbella's husband, 'that the Lady Arbella be not given in marriage without the king's consent'. James was obviously aware that if Arbella should marry a man ambitious to promote her royal blood, James might not succeed Queen Elizabeth after all.[13]

James's assertiveness and overconfidence must have infuriated Queen Elizabeth because she promptly and openly acknowledged that there was another in the running. She then invited Arbella down to London to the royal court. James was getting his comeuppance; that would teach him a lesson for daring to presume too much. The queen's successor was going to be Arbella Stuart.

7

ARBELLA AT THE
ROYAL COURT

Although Arbella had been born in London, she had not been there since she was three. She was now in her twelfth year and about to face the most daunting and exciting challenge of her young life. Aunt Mary Talbot would have shown her how to curtsy to the queen and told her the correct way to address the important people she would be meeting. She was warned to be discreet as Queen Elizabeth had sharp ears, sharp eyes and could winkle out gossip at fifty paces. She was advised to be aware of the lackeys of Milord Leicester, who could be found, all ears, in forgotten corners. She was told to be watchful of William Cecil, mild-eyed and soft-footed, and Master of Court since 1561.

A court visit was time for finery and new clothes. Even Bess, who was known for her contempt for show and splendour, agreed that Arbella must be richly dressed, so she was allowed seven yards of green velvet to have a dress made. In her naivety, she thought this was very grand and extravagant, until she realised that an appearance in court meant that an outfit could be worth more than an estate. Ben Jonson summed it up when he wrote, 'Four or five hundred acres of best land were turned into two or three trunks of apparel.'

The queen had 300 formal gowns and it was not unusual for her to have pearls worth £400 embroidered onto one gown. Ladies of her court had dresses decorated with ornamental buttons, knots of ribbon, elaborate embroidery, the fabric pinked or paned (cut in a decorative arrangement of holes or slashed to show a different material underneath).

A twelve-year-old would be dressed simply but equally extravagantly. Her hair would have been left plain to emphasise her virginity, she'd wear no cosmetics but a faint marjoram scent. Perhaps she was allowed to wear a magnificent double rope of pearls around her neck, and outsized pendants in her hair and ears, which would belie any suggestion of economy. Bess knew when to spend money where it counted. From the skin up, a lady would wear a chemise or smock of cambric or silk, finely embroidered and perfumed. Over that would come a corset, made in two parts and thus described as a 'pair' of bodies, stiffened with wood or whalebone and with a rigid centre piece projecting the long line of the stomacher downwards. Then there were the petticoats, tied by points or laces to the bodies. The petticoats were held out by the bell-shaped farthingale, which was itself supported by a strip of padding or rope tied around the hips below the waist, commonly known as a 'bum roll'. Over this went the gown itself, a sleeveless coat-like garment hooked onto the stiff front panel. The huge padded sleeves were attached separately before the ruffs and cuffs were pinned into place.

Court was the arena where people went to see and be seen. This was where power, contacts, position and lucrative employment were won. The court was the centre and fountain of patronage. It drew the brilliant and clever, the ne'er-do-wells and the hangers-on in search of whatever could be picked up.

When Arbella appeared at court every officer and suitor was eager to see her, the only princess of royal blood, who had been hidden away in remote Derbyshire for years. They knew that this apparently unsophisticated and unknown girl was of great diplomatic importance as she could be their next sovereign. Queen Elizabeth had spent almost thirty years as queen, and as Arbella approached the carved and canopied throne on which she sat, everyone was aware that she was confronting a representative of the dynasty that would succeed her, a living reminder of her own mortality. Likewise, Arbella knew that this was the woman who held her future in her hands.

Everyone paid homage to the queen with blatant adoration as she sat there surrounded by her admirers and favourites. Her eyes were still piercing, shrewd and bright, but her face had lost its youthfulness and sagged into the characteristic contours of age. In stark contrast, an exquisitely delicate, stiffly starched collar of lace rose up behind her head. Her long slender fingers were adorned with rings that glowed and throbbed in the lights from the lanterns, and as Arbella lowered her eyes and curtseyed before the terrifying figure, she tried to forget that only five months earlier this woman had ordered the beheading of her arch-rival Queen Mary, her cousin and next of kin.

The English court was like nothing Arbella would have ever encountered. It was a brilliant, noisy extravaganza, a spectacular with music, pageantry, dancing and feasting. It wasn't long before court life whirled around her young head, intoxicating her with its life. There were vast numbers of servants, courtiers and ladies in waiting, but as the only princess of the blood in England, she took precedence over all the other ladies and was treated with all the deference due to her rank. She may have got a bit above herself, but that was to be expected. She enjoyed speaking to foreign dignitaries in their own tongues and pitting her wits against learned scholars. The fact that she made such an impact at court with her lively mind and eloquence was thanks to the education her grandmother Bess had insisted upon. She was keen to put her knowledge to good use.

She met lots of important people. John Harrington paid a visit to Shrewsbury House in late June. He was a relative of the queen and of the Zouches of Derbyshire, the family whose household Bess had lived in when she was not much older than Arbella. John Harrington's father was a poet, his mother, Isabella Markham, a gentlewoman of the queen's privy chamber, and he had the honour of being one of the queen's 102 godchildren. Although he had studied law, John Harrington was attracted to life at the royal court, where his free-spoken attitude and poetry gained Elizabeth's attention. He was a writer of fantasy and satire and the queen encouraged his writing, but Harrington was inclined to overstep the mark with his risqué pieces, grotesque, bawdy jokes and ribald songs.

Angered by the raciness of his translations of Ariosto's *Orlando Furioso,* the queen told Harrington that he was to leave court and not return until he had translated the entire poem. She chose this peculiar punishment rather than actually banishing him, assuming that he would find the task so difficult that he would not bother to comply. She was wrong. Harrington chose to follow through with the request and completed the task in 1591, gaining him much praise and admiration.

Arbella was intrigued and asked him to read some of the Italian verse he was translating at the time. A friendly debate ensued as they battled over certain terms and phrases; later he was to say, 'She comprehended the whole with a gravity beyond her years.'[1]

Harrington explained how he had made and perfected Britain's first flushing toilet. True to form, he had chosen the name Ajax (as 'jakes' is an old slang word for toilet). He had the Ajax installed at his manor in Kelston and was trying to persuade Queen Elizabeth to have one.

Arbella dined with the queen and supped with Burghley at his own court. There she met and talked to Sir Walter Raleigh, who was at that time Captain of the Guard, a position that Bess's third husband, William St Loe, had previously held. Raleigh had been granted a royal patent to explore Virginia, which paved the way for future English settlements in North America. He told Arbella exaggerated accounts of his experiences searching for El Dorado, the empire of a legendary golden king in South America. She told him that she had read about the legend of El Dorado and, much to his surprise, gave him a brief outline in Spanish. Sir Walter was the second lord to tell her she had intelligence beyond her years.

One of the main topics on everyone's lips at the time was the offensive against England being planned by Philip as a direct result of the execution of Mary, Queen of Scots. War was not unusual on the Continent with countries forging and reforging alliances, looking for opportunities to gain power, territory or influence, sensing each other's vulnerabilities and assessing each other's strengths. Issues of succession were particularly likely to erupt into conflict, but Queen Elizabeth was not anxious to subject her people to the financial and human suffering a war would entail.

Elizabeth considered war to be a wasteful extravagance, to be avoided if at all possible, so she was looking for a way out of a costly struggle – and that's where Arbella came into the scheme. The queen suggested a betrothal between Arbella and Ranuccio Farnese, eldest son of Alexander Farnese, Duke of Palma, and Maria of Portugal. The Duke of Palma was the Spanish Governor General of the Netherlands and general of the Spanish army fighting against the English armies and its allies. The proposed marriage was a cunning ploy to avoid the threatened offensive, and Arbella's visit to court was to let Spain know that the queen was serious. Apparently she said to de Chateauneuf, the French ambassador, knowing that it would get back to Philip, 'Look at her well. She will one day be even as I am.'[2] It was probably the nearest the queen ever got to actually announcing that Arbella would be the future queen of England, but she was making sure that the right noises were being conveyed back to Philip of Spain and the Duke of Parma by their contacts at court.

This was of great significance. Queen Elizabeth was offering Arbella and the throne of England in exchange for peace with Spain; but Queen Elizabeth liked to play her cards close to her chest. The people who needed to know about the proposed marriage alliance were informed, but it's doubtful that it was common knowledge. James would not have known – Elizabeth was too cunning for that.

When the queen had crushed James with her bruising comment about there being another in the running for her throne, Arbella must have assumed that she meant her. But she was then informed that the queen could have been referring to Ranuccio Farnese whose mother, Maria Alexander Farnese, Duchess of Palma, was a member of the Royal House of Portugal and could, too, be in line to the English throne.

It was obvious that Queen Elizabeth was playing one against another. Arbella's claim and that of Ranuccio would most certainly be strengthened if tied in marriage, but there was no certainty at that stage that the proposal would be acceptable. Once the queen and her ministers had set the plans in motion, those involved had to wait for the reaction from Spain and further developments. Arbella was being used like a pawn in a game, and it was the turn of the Spanish to make the next move. That could obviously take some considerable time, and the court was on the move out of London to Theobalds, the home of the Lord Treasurer, William Cecil, 1st Baron Burghley, on the summer progress.

The newly built moated house near Enfield in Hertfordshire was located just off the main road north from London to Ware. It was known as an Elizabethan 'prodigy house', large as a village, dramatic, sumptuous and extravagant. Burghley's intention in building the mansion was partly to demonstrate his increasingly dominant status at the royal court and also to provide a palace fine enough to accommodate the queen. She visited eight times between 1572 and 1596. Luxury abounded: the formal gardens of the house were modelled after the Chateau de Fontainebleau in France; the great chamber was 60 feet long, 22 feet wide and 20 feet high with a ceiling laid out with sun, stars and signs of the zodiac. By some ingenious concealed mechanism, at night the ceiling glowed like the midnight sky with moon and stars shining brightly, functioning like a planetary clock. The gallery off the great chamber was 126 feet long and the roof had a great fretwork like the low gallery at Chatsworth.

Mealtimes at court were pure theatre. No member of the court was allowed to arrive late as this incurred the displeasure of the Chamberlain of the Household. While the queen said her prayers in the Privy Lodge, two gentlemen entered the Great Hall, one bearing a rod, the other a tablecloth. With great solemnity they advanced the length of the room, kneeling three times on the way, and then with utmost veneration carefully spread the cloth upon a small table. Having knelt once more they backed from the chamber. Two more gentlemen appeared, one again carrying the rod, the other this time with a salt-cellar, a plate and some bread. When they had kneeled, as the preceding attendants had done, they too retired with the same ceremony.

Next came the turn of two countesses, one married and one unmarried. The unmarried lady, dressed in white silk, curtseyed three times and rubbed the plate with bread and salt. After a while, the yeoman of the guard entered, bare-headed and clothed in scarlet, bringing in at each turn a course of twenty-four dishes served on gilt plate. These dishes were received by a gentleman and placed upon the table.

The married countess, who carried a small knife, gave each of the guard a mouthful of the particular dish he had brought in, to make sure the food had not been tampered with on its long journey from the kitchens. While all this was going on, twelve trumpets and two kettledrums made the hall ring for half an hour. At the end of all this noisy ceremonial, a number of unmarried ladies lifted the meat from the table and conveyed it to the privy chamber. There the queen chose what she wanted for herself; then the rest went to the guests. By the time the food was actually eaten it was barely warm.

Arbella was given precedence over everyone else. The household staff addressed her as 'Your Highness', and she was served first at table on bended knee after the food had been tasted for poison. When they curtseyed to her, the curtseys were as low as those to a queen. There could have been no greater contrast between the sombre ambience of Derbyshire life and the colour and pomp of life at Theobalds.

Dancing was encouraged and Arbella had been taught to dance with good grace. The queen had been a competent dancer and, although no longer light on her feet, she remained a critical spectator watching the dancers display their finery and their fancy footwork. As the newcomer, Arbella had no shortage of partners or attention from the grandees of the court. She didn't realise at the time, but the court was in flux. The old guard – men like Leicester, Walsingham and Burghley that Bess knew well – were fading. They were either dying or retiring, and a new generation of men at court were making the decisions. Leicester, father of the 'noble imp' and step-father of Milord Essex, died at his home in 1588, the first of a series of deaths. Walsingham died in 1590, and until his death in 1598 William Cecil, Lord Burghley, was increasingly handing over power to his son Sir Robert Cecil.

Arbella did not perceive the falsity that existed in the court and its social intrigues – how yesterday's friend could be tomorrow's enemy. Over the years she was to realise that the fair words she heard from courtiers and counsellors one day were likely to dissipate into the ether the next. Looking back, 1587 seemed a time of absolute personal triumph for her, but she was young and naive.

It would have amused the queen to mould her into her own image if she had so wished. She had kept one foreign power after another in line with the promise of her own hand and her kingdom along with it. This had been an invaluable tool in her lifelong game of diplomacy, and now that she could no longer play that game, she could offer an alternative: Arbella. She saw no reason why Arbella could not be displayed and given a brief moment in the limelight, with a visit to the court when diplomatic necessity required it. An acknowledgement of her rank as the queen's dear cousin whom she intended to make her heir and successor increased Arbella's value. The queen was letting it be known that she would give Arbella as wife to Ranuccio, and with her the succession to the throne.[3]

When the court moved to Greenwich on 13 August it was decided that there was no need for Arbella to remain at court, but she stayed in London nevertheless in the care of her aunt and uncle, Gilbert and Mary Talbot, at their home in Newgate Street. They later moved to a house called Fines in Coleman Street, at that time a fairly large street that ran from Moorgate to Lothbury in the City. Arbella wrote to Bess regularly from London keeping her up-to-date with events. She also had the ends of her hair cut on Saturday, the sixth day of the waning moon, and, as she had been instructed, she sent these to her grandmother Bess who could use the hair to cast a spell for Arbella's continued good fortune. Both placed a lot of importance on such superstitions (as did most people) and Arbella made sure never to comb and dress her hair after nightfall as that was believed to bring disaster.[4]

Bess had had an epiphany. It's unsure whether it was a vision or whether she experienced a sudden and striking realisation, but she was adamant that Arbella was destined for greatness and that she must provide the means and opportunities to help her achieve it. She was no doubt struck by the prediction and would refer regularly to it – and not just in a playful manner. Arbella learnt later that her grandmother had consulted a famous fortune teller and had her birth charted in the hope that it would show auspicious signs. She exhibited more faith in the crystal ball than in divine providence, and was certain that there was a great future before her granddaughter.

Arbella's star was on the ascent and grandmother Bess was determined that she should have the best of everything: the best that money could buy in the way of education, culture and polish. She was to stay in London so that she was exposed to the way of life of some of the richest and most cultivated members of society in order to widen her horizons. She became skilled at playing instruments, dancing and all the other arts a young woman needed to shine in society. She read widely, embroidered, developed the art of conversation and learnt to drive her own carriage. She was endowed with great natural gifts, but needed to learn the importance of discretion, discipline and self-control.

As winter approached and no decision on Arbella's proposed marriage had been reached, things were looking rather uncertain. Astrologers had predicted that 1588 would be a year of 'most wonderful and extraordinary accidents', but the mood of the country was dark. Spain's mighty Armada of 130 ships was already on the seas and England moved onto a war footing, building ships, requisitioning stores and erecting warning beacons on hilltops across the land.

8

ARBELLA RETURNS
TO DERBYSHIRE

With her head crammed with unfulfilled dynastic ambitions, in the early summer Arbella returned to the royal court, which had meanwhile moved to Greenwich. The atmosphere had changed from the pursuits of pleasure and all the joys characteristic of fashionable society to one of sombre concern. The difference was palpable. In the effort to conduct peace negotiations tempers were easily frayed, and nowhere was that more noticeable than with the queen.

Arbella was twelve years old and obviously growing up: she was noticing young men. She was painfully aware of the most handsome man at court, Lord Robert Devereux, 2nd Earl of Essex. He was twenty-two, tall, attractive, courtly and exciting. His skills as a showman and flatterer no doubt made her laugh and blush. He could be very ardent. He remembered that they had met previously when he accompanied his stepfather, Robert Dudley, 1st Earl of Leicester, when they visited the spa at Buxton; it had been his half-brother, whom they called the 'noble imp', that Leicester and Bess had tried to promote as a bridegroom for Arbella when she was eight.

Born into an ancient but impoverished family, Essex set much store by his noble birth. He was the great-grandson of not one but two of Henry VIII's mistresses, Anne Stafford, Countess of Huntingdon, and Mary Boleyn, sister of Queen Anne Boleyn, the mother of Queen Elizabeth I. Some believe that King Henry fathered Mary's daughter Katherine Carey, who was Essex's grandmother. If so, this would have made Essex a great-grandchild of Henry VIII and first cousin twice removed of the queen, although that was never officially recognised.

The son of Walter Devereux, 1st Earl of Essex, and Lettice Knollys, Essex was brought up on his father's estate at Chartley Castle, Staffordshire, where Mary, Queen of Scots was imprisoned after leaving Tutbury. He was nine years old when his father died and he inherited the title 2nd Earl of Essex. He became a ward of Lord Burghley and moved into his household; shortly thereafter, in 1578, his mother married Robert Dudley, Earl of Leicester, Elizabeth's long-standing favourite.

When the Earl of Leicester died that September, Essex replaced his stepfather in the affections of the ageing queen. He could be utterly charming, but was also egotistical and displayed the arrogance of a spoilt brat. He could be touchy and hot-tempered – his hysteria was never far below the surface – and the fact that he possessed no wealth enraged him.

He took an instant dislike to Sir Walter Raleigh, who 'glittered with jewels and could afford to wear jewels on his shoe strings worth 6,600 gold pieces'. These gifts from the queen were enough to antagonise Essex and they fought a duel, although later they became friends. Raleigh, like Essex, was a soldier of fortune, but had a totally different background; three years previously, 'Raleigh had been nothing more than the youngest son of a Devonshire squire with the broad Devon accent of a peasant.' He married Bess Throckmorton, granddaughter of Adrian Stokes, second husband of Frances Grey, mother of the Grey girls.

For Arbella, falling for the charms of Essex was undoubtedly a problem. Everyone knew that the queen would have no rivals.

Not that a twelve-year-old girl could be considered a rival to the queen or command the affection of a distinguished courtier, who had in 1584/6 performed military service under the Earl of Leicester and attained prominence by fighting against the Spanish in the Netherlands in 1586.

She was nevertheless young, enthusiastic and in love with the Earl of Essex. It must have been obvious to all in attendance, and this prompted various people to warn him of the queen's displeasure: he was told to divert his attentions elsewhere or fear being displaced. It had the desired effect. Essex had no wish to be displaced, so he could see no profit in wooing Arbella. Seeing the change in him, she felt dejected and deeply depressed. As she confided tearfully to her Aunt Mary, 'the Earl of Essex durst scarcely steal a salutation in the privy chamber where it pleased her majesty I should be disgraced in her presence.'

By the end of June it was clear that the offer of Arbella's marriage to Ranuccio Farnese was of no consequence and would not stop the Spanish fleet set to attack Britain. Elizabeth was frantically trying to conduct peace negotiations until 17 July, two days before the Armada was sighted off The Lizard, but Arbella's presence in court no longer had any significance. Some said it was because the offer of marriage was no longer valid or the fact that she could be taken hostage. Others said it was because of her childishly assumed airs or because she was mooning over Essex. It was most likely because she had served her purpose and the queen and council simply had no further use for her.

On 13 July Arbella left London, away from the danger and also away from the activity, and returned to South Wingfield Manor. As they travelled north that July, the Spanish Armada sailed up the English Channel and dropped anchor off Calais. Arbella had been an important figure in trying to prevent this attack, so if the Armada did land in Kent or sail up the Thames to take London, she might have been a target for the invading army.

That was quite a scary thought for a twelve-year-old, but South Wingfield Manor was an impregnable castle built to withstand attack. It was less than three years since it had been vacated by Mary, Queen of Scots, and in her solitude Arbella often felt her presence there.

In landlocked Derbyshire there was no hint of the possible invasion, and on the night of 28 July the Armada was scattered by an English fire ship attack. One of the ships involved was the two-hundred-ton, Shrewsbury-owned bark *Talbot*, with ninety men on board. The ship had been something of a financial burden to Shrewsbury, so he was quite happy to accept £900 in compensation for its loss. In the ensuing Battle of Gravelines the Spanish fleet was damaged, although the Armada managed to regroup and, driven by southwesterly winds, withdrew north with the English fleet harrying it up the east coast of England. The commander ordered a return to Spain, but the Armada was disrupted during severe storms in the North Atlantic, and a large portion of the vessels were wrecked on the coasts of Scotland and Ireland. Of the initial 130 ships, over a third failed to return.

In November, the month of the official victory celebrations, Arbella celebrated her thirteenth birthday at Wingfield Manor alone but for her servants. Nicolas Kinnersley, one of Bess's gentlemen stewards at Wingfield Manor, wrote to Bess at Hardwick informing her that Arbella was wild and out of hand and had refused to look at her schoolbooks for six days. Arbella had been at the heart of the court, surrounded by activity and intrigue, but since her return to Derbyshire she had been abandoned, alone and ill-informed. Everyone had forgotten her.[1]

Prompted by Kinnersley's missive, Bess arrived and took Arbella to Hardwick Hall, where she was just as isolated. Bess was living at the old hall, finishing off work started by her brother James who had been unable to finish what he had started. The place was like a building site as Bess was completing the top floor of the central block. Her solution was to employ tutors and insist that Arbella studied hard. Arbella was soon eager to return to South Wingfield Manor and the prospect of a new tutor, Thomas Morley, who became known as the 'singing man'. He had been attracted by the promise of an annuity of £40 a year but found himself unpaid and out of pocket. Looking for a means of making money, he took to spying for the Catholics but, it was later claimed, 'brought divers [people] into danger' by his indiscretions.[2]

Tutors always seemed to need to supplement their incomes. Earlier, Alexander Hamilton, a tutor of the younger Talbot children, was arrested on suspicion of carrying messages from Mary, Queen of Scots.

Arbella was unaware that she was still the subject of marriage negotiations, being (literally) mentioned in dispatches, in the conversations of ambassadors and reports of spies. Bess obviously realised and commissioned a full-length portrait of Arbella wearing a long white dress. In it, her skin looks unhealthily white – though that was considered beautiful by the standard of the times – and her hair hung loose as a symbol of virginity and eligibility for marriage. She wears a long rope of pearls, doubled and wrapped round her throat then brought forward and tied with a black ribbon that brought them to the centre so that they could cascade down to her waist. She wears pearl drops in her ears and a central drop in her hair. She didn't realise at the time, but Bess was still trying to reclaim the Lennox jewels for her. At the beginning of 1589, Burghley and Walsingham had reminded James about them, but had been put off.[3]

After hearing two different versions of their fate, at the third attempt they learnt that the jewels were detained by James, in recompense, he claimed, for legacies that he had never received from the old countess. Bess had been prodding Burghley to take action in this matter, and William Fowler, who seems to have felt guilty at the defalcation of his father, later made efforts to recover them.[4]

In the top-left hand corner of the portrait, above where her hand rests on a writing table, is a cartouche in which is written 'Arbella Stuart, Comitessa Leviniae Aetatis Sva 13 et', and the year 1589. It was a not so subtle reference to her lost title, just in case anyone should be labouring under the impression that Bess had accepted someone else now held it.

Arbella was moved between the unfinished old hall at Hardwick and the manor at South Wingfield. The family in general paid little attention to her welfare even when they were in residence at South Wingfield, which was rare. The Shrewsbury quarrels had long been a public scandal, and the family were permanently estranged by 1589. Bess was busy with her business interests and anxious to finish the building at the old Hardwick manor house.

News was received on 20 August 1589 that James of Scotland was to marry Anne of Denmark, daughter of King Frederick II and sister of Christian IV, King of Denmark, by proxy at ceremonies held simultaneously in Edinburgh and Denmark. Not only would he obtain a substantial sum from the English Privy Council, Anne was to bring him a dowry of 75,000 silver thalers, with an additional bridal gift of 150,000 more. Anne set off for Scotland in the care of the Earl Marshal, but the voyage ran into terrible storms that the admiral of the escorting Danish fleet blamed on witchcraft. Determined not to be thwarted by the evil powers, James left Scotland for the first time in his life and braved the supposed black arts. He arrived in Norway, where Anne had been cast ashore, and the wedding ceremony took place on 23 November.

The newly-weds spent that winter at the Danish royal court and arrived back in Scotland on 1 May 1590, but by this time James had become more interested in witchcraft than a wife. During his stay in Denmark he had been a witness at the witchcraft trials of six women who confessed that they had sent devils to climb up the keel of Queen Anne's ship, and had been guilty of sorcery in raising storms that menaced her voyage.

When James heard this, he decided to set up his own tribunal – the first major witchcraft persecution in Scotland. Very soon more than a hundred suspected witches in North Berwick were arrested. Many confessed under torture to having met with the Devil in the church at night and devoting themselves to doing evil, including poisoning the king and other members of his household, and sending storms in an attempt to sink the king's ship. The incident had given James a confidence in his own ability and he was convinced that few earthly princes had been permitted to put the Prince of Darkness to the test and defeat him. Apparently James learnt that the Devil had announced to the witches at North Berwick that the king was the greatest enemy he had in the world.[5]

James was sure that not only was he divinely ordained, he was unique in having divine protection, and in a series of trials that lasted two years he personally supervised the torture of over seventy women accused of being witches. James became obsessed with the threat posed by witches and inspired by his personal involvement in 1597 he wrote the *Daemonologie,* a tract opposed to the practice of witchcraft and which provided background material for William Shakespeare's *Tragedy of Macbeth*.

George Talbot, 6th Earl of Shrewsbury, died in November 1590 and his son and heir Gilbert became the 7th Earl. There arose new and different conflicts within the family. Bess was now the richest woman in England after the queen, and she immediately started building a new and magnificent hall within a few hundred yards of the first. Skilled and much sought-after craftsmen were hired and an overseer of the building appointed.[6]

The date of the start of the new build can be pinpointed almost exactly. The fortnight's accounts beginning on 26 October show ten labourers for the first week, increasing to twenty-three by 21 November. This sudden increase in labour was required for digging through to the bedrock of a bleak and windswept Derbyshire hilltop and laying the foundations.[7]

Materials were being accumulated: sandstone from the quarry at the base of the hill, alabaster from Tutbury, limestone from Skegby and Crich, timber from woods at Teversal, Pentrich and Heath. Chatsworth's neighbouring manor of Ashford-in-the-Water, which Bess and Sir William had bought in the 1550s from the Earl of Westmoreland, provided Bess with the black marble for fire surrounds and columns in the chapel. Everything was owned by Bess and came from within twenty miles of Hardwick, but as everything had to be hauled in carts pulled by oxen or carried on packhorses, it was a major project.

Hardwick Hall could not be called a prodigy house – one of those extraordinarily lavish constructions such as the aforementioned Theobalds, built by sycophantic courtiers to entertain the queen. Hardwick was a house of substance, a simple but ingenious platt (plan) based on a Greek cross, a rectangle surrounded by six turrets. To give shape to her vision Bess employed the services of Robert Smythson, who had worked on some of the most exuberant, inventive and romantic houses of sixteenth-century England. By the end of December, the fleaks or hurdles which formed a rudimentary scaffolding for the ground floor were in place. Bess was in her element. She had more in common with her architect and builder than she ever had with her husband, the late Earl of Shrewsbury.

Two features of Smythson's platt, unusual for its time, are the use of symmetry and glass. Both are displayed to maximum effect at Hardwick, which glories in great expanses of status-enhancing glass; the state rooms on the second floor are large and light due to the sheer amount. Medieval glass had been limited to the small-scale production of forest glass, and, although it remained extremely costly, the quality was vastly improved by the skills of French glassmakers, imported into Sussex in the 1560s. Bess used this knowledge to set up her own small-scale glasshouse at South Wingfield producing clearer glass than the forest glass with its characteristic variety of greenish-yellow colours.

The glasshouse and neighbouring ironworks were under the supervision of Sylvester Smith, who had the responsibility of turning wood ash and sand into window glass. The precious glass was then carefully packed and transported to Hardwick, where Richard Snidall, the glazier, was paid £290 for cutting and setting it in the metal window frames of the new hall. As Francis Bacon wrote: 'You shall sometimes have faire houses so full of glasse, that one cannot tell where to become to be out of the sunne or cold.'

The new hall was to have a suite for fourteen-year-old Arbella and her household on the first floor. Arbella occupied the comfortable bedchamber in the south-east turret with an unheated chamber for her lady-in-waiting, Bridget Shirland (now two bathrooms). Arbella called her chamber her 'quondam study'. Later it became known as the 'lawn room' as it overlooks the rear garden. The fire surround in this room displays Arbella's coat of arms.

Bess was confident that her granddaughter would be Queen Elizabeth's successor, so the new hall had to reflect the glories of the Cavendish dynasty – it had to be a building fit for the Queen of England.

9

MARRIAGE NEGOTIATIONS AND BROKEN PROMISES

In late summer of 1591 Arbella was again called down to London in another visit dictated by politics. The war in the Netherlands continued to sap England's resources, and because Elizabeth was reluctant to send more money and troops to the French king, it was decided to use Arbella again as an economical means to secure peace. This time the stay was going to be for eight months because Bess had to consult legal counsel over the highly public lawsuit that had been occasioned by the dispute over the Earl of Shrewsbury's legacy. She also needed to shop. The building of the new hall and the furnishing of the old hall demanded an extensive spending spree on splendid hangings and gold and silver plate.

The party that left Derbyshire for London on 18 October 1591 was a large one including William and Charles with their wives and servants. There were Bess's servants, ladies-in-waiting and personal maids, and Arbella's own personal maids, Mrs Abrahall and Mrs Digby. In total there were about forty people. They went by two heavy coaches, the ladies travelling within, the rest on horseback. The journey took seven days, allowing twenty miles per day, via Market Harborough, Dunstable and Barnet. It was slow progress owing to the heavy, lumbering and uncomfortable coaches. As they approached the important market towns, the bells rang out to welcome the travellers, and the party was entertained by musicians and players when they were put up at inns overnight.

Shrewsbury House at Chelsea was to be their headquarters for the next eight months. It was a great three-sided structure facing onto the river and surrounded by pastures. To feed the household, forty sheep and two oxen had been driven down from one of Bess's estates in Leicestershire and put to pasture in the neighbouring fields. Hasty building work had converted the stables into dormitories to house the extra staff, and revenues were diverted to Chelsea from some of Bess's distant estates.

The Duke of Parma was offered English support in exchange for a separate princedom in the Netherlands, ruled over by Ranuccio Farnese and Arbella. It was obviously a handsome offer, and the Duke of Parma asked to see Arbella's likeness. For convenience it had to be a miniature so that it could be carried easily and if necessary secretly; the best portrait painter of the time was the court painter Nicholas Hilliard.[1]

Thomas Barnes, who had the same task back in 1586 when the marriage negotiations were first opened, was the man trusted to negotiate this arrangement, and on 31 October 1591 Walsingham's right-hand man Thomas Phelippes drafted for Barnes a letter to Charles Paget, leader of the exiles in France, introducing himself as one 'sought as a practiser of a marriage between Arbella and the Duke of Palma's son'.[2]

At the same time, Michael Moody, another spy in the services of Walsingham, was interested in the Palma matter, but it was generally considered that Moody was too boastful a character to be given any real responsibility. His information was often out of date and 'such things that come to every man that harkens to news'.[3] He was warned to keep a guard on his tongue, but in

April 1592 it was reported to Cecil that Moody was engaged in promoting Arbella's marriage to Palma's son.[4]

Bess also considered it a good time to ask for an increase in Arbella's income. The £200 allowed for a baby princess was by no means adequate for a fifteen year old. Bess felt that Arbella's rank carried the right to a royal allowance. If her marriage to Ranuccio Farnese became reality, someone would have to provide a dowry and estates for her support; the queen could no longer avoid the issue.

That Christmas court was hosted at the royal palace at Whitehall. It had all the appurtenances for an impressive ceremonial, and was also the most public of all the royal palaces, for the main road from Westminster to the City ran right beneath the Holbein Gate. For entertainment it had a tennis court, tiltyard and cockpit. The privy garden had thirty-four coloured pillars on top of which sat thirty-four animals. In the centre was a sundial that told the time in thirty different ways and, to catch the unwary, a strong, multi-jetted fountain that could suddenly and unexpectedly start spraying. Queen Elizabeth's apartment overlooked the river.

Shrewsbury House was convenient for the court at Whitehall. It was only a short distance up the road to the City of London and conveniently situated by the river for access by water transport – upriver to Richmond Palace, downriver to Whitehall or to Greenwich. They had loan of the Bishop of Bristol's barge to move them to and fro on the river.

Once they were established at Chelsea and before they could make their debut at court the ladies needed new clothes. Fifty yards each of velvet, damask and satin were bought for their dresses. Discussion of the design and materials was an exciting distraction from the norm for all of them. Yards of black taffeta and cobweb lawn were bought for Bess, although the design of her dresses varied little. Tasker, the household's London tailor, was summoned to refurbish country wardrobes. Blue and white starches were bought to stiffen the lace collars and ruffs of the new fineries; the blue was a means of flattering the ladies complexions to make them appear whiter. Fine shoes of velvet, Spanish leather and neat's leather were purchased.

Two hundred pounds was spent on jewellery. Bess bought a pair of bracelets set with diamonds, pearls and rubies for £21, and a heavy gold chain worth £26. Johns, the queen's own tailor, was commissioned to make the magnificent dress designed for the queen as a New Year's gift. It cost £59 14s plus another £50 for embroidery.

The Shrewsbury party timed its first appearance in court to coincide with the twelve days of Christmas, commencing on Christmas Day. This was the great party of the year. Plays were put on in the banqueting hall, dancing, music and gaming were all mixed up with the official business of state and the nation. It is unlikely that the matter of Arbella's marriage was discussed during this period, although she had numerous sittings so that Hilliard could paint a miniature of her. The portrait cost £2, and Rowland Lockey was paid £1 to copy it. Until the Duke of Parma had given his answer, the finer points of the negotiations could not begin. They just had to wait.

Arbella only made occasional visits to the court, which had moved to Westminster by the end of January and by the end of February was situated at Richmond Palace. Elizabeth liked to spend time at Richmond as she enjoyed hunting stags in the neighbouring New Park; she was obviously not influenced by the fact that she was held prisoner there in 1554 on instructions from her sister Mary (though admittedly only for one night), who had that year become queen. Henry VII had built the palace in 1501 on the site of the former Sheen Palace and given it the name Richmond Palace after his earldom and his ancestral home, Richmond Castle in North Yorkshire. Richmond is a Norman name, *Riche Mont* meaning 'strong hill', which is not at all appropriate for the riverside setting of Richmond Palace. From Richmond the court went on one of the queen's progresses for the summer, to Osterley, Wimbledon, Croydon and Greenwich.

The circle of people Arbella was meeting was certainly more interesting than any she met in the country. Bess spent time with the lawyers who were sorting out the lawsuit that had resulted from the legalities after the Earl of Shrewsbury's death. That cost her £40. She also paid £321 16s to the heirs of the bankrupt Sir Christopher Hatton for seventeen Gideon tapestries, which would eventually line the long gallery at Hardwick Hall. She managed to get a £5 reduction because the Hatton arms needed to be replaced with her own. She had the arms re-embroidered but left his supporters, two does, thriftily transformed to two stags by the addition of antlers.

Just after Easter, more velvet and lace was purchased, along with pairs of perfumed gloves, Spanish leather shoes and a powdered ermine gown for Arbella. By June Bess was ready to leave London and get back to building her new Hardwick Hall; work had already been suspended eight months. She finally set off on 31 July, but Arbella stayed behind as no decision had yet been made regarding her marriage to Ranuccio Farnese.

One major stumbling block to the marriage going ahead was religion. Ranuccio was a Catholic and Arbella wasn't. Her Aunt Mary, with whom she spent so much time, had become a Catholic, much to the annoyance of her husband Gilbert, who had inherited the title 7th Earl of Shrewsbury on the death of his father. Mary was just one of the people who tried to influence Arbella to change religion, and rumours of her conversion were constantly being circulated. If Arbella had declared herself a Catholic, she would have attracted an enormous amount of support from Catholics at home and abroad. The temptation to adopt the old religion must have been immense, but she knew that it could also be disastrous. She had seen first-hand how it had wrecked the life of the Scottish queen, despite all the bold talk that it was necessary to restore England to its true faith.

The English Catholics hoped that James might be lured to convert, but James was quite happy to sit on the religious and political fence. The only thing that motivated him was his overwhelming desire to inherit the English throne, and he was not prepared to jeopardise that. Arbella was a different matter. The diverse influences of her background encouraged her to be a free thinker with no religious alliances through mere expediency. It bred in her a broad tolerance and genuine indifference to doctrinaire religious thought. In that she had the support of men like Sir Walter Raleigh and others who preferred to stay neutral.

On 15 October it was rumoured that Sir William Stanley, an English Catholic renegade living at the Spanish court, had warned a companion that two Scottish Catholic conspirators, John Semple and Herbert Rowlston, were going to kidnap Arbella and convey her by stealth out of England to Flanders and into Spain. Once she was in their keeping, Sir William Stanley, a descendant of the earls of Derby, would assist the organization of an armed assault on England by Spanish forces. When the 'Stanley Plot', as it became known, was successful, Arbella would be proclaimed queen.[5]

Well connected, able and energetic, Sir William Stanley soon became a leading figure amongst those Catholics who were eager to restore England to the faith. Rather surprisingly, Arbella was sent back to the comparative safety of Derbyshire. The fact that the Privy Council thought Derbyshire was a safe place for her seems quite ridiculous when in the last quarter of the sixteenth century, it was the epicentre of covert Catholic activities. This fresh wave of activity was partly due to the arrival of well educated and highly motivated men who were in fact disguised missionary priests. They found hiding places in the homes of sympathetic gentry within miles of Hardwick, and many ladies of the gentry and nobility soon found their old faith renewed by these persuasive young men.

Anthony Fitzherbert, a former judge under Henry VIII, was a leading Catholic, then in gaol for harbouring priests. He had a large and active family in the Derbyshire area, and he knew the Hardwick countryside well. He advised Rowlston and Semple on the best way to approach Hardwick and capture Arbella, but before the plans got underway, in August 1591 Semple was arrested in Flanders and shipped to England, where he was questioned. He revealed nothing about his mission but his capture blocked the kidnapping of Arbella.[6]

A month after Arbella left London, news reached Derbyshire that the Duke of Parma had died on 22 November 1592, at Arras. With him died any hope of an immediate peace in the Netherlands and Arbella's marriage to his son. Without his father's power Ranuccio Farnese was useless, so Arbella was to remain in Derbyshire until another suitable political gambit arose. As long as Elizabeth lived and the succession was left an open question, refusing to name her heir gave the queen plenty of room for political manoeuvre.

The possibility of a marriage to Ranuccio Farnese was over and the Stanley Plot had been foiled, yet many still tried to persuade Arbella to become a Catholic and reinstate the Catholic Church in England, sharing the throne with a suitable Catholic husband. Henry Percy, who inherited the title 9th Earl of Northumberland on the death of his father in 1585, sought her for his wife. The Percys were powerful Catholics and wielded great influence in the North, where their family seat was Tynemouth Castle in Northumberland. Queen Elizabeth knew the Percys as potential troublemakers with a family history of plotting and double-dealing. Henry's mild deafness and slight speech impediment did not prevent him from becoming an important cultural and intellectual figure for his generation, and although he was a grandee and one of the wealthiest peers of the court of Elizabeth, Henry Percy had no cause to love the Protestant ruler of England.

There were rumours that Henry Percy and Arbella were secretly married, and more dangerous were the rumours that any day he would proclaim her queen and restore England to the old faith. Arbella had nothing against Henry Percy personally, although he did show an unhealthy interest in alchemy and science. Because scientific instruments and witchcraft were considered synonymous, his dabbling in the realms of the unknown earned him the sobriquet 'the Wizard Earl'. Despite all the rumours, Arbella didn't marry the Wizard Earl; in 1594, he married Dorothy Devereux, sister of Milord Essex.

Arbella was used to Bess consulting the oracle, and it was no secret that the queen had her own consultant, the remarkable John Dee, the noted mathematician, astronomer, astrologer, occultist, navigator and imperialist who also devoted much of his life to the study of alchemy, divination, and Hermetic philosophy. Dee straddled the worlds of science and magic just as they were becoming distinguishable and was one of the most learned men of his age. A respected astronomer as well as a leading expert in navigation, John Dee trained many of the men who conducted England's voyages of discovery. His status as a respected scholar also allowed him to play a role in Elizabethan politics, nurturing relationships with Walsingham and Cecil. Simultaneously with these efforts, Dee immersed himself in the worlds of magic, astrology, and Hermetic philosophy. He devoted much time and effort attempting to commune with angels in order to learn the universal language of Creation and bring about the pre-apocalyptic unity of mankind. He did not draw distinctions between his mathematical research and his investigations into Hermetic magic, angel summoning and divination.

In 1594 Arbella's personal servant, Mrs Abrahall, left to take up a position in a more lively household. Arbella would have liked the chance to go, too, but when this was suggested to the queen she was emphatic that Arbella stayed at Hardwick where she knew she would be safe. As a reason for her continuing to live within the limits of Derbyshire, this was wearing rather thin after some five years. While Arbella sat at Hardwick amongst her books, other candidates were corresponding, manipulating, offering, doing deals and demonstrating royal authority.

In 1594, when a book entitled *A Conference about the Next Succession to the Crown of England* was published in Antwerp, it caused quite a stir. It was written under the pen name 'Doleman', purportedly expressing the opinions of gentlemen of diverse nations, qualities and affections, although the author behind the name and the opinions expressed within were generally accepted as being the leading Jesuit commentator and agitator, Father Parsons. Despite its subtle impartiality, it was highly controversial and was banned in England during Elizabeth's reign, but it did surreptitiously filter into English circles.

The first part of the book was devoted to a discussion on what constituted a claim to the throne, supported by examples from ancient history. Doleman claimed that primogeniture and nearness of blood were not the first requisites, and because the parliamentary Third Act of Succession 1544 mentioned no heir after Elizabeth and her children (if any), the Crown should be allocated because of suitability rather than lineage.

Doleman studied the family line of Henry VIII's younger sister Mary, which he described as tainted stock and piously averted his eyes from contemplating their position on the throne of England. He also dealt with the Plantagenet claimants that included the son of the Duchess of Palma and the infanta, described as 'a princess of rare parts, both for beauty, wisdom and piety'.

He then studied the family line of Henry VIII's older sister Margaret who had married into the Scottish royal family. This raised several important issues; the 1547 will of Henry VIII prevented his Scottish relatives from succeeding to the throne, and the Statute of Association, formed in October 1584, disallowed the claim and legal rights of any person who might conspire, depose or connive to depose Queen Elizabeth. Although this applied directly to Mary, Queen of Scots, who had been executed in 1587 for her involvement in Catholic assassination plots against Elizabeth, this should also have stopped James, as Mary's son and potential beneficiary of her actions, from inheriting the Crown and its estates.

Doleman also pointed out that since 1351 foreigners were forbidden to inherit English lands, so the fact that James was born in Scotland should have further blocked him from inheriting the Crown and its estates. This impediment was acknowledged by both the Protestants and Catholics, and in English law James's claim was therefore very uncertain. (Robert Cecil, Secretary of State, abolished this law in 1606, three years after James became king). Doleman then attacked James's pedigree. As he was descended from the third discredited marriage of John of Gaunt to his mistress Katherine Swinford, he maintained that her issue were illegitimate and banned by law from inheriting the throne. Doleman maintained that James had very little support in England. His only advantages seemed to be that he was male and already a monarch. After forty years of spinster rule, a male monarch offered a welcome return to what many people considered to be normality. James was a married man with a young family that promised long-term dynastic stability.

Rather surprisingly, no serious effort was ever made to stigmatise James despite bastardy being a frequent allegation. His parents were first cousins, and prior to 1560 it was illegal for first cousins to marry. The papal dispensation permitting the marriage of cousins did not arrive until after his birth in 1545.[7]

Doleman turned his attention to Arbella, ten years younger than her cousin James and sharing the same royal grandmother, Meg Lennox. Arbella Stuart was English-born and therefore exempt from the 1351 statute forbidding monarchs not born in England. But Arbella's claim to the throne was scrutinised and found lacking when Doleman found bastardy twice against her great-grandmother Margaret Tudor.

He also pointed out that she was not allied to the nobility, except to the Earl of Shrewsbury, so there was no band of kinsmen to promote or follow her. Her kindred on her father's side were Scottish, so she had only the Cavendishes, who were a mean family for a princess. It was his opinion that to see them so greatly elevated might cause considerable resentment. Doleman stated that Arbella's religion was no great motive either for or against her. Presumably being young and unmarried, she was tender, green and flexible, and he suggested that by her marriage she could join some other title with hers to gain support.

According to Doleman, Arbella seemed to be the obvious successor to Queen Elizabeth; but as the years passed Arbella's life was becoming more isolated from her own generation. It was quite normal for a girl of Arbella's station to live with her closest relative until a husband of equal wealth and rank had been selected for her. It was just so frustrating that Arbella's closest relative was her elderly grandmother Bess. Although she had the power and wealth to choose a husband for her granddaughter, her hands were tied. She respected the queen's wish to avoid making any matrimonial arrangements, but there was no indication that any new marriage proposals were being considered by the queen, who wouldn't play her ace in the hole. Arbella begged her grandmother to talk to the queen about this. She did, but it made no difference: the queen was in no hurry to make a selection. Despite the frustration, Bess and Arbella had no choice but to await the royal summons.

Arbella still received the kind of rigorous, classical education enjoyed by only the most high-ranking young women, and one that had certainly not been available to her grandmother Bess. Her education was fit for a queen. Learning was encouraged and Queen Elizabeth was considered a role model. Arbella had lessons in French, Italian, Spanish, Hebrew, Greek and Latin and in later years would no doubt have learned from the great philosopher Thomas Hobbes, tutor and friend to the household. He favoured a method of double translating, turning one language into another then back again. Arbella's uncle William Cavendish promised his eleven-year-old son William a rapier, a dagger, an embroidered girdle and a pair of spurs if he would speak to Arbella in Latin until Lent Assizes next. For recreation, Arbella studied music, dancing and played the lute, viol and virginals. She called her books her 'dead counsellors and comforters', but they were poor consolation when life was passing her by.

In 1596 Arbella came of age and her grandmother Bess presented her with land and property, which gave her the opportunity to be independent and run her own household. She was not yet betrothed, which was a source for constant rumours, but the responsibility for her marriage rested with the queen and her advisers.

She was still held in considerable regard abroad, and there was every possibility that she would marry a foreigner with the English crown as her dowry. There was a popular rhyme at the time: 'After hempe is sown and grown, King's of England shall be none.' To speak of the downfall of the English throne was treason, but this was a thinly disguised reference: 'Hempe' was to be read as the initials of the Tudor monarchs, Henry, Edward, Mary & Philip, and Elizabeth. The royal families of Europe were inextricably entangled and all the great names of Europe were at one time coupled with Arbella's, but the catalogue of husbands invariably took no account of her feelings.

Cardinal Farnese, brother of Ranuccio Farnese, was suggested by the Pope, who was prepared to release the cardinal from his vows of celibacy in order for him to marry Arbella. Nothing came of this plan. In 1599 Duke Mathias, the brother of Cardinal Archduke Albert of Austria, heir to the Holy Roman Empire, was proposed. Albert had married the former Spanish Infanta Isabel and together they ruled the Netherlands. This liaison did not please Elizabeth and it was rumoured that in retaliation she wanted to ally England and France against Spain.

There were speculations that Arbella was to marry the Prince of Condé, nephew of King Henry IV of France. Henry had freed himself from his barren first wife, Marguerite de Valois, and as his mistress was dead there were rumours that he intended to make Marie de Medici, niece of the Grand Duke of Tuscany, his queen. Then it was said that 'the marriage treaty between the French King and the great Duke [Tuscany] cools, for the Queen of England has promised a near cousin of her own, whom she loves much and who she intends to make her heir and successor'.[8]

Elizabeth was again using Arbella as she had once used her own person, to sweeten the relationship with a foreign power. The notion of an English Queen of France and England was a prospect that appealed to Elizabeth. Arbella's uncle Gilbert Talbot was a friend of the King of France, and although Arbella had never been to France, she spoke the language fluently and admired French literature.

It seemed almost certain that Arbella was about to marry the French king and take the English throne, but King Henry of France was not so sure. He'd heard Elizabeth's promises before, and Marie de Medici had one undeniable advantage: her Medici wealth, which was a definite attraction when weighed against an uncertain promise. He told his minister Sully:

I should have no objection to the Infanta of Spain, however old and ugly she might be, provided that with her I marry the Low Countries; neither would I refuse the Princess Arbella of England, if, since it is publically said the crown of England really belongs to her, she were only declared presumptive heiress of it. But there is no reason to expect either of these things will happen, for the Spanish King and the English queen are far from making such plans.[9]

However, Henry did not want to lose sight of the bride and offered one of his bastard sons as the groom. Sir John Harington perhaps expressed the general opinion with the words, 'A goodly young lady, aged about twenty-four years should be so disparaged as to be matched with a bastard of France under fourteen.'[10]

IO

CUNNING AND DECEIT

In 1596, Essex became a national hero when he shared command of the expedition that captured Cadiz from the Spanish. The following year, he was joined by Sir Walter Raleigh and Charles Blount, who on the death of his unmarried older brother William, in 1594, had inherited the title 8th Baron Mountjoy. Arbella had met Charles Blount, 8th Baron Mountjoy, at court, where the favours that his natural good looks procured for him from Queen Elizabeth aroused the jealousy of Essex. This led to a duel between the two hot-headed young courtiers – who later became close friends.

Their expedition to intercept the Spanish treasure fleet off the Azores failed, but it was rumoured that it was fixed to discredit Essex; and no one wanted that more than Robert Cecil. They had both been brought up in the household of William Cecil, Lord Burghley, Master of Court from 1561. Robert Cecil was his son, Essex his ward, and their dislike for each other was notorious. The feuding boys had grown into feuding men who clashed at every turn. It wasn't helped by their rivalry for power and the queen's uncertain favour. Essex represented noble and martial valour: he was impulsive, an adventurer and a charmer. His relationship with Elizabeth was amorous, dramatic and tempestuous. There were many quarrels but his charm ensured that she continued to grant him royal favours. Being the queen's favourite had made Essex many enemies amongst the Privy Council, the greatest among them Robert Cecil.

Increasingly as Cecil rose in prominence, Essex sought pre-eminence. Cecil was essentially a career courtier: cautious, undemonstrative and sly. He made sure that letters on every conceivable matter came regularly and frequently from his agents all over England and the Continent. No man in England knew more than he and, more important, he knew how to use the precise and detailed knowledge placed in his hands. His mind was essentially cunning rather than creative.

Essex returned from Cadiz to find that Cecil had succeeded to his ageing father's position and now wielded major influence and control over the queen and the royal court. Age hadn't mellowed them, and the two men who had been brought up in the same household now faced each other across the council table as sworn enemies. With the help of Anthony and Francis Bacon, Essex set up his own intelligence service in direct competition with Cecil's, and in July 1597 received news that English exiles in Munich were planning to kidnap Arbella and convey her out of England. Nothing come of it, but for showing his diligence Essex became on good terms with Arbella's uncle Gilbert Talbot, 7th Earl of Shrewsbury.

There was still a lot of interest in Arbella and the question of who would succeed the ageing Elizabeth, who remained obdurately silent on the topic of her succession. This was one matter on which Cecil was not able to sway the queen, and he had warned James that the queen might 'cut off the natural branch and graft upon some wild stock'. In 1600, Thomas Wilson, a member of Cecil's staff, compiled a list of possible candidates in a publication entitled *The State of England, Anno Dom. 1600*. He also made the rather obvious remark that 'the crown is not like to fall to the ground for want of heads that claim to wear it, but upon whose head it will fall is by many doubted'.

In 1600 the Fugger Newsletters were referring to Arbella as successor to the throne and heir to the English kingdom. In February 1601, they stated that the queen had issued a decree excluding James, 'so that she could transmit her crown to one of her blood relatives and assure her of undisputed possession'.[1] A bill was immediately drafted to prevent the publication of any more succession theories, but it was secretly rumoured that Cecil now favoured the infanta. Her proximity in the Netherlands encouraged those who wished to press her claim, and that included all those who were Catholic at heart. With Cecil's support her following would be in the millions – a huge foreign army that at a moment's notice was ready to ride into London.

Needless to say, if Cecil was supporting the infanta, Essex was determined to place his allegiance elsewhere. He favoured James of Scotland, who, consumed by his ambition to succeed Elizabeth, was increasingly showing signs of frustration. Essex sent his sister as an intermediary, but James made it quite clear that he preferred the brother to the sister.

He welcomed Essex's friendship and support, and it is believed that in a moment of rashness James told Essex about the money he received from the English government. It was categorised as his entitlement from the English estates of his grandmother, Meg, Countess of Lennox, that had remained with the English Crown. This obviously gave Essex the idea that if James was given the English lands instead of the payments, the possession of estates in England would make him an English landowner and would counteract the charge that he was a foreigner and ineligible to succeed. At Essex's suggestion James impudently asked the queen for these lands, but Elizabeth was not prepared to negotiate and gave his delegates short though polite shrift.

After the death of William Cecil in 1598, his son Robert Cecil became the queen's principal Secretary of State and most influential privy councillor. His wife Elizabeth (*née* Brooke) had died the previous year, and it was said that Robert Cecil was considering Arbella as his new wife. Robert Cecil had never previously shown any interest in her, and Arbella didn't want or need his attention. She was horrified at the prospect of being his wife, but Robert Cecil was ambitious and possessed great power and influence. He was undoubtedly the most influential English privy councillor and, like many of his contemporaries, he was friendless and formidable. Though he could be quite treacherous, he served the queen with an ardent determination. He was free to re-marry, and if he could persuade the queen to allow him to marry Arbella, there was nothing and no-one standing in the way but divine intervention.

It was soon reported that 'Sir R Cecil intends to be king by marrying Arbella, and now lacks only the name ... Lord Shrewsbury who can remove the blocks from the way of the marriage is for him, thinking he can't better establish his house.'[2] Known as 'the great survivor', the queen referred to Robert Cecil affectionately as 'my elf' or 'my pigmy' due to his uncommon appearance (the handicap of a malformation of the spine had retarded his growth, humped his back and splayed his legs). One contemporary at the time described him:

A slight, crooked, hump back young gentleman, dwarfish in stature, but with a face not irregular in feature, and thoughtful and subtle in expression, with reddish hair, a thin, tawny beard and large, pathetic greenish-coloured eyes, with a mind and manners already trained to court and cabinet. Apart from the gross deformity of his body, his head was overlarge with a high, square forehead, this proud and terrible hunchback who would virtually rule England.[3]

It was only a matter of time before it became common knowledge that Cecil was seeking Arbella's hand in marriage. He was showing excessive friendship towards Arbella's uncle Gilbert, the 7th Earl of Shrewsbury and the only influential relative that Arbella had. Arbella made it very clear that she had no desire to be joined in matrimony with Cecil, but she knew she could do nothing if it was the queen's wish. She must have been grateful that once again the queen remained silent on the matter.

In 1598 almost 1,000 English soldiers were massacred at the Battle of Yellow Ford in Ireland. Subsequently, in 1599 Essex was appointed Lord Lieutenant of Ireland and was sent to lead a campaign to put down a rebellion by the Earl of Tyrone. Essex set off at the head of a massive army, but the mood was pessimistic, particularly as it was rumoured that the Spanish were getting involved on the side of the Irish. Many had tried and failed to subdue the Irish, and throughout the Tudor period Ireland had remained a trouble spot. Essex's father had died there, trying to claim Ulster for the English and Protestant colonists. Powerful Irish Catholic lords under the Earl of Tyrone had been in open rebellion since the middle of the 1590s, and Essex's ensuing campaign was so disastrous that three-quarters of his men were killed without even engaging with the main body of the enemy.

Against orders, Essex agreed a truce with Tyrone, then abandoned his post to return to London to explain to the queen in person. He reached the court at 10.00 a.m., brushed his way through the layers of courtiers and forced his way into the queen's bedchamber, where she was in a state of undress. This was unpardonable conduct, but as the queen's favourite he assumed all his misdeeds would be forgiven. Contrary to all his expectations, instead of listening and appreciating his position, the queen was not prepared to forgive his behaviour. Essex was immediately deprived of his offices and placed under house arrest at York House. The queen's favourite was out of favour and there was no royal pardon.

Unable to believe that Elizabeth was inflicting such punishment on him, Essex was convinced that he was being penalized by Cecil and other factions conspiring against him in the Privy Council. He became paranoid in this belief – but he was not without reason. He knew that Cecil genuinely hated him and had been looking for a way to get rid of him, and he also knew that Cecil was a cunning and bent character. In retaliation, Essex decided to rid his queen of the self-interested councillors surrounding her. Essex and his supporters thus planned a coup and appealed to James of Scotland for armed support. It was not forthcoming. James may have enjoyed Essex's friendship, but he was not prepared to alienate Cecil or Elizabeth and lose the English crown.

But Essex held a trump card – or so he thought. He knew that between 1586 and 1600 James of Scotland had received £58,500 sterling from the Privy Council and Cecil. Most of that money did not pass through the hands of government officers and detailed records were not kept. This should have been enough to permanently disgrace Cecil and put him out of office, but it didn't. Neither did the fact that in 1596 James' efforts to have himself declared heir apparent to the English throne had culminated in a formal alliance named the Treaty of Berwick. Despite the fact that the whole succession was fixed, it was argued that the Privy Council were simply taking every precaution to ensure stability.

Essex had misjudged and mismanaged the issue. So, in typical swashbuckling fashion, he took to the streets in an attempt to raise the people of London in revolt against the government. Essex and his supporters, a band of brothers, many related by blood, were aroused by the old and noble code of honour; but it was not enough. Cecil was in charge and there followed reprisals that Cecil used with great cunning to remove most of his enemies for good. Essex was imprisoned in the Tower, and at his trial for treason on 1 February 1601, he and his colleagues were found guilty. After the sentence of execution was passed on Essex, he said to the judges,

'Although you have condemned me in a court of judgement, yet in the court of conscience you would absolve me.'[4]

It was now clear that Cecil was undeniably in charge and was running the country. Essex was executed for treason on Ash Wednesday, 25 February 1601. He had always been a favourite of the people, and they were unforgiving of Cecil, who was publicly blamed for his downfall; no one could understand why the queen had allowed Essex to die. She was openly criticised for her hardness of heart. One of Bess's neighbours, Sir John Byron of Newstead Abbey, wrote to Bess saying that at their local town of Mansfield, there was a lot of anger against Cecil. The townsfolk had labelled him 'Robin with the bloody breast', and armed vengeance was threatened.[5]

It was probably this show of aggression by the townsfolk of Mansfield that prevented Cecil promoting any further matrimonial ties between himself and Arbella. The people of her local town would not have viewed the alliance favourably – his appearance might prompt a lynch mob. Cecil was detested, and the people were growing weary of an old woman's rule. The queen's public appearances were no longer greeted with the old jubilation.[6]

James of Scotland must have panicked when he heard about the execution of Essex, and in April 1601 he sent two envoys south to repair what he considered the damaged relations caused by Essex's revolt. Cecil immediately indicated his willingness to cooperate in making James the recognised heir to Elizabeth, and an exchange of coded letters began. This was official malfeasance – a secret correspondence with a foreign monarch was a treasonable offence – but Cecil was so sure of himself that he considered this held no threat for him. In the correspondence, Cecil was referred to as '10', Elizabeth '24', James '30'.

James was reassured by his new-found alliance. Although Elizabeth remained silent on the succession, once James had clandestinely joined forces with Robert Cecil, all other possibilities seemed systematically closed off. Even though Elizabeth had previously refused to openly acknowledge any payments, she wrote to James in May 1601, indicating he would get an extra £2,000 per annum – a substantial increase on top of what he already received. James was secretly the King of England by prior arrangement.

Arbella was an important figure in the tide of intrigue that ebbed and flowed at the royal court, but she hardly left Derbyshire. She continued to live at Hardwick, withdrawing to her study chamber where she strained her eyes reading by rushlight during the long evenings. She learnt Greek and Hebrew: Greek was an unusual accomplishment for a woman, but with Hebrew Arbella put herself amongst the advanced scholars of Europe.

By playing the part the queen and Bess had assigned to her, Arbella's existence was more constrained than ever. She had no company of her own age and rank, no one who could share her fears and hopes. When her name was mentioned, they could only speculate and make statements about her that were rarely confirmed; this applied particularly to her religion. She should have had an agent to promote her and provoke public interest in her, but she didn't. Arbella always maintained a low profile. She should have had someone who could report on her daily pastimes, her accomplishments, her skill at hunting and hawking, her brilliance at conversation, but she didn't. Her accomplishments were only known by her family, and a few local friends. Arbella had no family support on the scale that previous queens had enjoyed. Anne Boleyn and Jane Seymour had had the estimable Howards and Seymours; she had no one and nothing but long, lonely years. She was, in short, uninformed and unhappy. Her only advocate was the cynical and capricious queen.

She was twenty-seven, and had been walled up at Hardwick for more than thirteen years. She had become a prisoner, buried alive. The rest of the country, the rest of the world in fact, had forgotten her. Even to contemporaries, her treatment seemed exceptional. As Harington said, 'We are not likely to be governed by a lady shut up in a chamber from all her subjects and most of her servants, and seen but on holy days.'

When Bess was twenty-seven she was a mother and had been married twice. By the time Elizabeth reached twenty-seven she had been queen two years. When Mary, Queen of Scots, was twenty-seven, she had been twice married, a mother, and made Queen of Scotland and France. A century earlier Arbella may have had the opportunity to enter a nunnery, but hers was a culture that saw marriage as the only successful destiny for a woman. She was expressing years of frustration when she wrote 'shall my hands be bound for helping myself in this distress?' It was desperation that made her decide finally to take her destiny in her own hands. It was a hopeless gamble, made by one who had little to lose and no other options.

11

A VIRTUAL PRISONER AT HARDWICK FOR THIRTEEN YEARS

Bess had never been good at showing emotion, so when she stepped in to sort out her granddaughter, her answer was to set Arbella to work, to give her something to do that would take her mind off things. Bess's time and energy were taken up with the profitable running of her many enterprises, and although Arbella did not share her fascination for building, she did enjoy watching the work as it progressed. Work on the old hall was complete, with its new wings of tall, grandiose proportions grafted onto the old core, but Bess was also building two more houses, the new hall at Hardwick and a much smaller house at Owlcotes (Oldcotes) near Heath, just three miles away and visible from the roof walk at Hardwick.

People have often queried why she decided to build Owlcotes and why she gave it that name. The public perception she preferred to nurture was that it was to give her son William and his family a home near Hardwick. William Cavendish was thirty when he married Anne Keighley, in 1582, the same year that Elizabeth Cavendish died, leaving Arbella a seven-year-old orphan. Possibly Anne was a substitute mother for Arbella, although they spent a great deal of time at their London house in Holborn with William looking after Bess's business interests in the capital. When in

Derbyshire they stayed at Hardwick Hall, where the school room was below Bess's drawing room; during the 1590s, Hardwick must have bustled with family life. Bess might have found this noisy, young family too boisterous, and so decided to build Owlcotes.

After giving birth to three sons and three daughters, of which only his son William and daughter Frances survived, William's first wife Anne died in February 1598, before Owlcotes was completed. There is no indication that the widowed William ever moved out of Hardwick. Bess's accounts in 1599 show the charges for the full furnishing of Owlcotes, so William may have moved there later with his second wife Elizabeth Wortley (*née* Broughton), whom he married in 1604.

There's a story that Bess built Owlcotes out of spite, right on the boundary of Sutton Scarsdale, the land of the elderly Sir Francis Leake, a cousin on her mother's side. Leake at the time was building a new splendid hall, itself completed around 1595, commanding views over the valley. The original hall at Sutton had formed part of a Saxon estate owned by Wulfric Spott, who died in 1002 and left the estate to Burton Abbey. In the Domesday Book the estate was owned by Roger de Poitou, and in 1225 the lordship of Sutton-in-the-Dale had been given to Peter de Hareston. An heiress of Robert de Hareston brought it to Richard de Grey, and a coheiress brought it to the Leake family in the reign of Henry IV; a later John Leake was made a knight by Henry VIII. The Leake family were the largest landowners in the Scarsdale one hundred of Derbyshire, and Sutton Scarsdale Hall became their main family seat.

It was just unfortunate for Bess that John Leake's son, Francis Leake, was not a charitable neighbour. He was a difficult man and a ruthless landlord who frequently quarrelled with others, including his cousin Henry Leake at Codnor, and Bess. He was not averse to throwing insults and belittling people, knowing that the Leakes could trace their ancestors back to the Norman conquest.

If the account is to be believed, apparently he went just that little bit too far when he reminded Bess of this and pointed out that she was from base stock. That was enough to make Bess a foe for life. He also made disparaging remarks about Hardwick's lofty position on the exposed ridge being better suited to owls than men. The comment perhaps possessed some truth, but Bess saw it as a personal insult to her, and in a fit of anger she decided to build another mansion in the valley on the very edge of Sir Frances' land, not half a mile from Sutton Scarsdale Hall. Her chosen site was an old carboniferous forest where owls lived, often in old hawk or squirrel nests or in tree cavities. Bess then announced that she would build a house, 'as splendid for owls as his house was for men', and she called it Owlcotes. It wasn't just built in a pique to show off: she wanted to teach Sir Frances a lesson he would never forget. Owls were considered to be birds of ill omen, generally disliked and feared in popular folklore; she was putting a curse on the old man.

Just as perfidy was penalized, loyalty was rewarded. Some of Bess's workmen had been with her since the building of Chatsworth House. Thomas Accres had worked for her since 1576. Abraham Smith had first come to her at Chatsworth in 1581. Both had leases of farms from Bess. Smith had fifty-five acres at Ashford-in-the-Water, where the blackstone used for the overmantles came from; it was at his farm at Ashford-in-the-Water where he had devised an engine to cut the blackstone and the sandstone that was quarried below Hardwick Hall. There was John Balechouse, known as 'Painter' for obvious reasons. He worked with Renold Plumtree and Robert Ashmore. Bess also wrote to Sir John Thynne at Longleat asking if he could 'spare me your plasterer that flowereth your hall'. Skilled craftsmen like Thomas Accres the stonemason and Abraham Smith the plasterer were in great demand and moved around the country working for various patrons. They were all craftsmen whose work has been admired over the centuries.

Although it would take another two years to add the finishing touches and furnish Hardwick Hall, when John Good had finished laying the matting in the long gallery, Bess decided that the hall was ready for occupancy. She dressed seventy-four servants in her stylish blue livery in readiness for the move into the new hall, and on Tuesday 4 October 1597, to an accompaniment of musicians, Hardwick Hall was officially declared finished and the family moved into their new home. There were fourteen principal bedchambers; servants slept on truckle beds or temporary pallets in the passages to be on hand, while yeomen and gentlemen slept in the old house, which acted as an annex.

Mary Talbot, Countess of Shrewsbury, who was at court at the time, informed the queen of the move. She then suggested that as Arbella now had a household of my own, could her two oldest daughters be appointed maids-in-waiting to their cousin Arbella? The right to have maids of honour was granted only to the heir presumptive, and the furious queen ordered the Talbot family home immediately. It was a blunt answer.

Now that Hardwick Hall was officially completed, a lot of the workmen moved on. Bess kept her most skilled masons because Owlcotes needed completing, and she began making plans to build almshouses at Derby, the building of which commenced in the spring of 1598. Work was completed in March 1600 and the first twelve lodgers moved in. One of them, Isabell Heyward, had been a servant of Bess. Each received 33s 4d (£1.66) and a livery upon arrival.

By 1600, the building of Owlcotes was also completed, and in April 1601 Bess decided to enlist Arbella's help in making a new will. She bequeathed to Arbella £1,000, a crystal glass cup set with lapis lazuli and precious stones, her sable and her pearls. She left the queen £200 to buy a gold cup and a request for her to take Arbella back to court and find her a husband. She reminded the queen that Arbella had been taught all the skills necessary for a lady and wife of a great man. The family chaplain, the Reverend James Starkey, witnessed Bess's will and the letter to the queen dated April 1601.[1] At the same time, Bess decided to have a full inventory made. It's possible that this task was also undertaken by Arbella, giving her the responsibility for all the sorting, categorising and cataloguing of Bess's houses and their contents.[2]

Arbella may have been assisted by James Starkey, who would have shown more concern and pity for Arbella than Bess or anyone else in the family. They often prayed together, read together and, when the weather was fine, walked together. They frequently spoke for hours on end, but the restricted company at the remote Hardwick encouraged small talk and idle gossip, and soon rumours were rife that Starkey and Arbella were more than just friends. She must have resented this, as she didn't have a real friend and desperately needed one.

In October, the family were making plans to go to London to attend a family wedding. Arbella's cousin Elizabeth Talbot, middle daughter of her Aunt Mary and Gilbert Talbot, 7th Earl of Shrewsbury, was marrying Sir Henry Grey of Ruthin at St Martin-in-the-Fields on 16 November. Born in 1582, Elizabeth was seven years younger than Arbella, which no doubt caused slight resentment on Arbella's part. She was twenty-seven and for the last thirteen years had been living with her aged grandmother, who by that age had entered her second marriage. At twenty-seven and unmarried Arbella was still being 'bobbed [smacked] and her nose played with which she could not endure'. Not that Henry Grey was such a great catch. Lord Henry Howard considered the match ill-advised, partly because 'the young gentleman is of my Lord Simple's house, and as silly as his father-in-law is shrewd'. It's difficult to know how seriously to take this remark. Grey was not necessarily deficient in intelligence or a fool, but may have been slow-witted and immature.

That Easter – in 1602, the first week in March – Arbella poured out her troubles to William Starkey, the household chaplain. She told him that she found her existence insupportable and was looking for a way to escape: 'She would use all the means she could to get from thence by reason she was hardly used, plagued and the butt of despiteful and disgraceful words.' She wanted a normal life but was denied it. As an unmarried woman, she had few opportunities in a culture that saw marriage as the only option for a woman in her class. Now she begged Starkey for his help and promised she would make him her chaplain. Starkey took pity on Arbella. He had noticed her state of nervous tension and depression, how 'being at her books, she would break forth into tears'.[3]

James Starkey was a kind man. He felt that the queen had used and abused Arbella most cruelly, and he also nursed a grievance. William Cavendish had taken him into the household with the promise of a living and a parish, but William's reputation for meanness was well known and well founded. Alongside his duties as household chaplain James Starkey was also expected to be tutor to William's children, Gilbert, William, James and Frances. He had spent eight years at Hardwick in regular contact with the family but was still without his promised living. Starkey found Hardwick and the meanness of William Cavendish unbearable and, by 1602, was planning to leave. The decision may have been due to William junior needing a more advanced tutor or being sent off to Eton like his father.

There is every possibility that whilst doing the inventory, amongst a pile of papers Arbella and Starkey discovered letters written by a London solicitor named Edward Kyrton, representing Sir Edward Seymour, 1st Earl of Hertford. Arbella may have dismissed the correspondence as something that could have happened forty years previously, when in 1562 the young Queen Elizabeth was critically ill with smallpox. With no obvious heir to the English throne, the situation had been serious and the country in crisis. The nobles had been in disagreement as to who would inherit, and there had been much plotting amongst themselves (as covered in Chapter One).

But on closer inspection, the correspondence that Arbella and Starkey found was more recent and dated from 1599. The situation had changed little. Queen Elizabeth was now old but there was still no obvious heir to the English throne, and the nobles were again plotting amongst themselves as to who would succeed Elizabeth. In 1598, the French envoy had reported to his master that the young men of the court grew restless under the petticoat government of an ageing woman. They would not submit to another female after being ruled for forty years by the unmarried Elizabeth I, but not everyone was anxious to have James VI of Scotland as the English king.

As Arbella read the letters, it became obvious that the Earl of Hertford and a small number of courtiers, anxious to prevent a Scot inheriting the throne of England, were planning a native Seymour/Stuart match that would strengthen the joint claims of Edward Seymour and Arbella Stuart to the throne of England.

THE STORY OF THE SISTERS JANE AND KATHERINE GREY

To understand the situation, it is necessary to go back to Mary Tudor (1498–1533), the youngest daughter of Henry VII (1455–1509) and Elizabeth of York (1466–1503), founders of the Tudor dynasty. Mary Tudor became the third wife of King Louis XII of France; after his death, she moved back to the English court of her brother Henry, where she fell for the charms of Charles Brandon, Duke of Suffolk (1487–1545). Brandon's father had been Henry VII's standard-bearer at the Battle of Bosworth Field and died defending the future king.

Henry VII repaid his loyalty by educating young Brandon with his own children, Arthur, Henry, Margaret and Mary. Charles formed a close friendship with Henry that lasted all their lives, ensuring him a succession of offices in the royal household and many valuable grants of land.

Charles Brandon, Duke of Suffolk, was also a ladies' man. His name was linked with Margaret Neville before he married his niece Anne Browne in 1508. Anne died in 1511 after giving birth to two daughters, Anne and Mary, and on 15 May 1513 Brandon entered into a marriage contract with his ward, Elizabeth Grey, *suo jure* Viscountess Lisle. He took the title Viscount Lisle, but the marriage contract was ended and the title forfeited when Brandon secretly married Mary Tudor, Queen Dowager of France, in May 1515.

When their daughter Frances was born in July 1517, Brandon's former wife was still alive so there was uncertainty about the legitimacy of Frances. The former wife had died when their second daughter, Eleanor, was born, making Eleanor unquestionably legitimate with a claim to the throne superior to that of her elder sister. Lady Eleanor Brandon married Henry Clifford, 2nd Earl of Cumberland; their only surviving child was Margaret Clifford, who married Henry Stanley, 4th Earl of Derby, to become Countess of Derby. Even Doleman could find nothing to denounce the claim of Eleanor Brandon as the indisputably legitimate younger daughter of the dowager Queen Mary, and when Eleanor died in September 1547, just eight months after Henry VIII, her place in the royal line was taken by her daughter Margaret, Countess of Derby. But Elizabeth hated Margaret, and when she became queen she accused the countess of plotting her death by magical practices, so the unfortunate woman was kept in custody for the greater part of Elizabeth's reign.

Meanwhile, Frances Brandon married Henry Grey, 3rd Marquess of Dorset, who took the additional title of 8th Duke of Suffolk when his father-in-law died. Frances gave birth to Jane Grey in 1537, Katherine was born a year later and Mary in 1540. Their main residence was Bradgate Park in Leicestershire, and it was to this household that Bess Barlow, as she was then, arrived around the time of Mary's birth. Being only ten years older than Jane and thirteen years older than Katherine, she must have been a lively young companion for the little girls.

It was at Bradgate Park where Bess met Sir William Cavendish, an elderly, distinguished and extremely rich government servant, already twice married with two daughters, and where in 1547 Bess Barlow and William Cavendish were married in the Grey family chapel. Bess and William Cavendish were Arbella's grandparents; Frances Brandon was the godmother of Arbella's mother, Elizabeth, so there was a strong link between the two families.

As the great-granddaughters of Henry VII, the Grey sisters were first cousins once removed of Edward VI and in line for the English throne. Henry VIII gave precedence to this branch of the family but Doleman saw them as tainted stock because Henry Grey, like his father-in-law, had a wife living when he married Frances Brandon. Although Henry Grey repudiated his first wife before he married Frances, the girls were considered illegitimate.

The exact date of Jane's birth is not known. Her arrival would have been overshadowed by the birth of her cousin Prince Edward, the first and only male heir to Henry VIII, on 12 October 1537 at Hampton Court Palace. The name Jane was uncommon in those times, and it's believed that she was named after Jane Seymour, the mother of Prince Edward, no doubt to gain royal approval. With children of the same age, the Greys may have nursed the underlying ambition that one day their daughter might marry her cousin, the future King of England, and with this in mind Jane was well educated in Latin, Greek, French, and Italian.

After the death of Henry VIII, his nine-year-old son Edward VI was crowned King of England and Ireland on 20 February 1547. With a sickly boy king on the throne, the entire system of succession could be manipulated by powerful noblemen. None was more powerful than Edward Seymour, Duke of Somerset, and the boy king's uncle governing as Lord Protector in his place. Edward Seymour's brother, Thomas, proposed Lady Jane Grey as Edward's bride, and in early 1547, nine-year-old Jane was sent to court under the guardianship of Queen Katherine Parr, the widow of Henry VIII, whom Thomas married in secret. In September 1548, at the age of eleven, Lady Jane Grey was the chief mourner at Katherine Parr's funeral. Edward Seymour remained a powerful force until he was overthrown and executed in 1552.[1]

John Dudley was made Duke of Northumberland in 1551. As the boy king's chief minister, he was the most powerful statesman in England, and he too tried to promote a marriage between Edward and Jane. If Edward produced a male heir, the succession problem would be solved; but nothing came of that suggestion because, in April 1552, Edward became sick with the measles. Soon he was stricken with tuberculosis as well, and by the following spring he was so ill that he was coughing up blood.

There was no point in trying to arrange a marriage between the dying king and Lady Jane Grey, but as Edward's first cousin once removed, if Jane was named as Edward's successor, it would mean pacifying both the Catholics who did not want Elizabeth and the Protestants who did not want Mary. A country with only an heiress to the throne was widely regarded as disastrous; and Protestants further believed that female rule was against the Scriptures, so if Jane was to be next in succession, she needed a suitable husband. John Dudley's plan was to marry Jane to his son Lord Guildford Dudley and instate him as the next King of England.

Because of the claim of illegitimacy against Frances, John Dudley convinced her to forego her claim to the crown in favour of her daughter Jane. He wasn't necessarily acting against the interest of the country, but he wanted to make sure that the next move was in his own interest. He realised that if Mary or Elizabeth were to take the crown, he would most certainly lose his high position – and possibly even his head.

On 25 May 1553, in John Dudley's London home, fifteen-year-old Jane Grey married Guildford Dudley in a triple marriage ceremony with her younger sister Katherine Grey and the daughter of the house Katherine Dudley. Katherine Grey married Lord Henry Herbert, and Katherine Dudley married Lord Hastings, son of the Earl of Huntingdon. The event was so rushed that the garments for the weddings had to be borrowed from the royal Master of the Wardrobe. A month later, fifteen-year-old Edward VI died without issue on 6 July 1553 at the Palace of Placentia, London, and the Privy Council agreed to declare Jane as Queen, thus subverting the claims of his half-sister Mary under the Third Succession Act.

Jane Grey did not want the crown and protested, 'The crown is not my right and pleaseth me not. The Lady Mary is the rightful heir.' On the afternoon of 10 July 1553, a parade of barges took Jane and her attendants to the Tower. There was no celebration; the populace were only just learning of Edward's death and could not believe that his young cousin was claiming the throne. This innocent usurper was reluctantly crowned queen, but the people began to revolt, so to save their own necks, on the eighth day the Privy Council publicly proclaimed Mary as queen.

In nine days between 10 July and 19 July 1553, Jane's status changed from queen to prisoner in the Tower of London. She was tried and convicted of high treason in November 1553. Her father-in-law, John Dudley, and her husband, Guildford Dudley, were executed, but the rest of John Dudley's sons, including Robert Dudley, later to be favourite of Queen Elizabeth, were spared. Seventeen-year-old Jane and her husband were beheaded on 12 February 1554 at the Tower of London. Mary was declared queen in July 1553.

Queen Mary's health was never good, and when she died on 17 November 1558 Elizabeth became queen. There were two heirs to the throne at the time of Elizabeth's accession: Jane Grey's younger sister, eighteen-year-old Katherine Grey, and Mary, Queen of Scots. One represented the Protestant faction and the other the Catholic, and Elizabeth couldn't stand either of her possible successors. In October 1559, it was reported that Philip II of Spain was considering an alliance between his heir and Katherine Grey. The English ambassador at Madrid in correspondence with William Cecil added that Katherine would probably be glad to leave the English court as she was in the queen's displeasure.[2]

Many considered that a married queen would be preferable to the unmarried Elizabeth, so if Katherine was to marry the heir of Philip II of Spain, this would strengthen her position as Elizabeth's heir against the pretensions of Mary Stuart, Queen of Scots, who, being married to the Dauphin of France, represented England's two enemies Scotland and France.[3]

In the summer of 1558, eighteen-year-old Katherine Grey had attracted the attention of nineteen-year-old Edward Seymour, the Earl of Hertford's heir and a descendant of Edward III. Katherine was a friend of Edward Seymour's sister Jane, who agreed to pass messages between the lovers. She was however told by her brother to 'break with the Lady Katherine touching marriage', possibly because Katherine Grey's name was linked with that of the Spanish king's heir, and because in the eyes of the law she was already married in the aforementioned triple marriage ceremony on 25 May 1553, when she was around thirteen.[4]

The growing rumours of the love affair between Edward and Katherine brought considerable risks and Cecil advised Edward to cool his ardour for Katherine; the political landscape was stormy enough without the Protestant heir being involved in a dangerous romance, when there were negotiations in progress to marry her to Phillip of Spain's heir. Cecil was not a man to be ignored. Withdrawing his affections to please Cecil, Edward Seymour distressed Katherine, who had heard that he was flirting with a girl named Frances Mewtas. Katherine sent him a furious letter, and he wrote back immediately swearing his love and his desire to marry her. He then approached Katherine's mother, Frances Grey, who readily gave her consent for them to marry. But the next obstacle was gaining the queen's permission.[5]

As a potential claimant to Elizabeth's throne, the law stated that it was a penal offence for Katherine to marry without the sovereign's consent, so it was suggested that Edward should acquire as much support as possible from the Privy Council before approaching the queen. As son of the Protector Somerset, Edward Seymour was a suitable candidate. He had a good position and was allied to powerful friends, but in November 1560, Edward Seymour gave Katherine Grey a pointed diamond ring and, in the most foolhardy move possible, they were married by an anonymous clergyman at Hertford House, Canon Row with just Jane Seymour as witness.

Under other circumstances their marriage should have been secure and blessed, but to keep the marriage secret, Cecil sent Seymour on a subsidised tour of Europe. While he was away his sister Jane died and Katherine found she was pregnant. She kept the secret until July, but when Elizabeth found out, she was furious and Katherine was ordered to the Tower under armed guard. Messengers were sent to France demanding Edward Seymour's immediate return, and, on 24 September 1561 while still in custody in the Tower, Katherine gave birth to a son, Edward Seymour, Viscount Beauchamp. Under the will of Henry VIII, he would follow his mother in line of succession as heir to Elizabeth, so at last England had a Protestant male heir to inherit the English throne.

Queen Elizabeth was not happy. She was bent on having the marriage declared invalid and the child declared a bastard. In February 1562, a commission headed by Archbishop Parker was set up to inquire into the marriage: they found that no banns had been read, the priest that conducted the service could not be located, no one formally gave the lady to the earl, and their only witness, Edward's sister Jane Seymour, was dead.

Against this background, in October 1562, as we have seen, Queen Elizabeth contracted smallpox, a potentially lethal disease, and she had not named her successor (Chapter One). Despite the queen's cousin Katherine Grey being the favourite to keep England a Protestant country, the Privy Council were loath to name Katherine as Elizabeth's heir when the commission had reached no decision about the Grey/Seymour marriage. The marriage could be a sham and Katherine's son and heir illegitimate.

They were equally reluctant to name Mary, Queen of Scots and the Catholic representative, as Elizabeth's successor. The country was in total disharmony and disagreement. Against all expectations, the queen recovered and the potential catastrophe was averted. When Parliament assembled in January 1563, it petitioned Elizabeth to name a successor, but Elizabeth ignored the appeal and continued to do so. (The story of the claim of Mary Queen of Scots to the throne is covered in Chapter One).

In May 1563, the Privy Council eventually declared the marriage of Lady Katherine Grey and Edward Seymour, Earl of Hertford, illegal. He was fined £15,000 for 'seducing a virgin of the blood royal', and the baby Edward, Lord Beauchamp, was officially declared illegitimate.

The kindness of Sir Edward Warner, Lieutenant of the Tower, in allowing Edward Seymour to visit his wife was exposed when Katherine announced she was about to have a second child. Elizabeth promptly had Sir Edward Warner locked up in his own prison for the lack of security that had allowed Katherine and Edward to enjoy their conjugal rights. Their second son, Thomas Seymour, was born in the Tower on 10 February 1563. In the eyes of the law he, too, was declared illegitimate despite the fact that the parents continued to proclaim themselves married.

In the summer of 1563 there was an explosion of cases of the plague in London, and for their safety Edward Seymour and his son Lord Beauchamp were sent temporarily under house arrest to his mother's home at Hanworth; Katherine and the newborn baby Thomas were allowed no liberty. They were moved between five prisons in seven years, until Katherine died in captivity on 27 January 1568. Only then were Edward Seymour and his sons finally let out of the Tower and allowed to reappear at court, but Edward faced ruinous fines of nearly £20,000.

From then on, he devoted his life to proving the legitimacy of his sons. He never ceased to believe that one day his eldest son,

Lord Beauchamp, would be the rightful King of England. After all, illegitimacy had not prevented Elizabeth being crowned queen. His plans were shattered when, in 1581, nineteen-year-old Lord Beauchamp married Honora Rogers, a girl far below his station and a wholly unsatisfactory wife for a potential future King of England. Their marriage was a deep disappointment to many, including his father, who did everything he could to end the marriage that had damaged all hope of Beauchamp inheriting the throne.

Together they had four children, William, Edward, Francis and Honora. As the years passed Edward Seymour, who had inherited the title Lord Hertford, began to consider a plan that centred on Beauchamp's teenaged son Edward Seymour. As a poor marriage had so damaged Beauchamp's claim to the throne, the reasoning went, a brilliant marriage could revive it with his son. The bride was to be Arbella Stuart, a great-grandchild of Margaret Tudor. A Stuart/Seymour marriage was a powerful combination that couldn't be ignored: they were both claimants to the throne. A marriage between them would unite the two lines of descendants of Henry VIII's sisters Mary and Margaret and create a joint candidacy capable of attracting widespread support. They would produce heirs with a very strong claim to Elizabeth's throne, but because it was a proposal that was not likely to have the agreement of the queen, the matter had to be conducted in total secrecy.

13

ARBELLA PROPOSES MARRIAGE

The letters that Arbella and Starkey found from Edward Kyrton, the London solicitor, outlined the plans for a marriage between Arbella Stuart and Edward Seymour to strengthen their joint claims to the throne of England. Kyrton was representing the boy's grandfather Sir Edward Seymour, 1st Earl of Hertford, but to whom were the letters addressed? Bess was the obvious recipient, but she had assured the queen that she would do nothing to promote her granddaughter's marriage prospects. Her allegiance to the queen was too strong to consider a marriage other than one that the queen might suggest, and she had stood by that decision for years.

Perhaps Bess realised, however, that as Arbella aged her chances of attracting a suitable husband, and her use to the queen, had diminished. The Seymour/Stuart marriage would have been kept secret to safeguard Bess's position of trust and loyalty to Her Majesty. Perhaps the people concerned were planning to have everything in readiness in order to act promptly when the moment came and the queen died. This seemed the obvious reason, but because the matter was not recorded until Dodderidge became involved, this can only be conjecture.

It may have been at Starkey's suggestion and with his encouragement that Arbella decided to take matters into her own hands. For the first time, the meek Arbella was asserting herself. Why shouldn't she contact Kyrton and resume the correspondence? Surely she had a right to know what was being planned for her future. She no doubt felt assured about dealing with Edward Kyrton, because Catherine Cavendish, daughter of her grandfather Sir William Cavendish by an earlier marriage, had married Thomas Brooke, and their youngest daughter Dudley Brooke had married Daniel Kyrton, son of the solicitor. A further link was provided by Frances Kyrton (sometimes written Kirton). Frances had married Daniel Kyrton after Dudley's death, and after Daniel died in 1594, she went to serve Arbella. She continued in her service until 1606 when she married Sir Robert Vernon, then living at Mitcham, Surrey. It may have been with the help of Frances that Arbella felt confident in contacting her father-in-law, Edward Kyrton.

Starkey was planning to go to London and offered to deliver letters and messages for Arbella, who gave him £75 for his expenses and to spend on her behalf. He left in the summer of 1602, and there is no further reference to the money or the contents and destination of the letters. Arbella waited with some impatience for Starkey's return, but whatever she had planned for Starkey to effect did not go ahead. He sent a letter via her aunt Frances Pierrepoint to say he would not be returning to Hardwick until the following Easter. About this time, she sent what money and jewels she had to an unknown destination in Yorkshire because Bess had threatened to take them from her.[1]

The letter from James Starkey must have been a huge disappointment to Arbella. She couldn't delay her plans indefinitely, so she confided in her uncle Henry Cavendish, who was out of favour with his mother Bess for evicting her from Chatsworth. Henry probably helped Arbella formulate the next part of the plan, but it was riven with misjudgements. Arbella was to send a messenger to Edward Kyrton at his home in Amesbury; three weeks before Xmas she approached Dodderidge, one of Bess's most loyal servants, and asked if he would go a little way on her behalf. When he seemed doubtful, she asked if he would go a hundred miles on her behalf and promised him her protection before disclosing the details.

Arbella told Dodderidge that the earl had commissioned Kyrton to sound out David Owen Taylor, one of Bess's servants, on the topic of a marriage between Edward Seymour, his oldest grandson, and Arbella. Now Dodderidge was to tell the lawyer that if Hertford still wanted this marriage, Arbella hoped he would take steps to bring it about. She suggested that the younger Edward Seymour and Hertford's agent were to come to Hardwick on the pretence of having land to sell, a pretext that would enable them to stay in the house and spin out the negotiations for as long as was necessary for Edward and Arbella to decide on the next step. They were to pretend to be uncle and nephew, and to prove their identity to her, she asked them to bring some picture, handwriting or item that had belonged either to Jane or Katherine Grey that only they could possess. Her uncle Henry Cavendish was to meet and accommodate the party of men that would accompany Edward Seymour and the agent at Mansfield, and if necessary he was prepared to assist Arbella's escape from Hardwick.

Then it was decided that, rather than going via Kyrton the solicitor, Dodderidge should go directly to the Earl of Hertford in London, where he was in residence at the family house in Tottenham. Henry Cavendish lent Dodderidge a horse and, on Christmas Day 1602, he set off. He arrived at Hertford House on the afternoon of 30 December and asked for a private interview with Hertford, but Hertford was suspicious of Dodderidge and his reception was contrary to all Arbella's expectations. Hertford suspected some deep underlying reason behind the visit and made Dodderidge repeat his message in front of two witnesses. He was then taken away, locked in a room overnight and questioned again next morning.

He did however manage to write a short note to Arbella informing her that 'entertainment here is contrary to all expectations'. It is doubtful that she ever got the note as it was produced later for the Privy Council. When Dodderidge insisted that he was speaking the truth and didn't crack by ten o'clock, he was sent under guard to Cecil and ways were used to frighten the truth out of him. Cecil was convinced that the proposal was some deep Catholic plot to overthrow Elizabeth, although despite the efforts of his network of spies they weren't able to find anything. Eventually, and after much interrogation, Dodderidge was thrown into the gatehouse jail at Westminster for fourteen days. He made a full confession to the Privy Council on 2 January 1603:

About three weeks afore Christmas, as I guess, my Lady Arbella asked me, if I would go a little way for her, and I answered, I would do the best I could; so she rested for that time. Not long after, she told me I must go a hundred miles for her; I made answer that I durst not, for fear of my Lady's displeasure and endangering the loss of my service. She said to me that if I did, I should not need to care, for I should find friends, whereupon I granted that I would go. Then she told me that I must go to a place called Amsbury [sic], in Wiltshire, where Lord Hertford owned the Priory, and deliver a message to one Mr. Kirton, my Lord of Hertford's solicitor of his causes; the effect of the message, as far as I can remember is as followeth: Mr. Kirton. You are my Lord of Hertford's ancient and faithful servant and reputed to be a discreet and honest man, your son married a [grand] child of Sir William Cavendish's ... [The son was Daniel Kirton whose wife was

Dudley Brooke, youngest daughter of Catherine Cavendish and Thomas Brooke].[2]

Because Dodderidge reported the part played by the Reverend James Starkey, he was arraigned for questioning. He admitted his involvement but pleaded his own innocence in the scheme. The whole affair obviously troubled him deeply.

David Owen Tudor was questioned in Wales on 15 January 1603. He had been a servant of Bess but had left her employment in 1601 when he had sent his son Richard Owen to be Arbella's page. David Owen Tudor admitted that three or four years previously he had been approached to 'move a marriage between the Lord Beauchamp's eldest son and Lady Arbella'. He was rather vague about the date. He had refused, but the Earl of Hertford's solicitor than asked for his help in approaching Arbella; the man again refused.[3] When questioned, Hertford did not deny that David Owen Tudor had formerly been a go between in the marriage, but he had changed his mind.[4]

On 3 January 1603, Sir Henry Bronker (sometimes written Brounker), the queen's commissioner, was sent to Hardwick to learn the facts behind the proposal. He arrived in the nearby town of Mansfield on 6 January and identified six men who he described as suspicious characters. Three of them were Henry Cavendish, Arbella's uncle, John Hacker, a former gentleman servant of Bess of East Bridgford, Nottinghamshire, and Lord Stapleton from Yorkshire. They were obviously there as planned to await the arrival of young Edward Seymour and his agent, unaware that things had gone drastically wrong.

Bronker's arrival at Hardwick on 7 January 1603 and was met with a mixture of surprise and apprehension by Bess, Arbella and William Cavendish. Bronker had Dodderidge's confession in his pocket, and although he hinted at what was going on, he didn't actually say what. He succeeded in separating Bess and

Arbella by tact and spoke to them individually. His interrogation of Arbella began with pleasantries, thanking her for the New Year's gift sent to the queen, but eventually he came to the point. Arbella at first denied all knowledge of the letters or her wishes to reopen negotiations with Hertford, but she was poorly equipped to oppose such a man as Bronker, who had distinguished himself by the ardour of his persecution of Catholics. He was a man without sentiment or pity and utterly loyal to Cecil. Bronker kept up his calculated pressure and they battled on for a while, until Arbella bowed and said she would tell him everything – but what she said was such a jumble of hysterical nonsense that Bronker could make nothing of it. Arbella was frightened and incapable of coherent thought. He promised to say nothing to Bess – another calculated lie – if Arbella wrote down what she had done.

Next morning, she offered him a letter. He found it confused, obscure and ridiculous. He told her to rewrite it, but the second attempt, according to Bronker, 'made me believe her wits were thoroughly disordered, either with fear of her grandmother or conceit of her own folly'. Finally, Bronker wrote the confession and Arbella signed it.

After two days, Bronker was satisfied that there was no grand plot, no Catholic involvement and no harm intended to the queen. His report states there were no strangers at Hardwick, Bess was completely unaware of Arbella's plan, and Arbella was waiting for a message from Hertford. The marriage suggestion was just foolishness on Arbella's part.

Arbella sent a letter to the queen, probably at Bronker's dictation, admitting all she was accused of and apologising. Bronker told Bess that she was in danger of losing her majesty's favour, so Bess also wrote to the queen exonerating herself from all knowledge of Arbella's folly. She claimed she was deceitful and asked the queen to take her off her hands, away to court, in marriage – anything to be rid of the responsibility of keeping the duplicitous Arbella. Bess wanted to make sure that she was in no way implicated.

The dramatic scenes and recriminations would have started as soon as Bronker rode away on the Sunday. In Bess's eyes this was a crisis because an unsanctioned royal marriage could be viewed as treason. She showed no sympathy or understanding despite having been a life-long friend of Frances Grey and her daughters, Jane and Katherine; the latter had been one of the godparents and sponsors of Bess's daughter Elizabeth Cavendish, Arbella's mother. Reports said that Bess was the person Katherine confided in when she discovered she was expecting her son Lord Beauchamp, father of the man whose name was now being linked with Arbella's.[5]

The reserved Arbella had asserted herself for the first time in her life, and now she felt betrayed. She had no reason to be grateful to the queen for her solitary and introspected life, but she had hoped to gain the support and sympathy of her grandmother. If Edward Seymour, Earl of Hertford, had been pressing Arbella's claim, why did he drop it and deny all knowledge? Why did he betray her? Of all people in England he should have understood her position, but he was an old and timid man.

Bronker reached London on 13 January, and, three weeks after he had left Hardwick, a reply was delivered from the queen stating that Arbella was to remain at Hardwick and was to be closely watched.[6] He suggested that Bess was to rid Arbella of base companions and appoint some discreet gentlewoman to be in her company and some honest gentlemen to attend her. The minister went on the say that the queen was pleased with the way she had dealt with the situation and was content that Bess was in no way involved.

On 15 January Arbella wrote a letter to John Hacker of East Bridgeford, one of the men that had been with Henry Cavendish at

Mansfield a week earlier. She asked him to contact her aunt Mary Talbot and to tell her to come to Hardwick with all haste. Arbella's lady-in-waiting Bridget Shirland managed to leave Hardwick with the letter, but when Arbella received no response, she wrote again. Hacker never received either of these letters, and others were also intercepted. Bridget Shirland also wrote to Edward Frank, the constable at Health, asking him to bring letters from London to a safe house in Sutton rather than Hardwick. In each case the messengers returned with feigned answers in the handwriting of Bess's steward Timothy Pusey while the letters went to Cecil in London. Arbella wrote volleys of letters. She appealed to Bronker, Cecil and Stanhope for her freedom, but her pleas fell on deaf ears. What Arbella didn't realise was that she was playing into her enemies' hands because the rumours were circulating that she was mad (with porphyria).

It had become an intolerable situation. Arbella was being kept like a prisoner at Hardwick, guarded by staff who reported her every move to Bess. They were constantly at loggerheads, each anxious to thwart the other.

On 11 February, Arbella received news that the Reverend James Starkey had hanged himself in his cell after prolonged questioning. He left a confession note asking for Arbella's forgiveness and for God's forgiveness for taking his own life, something that was abhorrent to a Christian and especially a man of the cloth. He gave an account of what had passed between them in 1602, 'being sorry that such a one should be made an instrument of the bad practices of others, whose device was to turn me out of my living and to deprive me of my life'.[7] It was a month before Venetian state correspondents reported Starkey's death, which soon became a sensation: 'In the house of Arbella Stuart they have found the body of her chaplain and tutor with his throat cut. Rumour says he killed himself because he was conscious of his own intrigues.'[8]

On 2 February Arbella informed Bess that she had a lover whose credit was great with her majesty. Bess told her to write down the details. The account was six pages long yet it did not name the mystery lover. Arbella said she would reveal that only if she was permitted to visit the Privy Chamber in London. She refused to eat or drink until she had heard from the queen, and Cecil wrote from the court at Richmond Palace saying that Bronker was on his way to Hardwick. He set off on 27 February and arrived on 2 March with a list of questions, no doubt devised by the Privy Council. Arbella was forced to admit that the secret lover was a stratagem and did not exist; although if she wished to alarm the council she had chosen a good way to do so.

She was requested to write and confirm this, and went on:

I am free from promise, contract, marriage or intention to marry and so mean to be whilst I live and nothing whatsoever shall make me alter my long determination, the continuance of these disgraces and miseries, and the peril of the King of Scots his life, and if her majesty continues her hard opinion of me, and I continue in my lady my grandmother's hands, then whatsoever befall, I have determined of a course which, if it pleases your majesty to like of, will be for her majesty's honour and best to my liking ... I will make a vow if it should please your Highness to command, upon condition that I may reobtain your majesty's favour, and have my dear and true liberty, I will never marry whilst I live, nor entertain thought nor conceal any such other matter whatsoever from your Majesty, which I shall think worthy for her majesty to incline her princely ear unto. [This letter, kept with the Cecil Papers, is smudged with tears.][9]

Bronker left Hardwick on 3 March, convinced that Arbella 'hath vapours on her brain'. The meeting had not gone well, but when she asked for her grandmother's blessing she was met with a volley of most bitter and injurious words. Retiring to her chamber through the great rooms at Hardwick, she was followed by her grandmother shouting and hurling abuse, frustrated and in despair at the failure of Bronker's visit. Cecil and Stanhope had assured Arbella that her chamber would be her sanctuary, but Bess and her son William followed her, screaming abuse. The promised privacy had not materialised.

She sat down to write another letter to Bronker while her tormentors stood over her reading it. Arbella described the tension and the intolerable position at Hardwick after he had left and, although the letter is mainly incomprehensible, amongst a string of bizarre sentences she asked:

> What will become of us? After my cousin Mary and I had spent a little breath in evaporating certain court smoke, which converted into sighs, made some eyes beside ours run a-water, we walked in the great chamber, for fear of wearing out the mats in the gallery (reserved for you courtiers), as sullenly as if our hearts had been too great to give one another a good word, and so to dinner.

Before they could stop her, she had left the chamber in search of a messenger. Some of the household staff were gathered around the fire in the upper great chamber. Amongst them was George Chaworth, who was a friend of Arbella's and acted as courier of her letters to Bronker. She wrote on 4 March, 'This gentleman Mr Chaworth can witness my many great and increased wrongs which if you will not believe, I cannot help.' She ends the letter by saying, 'PS I deal better with you than you with me for I do not torture you with expectation, nor promise better than I will perform.'[10]

She again wrote a series of letters to Bronker on 6 March and 7 March; the longest letter of all was written on Ash Wednesday,

9 March, the anniversary of the execution of Essex, as she reminded Bronker. The letter revealed a surprising amount of information about Essex and lends strength to the suspicion that she was rather too fond of the queen's favourite.

There was obviously a spy in their midst because Arbella's secret lover was a matter of general knowledge by 9 March, when Father Rivers wrote to Father Persons that 'Arbella has written to her majesty that she is contracted to one near about the queen, offering if he may be pardoned, to name him; whereupon some deem Mr Secretary to be the man, others the Lord Mountjoy; some forsooth, Grenville; some one some other'.[11]

Based on nothing but hearsay and conjecture, both Father Rivers and the Venetians were making false statements about Arbella. One such statement said she had been removed to the palace at Woodstock, where Elizabeth had been confined as a princess during Mary's reign. That was not true. The Privy Council did not propose to remove her from Hardwick, although they did suggest that William Cavendish should bear more of the burden than he had previously done, so she was taken to Owlcotes for a short period in William's care. At the height of her distress and frustration she wrote almost daily to Bronker. She repeatedly informed him that she could trust no man: 'All men are liars; they are dead whom I loved.' Arbella felt Hertford had betrayed her and wrote to the queen concerning the wickedness of Robert Cecil and Edward Seymour, Earl of Hertford.

Of the many visitors to Hardwick, the only one willing to help Arbella was her uncle Henry Cavendish, known as Bess's 'bad son'. It's likely that Arbella was able to tell her uncle about her desire to escape rather than writing an incriminating letter; together they planned Arbella's escape with the help of a Catholic named Henry Stapleton. The attempt was to be made on 10 March. The two Henrys with a party of eight men were to go to Ault Hucknall church to watch from the church tower for Arbella taking exercise outside Hardwick Hall (the grounds of Hardwick Hall stretch almost up to the church boundary and the road runs between). But they had been unable to get the key of the church from the vicar, and, at two o'clock after the plan had failed, the group presented themselves at the Porter's Lodge. They were refused admittance but 'Arbella was desirous to speak to Henry and he was allowed inside for just two hours'. He and Arbella walked down the stairs through the hall and out into the walled forecourt. They crossed to the gates, no doubt being watched by Bess from inside, but the porter at the gates prevented them from passing to the outside. Bess refused Arbella's request to speak to Stapleton and Arbella responded by asking if she was a prisoner. Eventually, Henry and Stapleton were forced to leave.

In trying to kidnap Arbella with a known Catholic like Stapleton, Henry Cavendish was very close to committing an act of treason; yet Arbella was a willing participant. She wanted to leave and had been prevented from doing so. Bess wrote of the attempt to Bronker, who returned to Hardwick for the third time on 17 March. He sent at once for Henry Cavendish. He interviewed Arbella and her servants, the vicar of Hucknall and the villagers, and anyone peripherally connected with the matter. He had with him a warrant instructing all deputy lieutenants, sheriffs, mayors, bailiffs, constables, headboroughs and all others of her majesty's officers to assist Bronker if called upon. This might seem extreme, but the timing was critical: Queen Elizabeth was dying, and such a measure might have been necessary in the event of the queen's death causing riots and rebellions over a disputed succession.

This may also have been why Bronker decided that Arbella should be removed from Hardwick to the care of Henry Grey, Earl of Kent, at Wrest Park in Bedfordshire. It is hard to decide why exactly Arbella was sent there. The Earl of Kent was an elderly man stricken with deafness and Wrest Park was not a merry place. He was however distantly related, his nephew having recently married Elizabeth Talbot, the second daughter of Gilbert and Mary Talbot.[12]

On 20 March, Bess signed a codicil cutting both her son Henry Cavendish and her granddaughter Arbella Stuart out of her will. Four days later, on the death of Queen Elizabeth, Arbella had left Hardwick, never to live there again.

14

THE DEATH OF QUEEN ELIZABETH

Elizabeth had become queen in 1558. For almost forty-five years Britain had been ruled by a queen who seemed to many to be immortal. At almost seventy years of age, which was ancient for her time, there were reports of her frailty. Elizabeth was old, and the illusion that she was otherwise was falling away rapidly. When visiting the house of a courtier she had to have a stick to walk up the stairs, and during the opening of Parliament she almost fell under the weight of her heavy robes. She had continued her annual routine of a short summer progress and Christmas revels, but by the late winter of 1602/3 Elizabeth was feeling unwell.

In early February she had caught a chill after walking out in the cold winter air, and complained of a sore throat as well as aches and pains. By the end of the month she had developed pneumonia. Bess was keeping Bronker informed of everything that was happening at Hardwick and he was passing the information to Cecil, but the timing was wrong. Elizabeth's end was fast approaching and it is doubtful that they bothered to inform the dying queen; she had shown no concern for Arbella Stuart and her problems in the past and was hardly likely to do so when she was dying.

In March 1603 Elizabeth had retired to Richmond Palace, her warm, snug residence. She was old, she was tired, and she was lonely. It was generally believed that the dying queen was asked if she wanted the King of France to succeed her. She made no answer. She was asked if she wanted the King of Scotland to succeed her. She made no answer. She was asked if she wanted Lord Beauchamp, the son of the Earl of Hertford, to succeed her and she replied, 'I will have no rascal's son in my seat.' Arbella was not mentioned, but her gender was against her. Elizabeth was still playing with her royal prerogative right up to the end.

Although they were all waiting on the outcome, it was a foregone conclusion. Cecil as head of the Privy Council had already prepared the proclamation announcing the transfer of the Crown and had sent it north for James's approval before Elizabeth's death. His elder half-brother Thomas Cecil was Lord President of the Council in the North, a key post facilitating contacts with Edinburgh.

Elizabeth stood for hours on end, then rested in a low chair by the fire, refusing to let doctors examine her. As the days passed her condition slowly worsened, until finally she was persuaded to lie on cushions on the floor in her private apartments. She rested there for two days, not speaking. A doctor ventured close and asked how she could bear the endless silence. She replied simply, 'I meditate.' For the third and fourth days, she continued to rest in silence, with a finger often in her mouth. She could not be persuaded to leave the cushions for the comfort of her bed.

Cecil visited and beseeched her, 'Your Majesty, to content the people, you must go to bed.' Elizabeth replied, with some of her old spirit, 'Little man, little man, the word "must" is not used to a queen.' Although nothing was said, she knew that those around her were preparing for the time when her reign would be over. Being a monarch had been a difficult, demanding, and often very lonely task, and Elizabeth was tired not only physically but emotionally. She herself had said. 'To be a king and wear a crown, is a thing more glorious to them that see it, than it is pleasant to them that bear it.'

Finally, Elizabeth grew so weak that they could carry her to bed. She asked for music and, for a time, it brought some comfort. As her condition deteriorated, Archbishop Whitgift, her favourite of all her Archbishops of Canterbury, whom she once called her 'little black husband', arrived to pray at her side. He was old and his knees ached terribly, but he knelt at the royal bedside until she finally slept. Those in vigilance around the queen's bed left her to the care of her ladies and, at last, as the courtiers watched and waited, the laboured breathing stopped.

The queen died in the early hours of Thursday 24 March 1603. It was the eve of the Annunciation of the Virgin Mary, perhaps an apt day for the 'Virgin Queen' to die. The Elizabethan calendar was different to ours, as they still used the Julian calendar, the New Year beginning on 25 March. Thus it was that the last day of the year 1602 also saw the last hours of the last Tudor monarch. (See appendix page 264, the Gregorian calendar.) The new year would bring a new reign, and there was going to be a new ruling dynasty, the Stuarts, and a new era in British history. With Elizabeth's death, the world as they knew it was about to change.

At dawn on Thursday 24 March 1603, the chief councillors left Richmond and rode to Whitehall where Cecil drafted the announcement of the queen's death and the proclamation announcing the transfer of the crown to James VI of Scotland, who was proclaimed King James I of England. The grandees of the land, heralds, privy councillors, lords and courtiers spread the news throughout the country. At ten o'clock on the green opposite the tilt yard at Whitehall, Robert Cecil read the proclamation aloud, proclaiming James king. The proclamation was read again at St Paul's and Cheapside Cross, then the councillors formally demanded entrance to the Tower of London in the name of King James I of England.

The new king received the news of his accession three days later on 27 March, for the ambitious Robert Carey had ridden at top speed to Edinburgh; his journey was so quick that its speed would not be matched until 1832. That same day, James wrote to Cecil praising him and his fellow councillors for their care in overseeing what he described as an unprecedented event, 'the translation of a monarchy'.

In the Parish Register of Mansfield, the local town for Hardwick Hall, it is stated that Gryffythe Markham (sic) was present on 31 March 1603 at the Market Cross at Mansfield, with Sir John Bryon, Mr Henry Chaworth and other gentlemen at the proclamation of the accession of James I to the Crown.

It was a peaceful transition of power, and to ensure this the English ports had been closed, extra watchmen patrolled the streets of London and known Catholics were kept under surveillance. It was reported that Beauchamp had left London secretly around 28 March and was in the west gathering support against James to proclaim himself king in his own right. Some claimed that his forces were 10,000 strong. It was alleged that Beauchamp was acting at the instigation of France, but on 13 April it was reported as a false alarm. The supporters of the unmarried Arbella and the childless Isabella did nothing. The speed and ease of the unchallenged transition evoked some astonishment. The London diarist John Manningham slyly noted that the proclamation was met with 'silent joye, noe great shouting', although there were bonfires and bell-ringing that evening.

As the queen had wished, there was no post-mortem. Her body was embalmed and placed in a lead coffin. A few days later she began her last journey, by water to Whitehall, and was laid in state, before being taken to Westminster Hall. There her body was to remain until the new king gave orders for her funeral. He left Scotland on 5 April but had not reached London by 28 April, the day arranged for the funeral of Queen Elizabeth.

Arbella, being the only royal princess, was ordered to attend the funeral but refused. She said her access to the queen had been denied during her lifetime; she would not be brought on stage for the public spectacle after her death. Elizabeth had never shown her cousin Arbella any love or support or concern. She had treated her badly and Arbella spurned the ceremony.[1]

The queen was given a magnificent funeral but the new king was not in attendance. The procession to Westminster Abbey was composed of more than a thousand mourners. Her coffin, covered in purple velvet, was drawn by four horses draped in black. Behind the queen came her palfrey, led by her Master of Horse. The chief mourner was Elizabeth's step-aunt by marriage, the Marchioness of Northampton. She led the peeresses of the realm, all dressed in black, and behind them came all the important men of the realm, as well as over two hundred poor folks. The streets were full of people, all come to pay their last respects to the queen who had ruled them so wisely and for so long as she made her way to her final resting place at Westminster Abbey.

An effigy of the great queen, dressed in the Robes of State with a crown on her head and a sceptre in her hands, lay on the coffin beneath a mighty canopy held by six knights. Many wept when they saw the lifelike effigy of the queen. John Stow, who attended the funeral, wrote:

Westminster was surcharged with multitudes of all sorts of people in their streets, houses, windows, leads and gutters, that came to see the obsequy, and when they beheld her statue lying upon the coffin, there was such a general sighing, groaning and weeping as the like hath not been seen or known in the memory of man, neither doth any history mention any people, time or state to make like lamentation for the death of their sovereign.

The grief of the nation was unprecedented, and was a tribute to the remarkable achievements of a remarkable woman. Her tomb in Westminster Abbey, where Elizabeth rests alongside her half-sister Queen Mary, was paid for by the new king. It was less impressive than that provided to his disgraced mother, and cost far less.

On 5 April 1603 James left Edinburgh on his journey south to take possession of his long-coveted new kingdom. He optimistically assured his people that he would return in three years, and rather typically borrowed 10,000 Scottish marks for his travel expenses. He crossed the border at Berwick, but travel was slow. He and his entourage were entertained at almost every great house on the way, and it was said that every person of consequence in the kingdom rode out to meet him.

There are many anecdotes about this journey, and almost all are rude and uncouth. In youth James's appearance was melancholy rather than distasteful, although few kings of England have looked less king-like. In later life he had large rolling eyes, a large tongue that could not be contained in his mouth so that he dribbled back into his cup as he drank, weak legs that meant he had to be assisted in walking by leaning on other men's shoulders, and was rather plump, ruddy in complexion with a sparse beard. He was a grotesque and shambling figure, narrow and coarse with the mind of a pedant, the manners of a boor, and the superstitious terrors of a savage. One has, however, to remember his parentage and his upbringing. He was intensely superstitious, and laid great stress upon the fact that he was born on 19 June; he first saw his wife on 19 November; his son Henry was born on 19 February, his daughter Elizabeth on 19 August and his younger son Charles on 19 November.

Gilbert Talbot, the 7th Earl of Shrewsbury, was one of the earls who on the death of the queen signed the proclamation of her successor James VI of Scotland. To show his allegiance, on 30 March he wrote a letter to his agent John Harper, from Whitehall Palace, London:

> Mr Harper, it may be I shall be very shortly in the country and perhaps may be so happy as to entertain the King our sovereign at Worksop. I would entreat you to let all my good friends in Derbyshire and Staffordshire know so much, to the end that I may have their company against such a time as his Majesty shall come hither. I know not how soon. If it so happen as I shall know when in a few days certain; but then it will be too late for your horses or anything else to be prepared unless you prepare them presently upon the receipt hereof. All things here are well and nothing but unity and good agreement. God continue it. Amen. At my chamber in Whitehall Palace, this 30th March being Wednesday night, in very great haste. 1603. Your friend, most assured, Gilbert. Shrewsbury. I will not refuse any fat capons and hens, partridges, or the like if the King comes to me. GSh.[2]

Worksop Manor was the showpiece Shrewsbury had built to entertain Queen Elizabeth. She never visited but now James stayed there overnight on 20 April, the guest of Gilbert and Mary Talbot. It was a convenient stopping place on the king's journey to London, and Gilbert Talbot obviously wished to show his hospitality and allegiance to the new king, particularly as his niece Arbella might be regarded as James's rival for the throne. Gilbert had obviously not backed Arbella.

Cecil made a fast journey north to meet his new master at York on 17 April. When the king arrived there, he delighted the crowd by walking through the streets to the minster for the Easter service. The ride south became a triumphant progress, with James feasting and indulging his passion for hunting. He thought he was witnessing an outpouring of spontaneous affection, but the overwhelming public emotion expressed relief at the peaceful succession mixed with a natural curiosity.

A contemporary account records:

> The 20th day, being Wednesday, his majesty rode [from Doncaster] towards Worksop, the noble Earl of Shrewsbury's house; and at Bawtry the High Sherrif of Yorkshire took his leave of the King, and there Mr Askoth, the High Sherrif of Nottingham, received him, being gallantly appointed both with horse and men; and so he conducted his Majesty on, till he came within a mile of Blyth, where his highness alighted, and sat down on a bank side to eat and drink.' After his Majesty's short repast, to Worksop his Majesty rides forward; but by the way, in the Park he was somewhat stayed, for there appeared a number of huntsmen, all in green, the chief of which, with a woodsman's speech, did welcome him, offering his Majesty to show him some game, which he gladly condescended to see; and he hunted a good space, very much delighted; at last he went into the house, where he was nobly received, with a superfluity of all things that still every entertainment seemed to exceed another. In this place, besides the abundance of all provision and delicacies, there was the most excellent soul-ravishing music, where with his Highness was not a little delighted. At Worksop he rested on Wednesday night, and in the morning stayed breakfast; which having ended, there was so much store of provision left, of fowl, fish and almost everything, besides bread, beer and wines that it was left open for any man that would, to come in and take.

There was extravagant hospitality given on behalf of Gilbert, who received nothing in return although James gave knighthoods to thirteen of the Earl of Shrewsbury's friends. That included his son-in-law Henry Grey of Ruthin, Elizabeth's husband, and no connection to the father of Jane, Katherine and Mary Grey.[3]

It is possible that Mary Talbot took the opportunity to inform James of Arbella's situation, and he wrote to the Earl of Kent:

> For as much as we are desirous to free our cousin the Lady Arbella Stuart from the unpleasant life that she hath led in the house of her grandmother with whose severity and age, she being a young lady, could hardly agree, we have thought fit for the present to require you as a nobleman of whose wisdom and fidelity we have heard so good report to be contented for some short space to receive her into your house and there to use her in that manner which is fit for her calling, having the rather made choice of you than of any other because we are informed that your nephew is matched with her cousin germain in which respect she will like better of that place than of a strangers until further order be taken.[4]

As the chosen one, James could afford to be magnanimous towards Arbella and free her from the unpleasant life she had led at Hardwick. Arbella wrote in all humility to James stating that she desired no other husband, no other state, nor other life than that which James, her cousin and lord, may assign her.[5] It was also reported that Arbella left Wrest Park on 1 May when she went to meet James with 300 horses.[6]

In May, Queen Anne followed the same route from Scotland, accompanied by her two elder children, Prince Henry, who had just celebrated his ninth birthday, and seven-year-old Lady Elizabeth; the two-year-old Charles was left behind in Scotland. Anne was plump through overfeeding and childbearing. Her hair was blonde, her skin was pale, her face plain and dominated by a sharp nose that ran down like an escarpment. Though she and her husband kept on good terms, she occupied a separate establishment.

The queen and her entourage were at Worksop on 20 June – a second royal visit for Gilbert and Mary. On Trinity Sunday, Toby Matthew, Bishop of Durham and later Archbishop of York, preached to the party. Worksop Church Wardens' Book records that three shillings were paid to six ringers when the queen's majesty came to Worksop Manor. The double honour of entertaining royalty can't have appeared as a double blessing for the new Earl and Countess of Shrewsbury when they totted up the cost. For a long time after they were perpetually short of money, but Gilbert did secure office as Warden, Chief Justice and Justice in Eyre of the king's forests beyond the Trent.

15

THE NEW KING AND QUEEN BEFRIEND ARBELLA

James arrived at Whitehall on 7 May, and on 11 May he wrote to the Earl of Kent suggesting that Arbella came to the court at Greenwich accompanied by her Aunt Mary, Countess of Shrewsbury, who had entertained him at Worksop.[1]

The meeting was successful. Arbella was told she could choose where she wanted to live, but at Cecil's suggestion this was to be Sheen with the Swedish-born Marchioness of Northampton, third wife of William Parr, Queen Katherine Parr's brother. From Sheen, Arbella started a correspondence with Cecil about her financial affairs. Cecil was no longer to be viewed as her enemy – he was the one responsible for sorting out the money. How was the newly independent Arbella going to support herself in this expensive environment? Her pension had ceased with Elizabeth's death and, being out of favour with her grandmother, it was doubtful she could count on an allowance from Bess. She wrote to Cecil, 'If I should name two thousand pounds for my present occasions it would not exceed my necessity.'[2]

The Venetians were received at court at the end of May. They were not impressed by James, and wrote scornfully, 'From his dress he would have been taken as the meanest among his courtiers,' although they did note a chain of diamonds and a single stone in his hat. They also took a special interest in Arbella, stating that 'she has returned to favour and they say that should the queen [Anne] die, she would be wedded and crowned at once'.[3]

The Venetians had misread the situation. Arbella had no option but to make peace with James, who was not only her closest living relative in age but as the new monarch also responsible for reissuing her pension. Being in favour was an essential prerequisite because she was reliant upon James, who had given no positive assurance on his plans for her future. He had never expressed cousinly sentiment or honoured the ties of blood, and with a ten-year age difference, the fact that they had never met until she was twenty-eight emphasised the cold fact that their relationship was not close. This was not surprising, considering James had never ventured onto English soil until he was declared King of England in 1603.

Arbella might have been his closest relative but she approached James in the posture of a suppliant. He expected self-interest in those nearest to him and was probably justified in thinking that Arbella might still intend to supplant him, so he was cautious. She may have nursed ambitions, but throughout her life these had been thwarted at every turn; she had been cheated of the throne, of her freedom, of marriage, of her titles and estates.

With the arrival of Queen Anne and her children at Windsor at the end of June, Arbella joined the court. Her relationship to the king was recognised and granted her precedence, but that cost James nothing. Being a first lady at court was a costly business, demanding a great number of expensive clothes as well as constant presents for the royal family. She wrote to the recently ennobled Sir Robert Cecil on 14 June asking him to remind the king's majesty of her maintenance.[4] When Cecil gave a noncommittal answer, she wrote again on 22 June, and when she received no response, she wrote yet again the following day. She had suggested a pension of £2,000 as being a sum that would not exceed her necessity.[5] Cecil sent her £666, and on 26 June she wrote stating that she was 'greatly bounded to his lordship'. But £666 was a ludicrously low figure on which she could not hope to keep herself, her household and servants. Someone in her position at court would ordinarily be responsible for a secretary, an usher, groom, embroiderer, waiting women, cook, baker, page, serving man, laundress and general domestic staff.[6] By 17 September, and seriously in debt, she learnt that she would receive a pension of £800 a year plus her diet (this allowance for diet meant that she was allowed a number of dishes from the king's table).[7]

A new life now dawned for Arbella. Anne of Denmark was a peer the same age as Arbella, although they were quite different in temperament and taste. Anne was a frivolous, pleasure-loving, empty-headed woman, but kindly enough when it suited her to be so. Arbella was studious and thoughtful, but they took an immediate liking to each other. Anne insisted upon keeping Arbella constantly with her, making her both a personal friend and the first lady at her court. As a princess of the royal blood, Arbella was placed in her appointments, table and rank near the king and queen.

On 2 July Arbella watched the installation of nine-year-old Prince Henry as a Knight of the Garter in St George's Chapel, Windsor. Soon after, his sister Princess Elizabeth was sent away to live at Coombe Abbey in the charge of Lord and Lady Harrington. Arbella moved with the court from Windsor to the medieval bishop's palace at Farnham in Surrey. At the time, the plague was raging through London with unusual ferocity, and for the next few months the court moved around the southern counties.

James was crowned on 25 July 1603 at Westminster Abbey, but due to the plague the coronation was cut short. All parts of the ceremony that were not essential were cut, and limits were set on the number of people attending the service. There was not the usual feast to follow. The royal couple travelled by barge from the Tower, where the monarch traditionally spent the night before the coronation. Road access to Westminster Abbey was barred by armed guards and no one was allowed to travel by river from the City. No doubt Arbella attended the coronation dressed like the others in crimson velvet. That week in London, 1,396 people died of the plague.

While James was initially welcomed peacefully and happily, his reign quickly turned sour. Even the powerful Robert Cecil who had promoted James as the future King of England saw his flaws before he was crowned: his profligacy with money, his intemperate attraction to young men, his Scottish favourites and Scottish habits. He was uncouth and crude. When told that his people loved to see their king's face, he replied, 'God's wounds. I will pull down my breeches and they shall also see my arse.'

Despite coming to the English throne with over thirty years' experience of kingship in Scotland, James was quite out of his depth in England. The Scottish court at Holyrood had been only an anteroom compared to the vast sophistication of the English courts at Whitehall, Hampton Court, Greenwich and all the other establishments held by the English royal family. By June 1603 the industrious Venetians had made an accurate assessment of the new king, who seemed to have all but forgotten that he was king except in his kingly pursuit of stags, to which he was rather foolishly devoted, leaving his statesmen in such absolute authority that they had more power than ever before. For a long time people spoke sneeringly of King Elizabeth and Queen James.

James saw no reason to educate women – he said it only made them more cunning. This may have been a personal insult aimed at Arbella, who insisted upon spending several hours a day studying. He thought a woman had a definite place in the home, and when faced with a learned woman he asked sourly, 'But can she spin?' He even encouraged the clergy to denounce women exhibiting signs of manliness like short hair, broad-brimmed hats, pointed doublets and mannish dress.

The accession of a new monarch with a frivolous consort, the general prosperity and extravagance, the numerous patents of nobility and other elevations of rank conferred or available acted as a blood transfusion to a court grown old and stale under the long rule of Queen Elizabeth. The new Stuart court was a place of luxury and overindulgence that bred avarice on an unprecedented scale. Vast expenditure went on buildings, clothes, banquets, tourneys, tilts and masques, and all this excess needed financing.[8]

Preening themselves with the honours James bestowed upon his favourites were Lady Hatton, Lady Walsingham, Countess of Derby, Countess of Bedford, and the beautiful Penelope Rich. These were the ladies of the court. Penelope Rich was the sister of Essex and married against her will to the elderly Lord Rich, who divorced her after the Essex scandal in 1605. Penelope Rich was the long-time mistress of Charles Blount, Lord Mountjoy. Described as handsome, courageous, honest, fair and, that rare virtue at James's court, incorruptible, Mountjoy married Penelope after her divorce. Young and ambitious, the Countess of Bedford, formerly Lucy Harington, at once set herself the task of capturing the foremost place at court and became the queen's favourite.[9]

Amongst the Scotsmen who had accompanied James to England was his favourite, James Hay, who was described as 'a most complete and well-accomplished gentleman, modest and courtlike'.[10] An equally biased opinion was expressed about James's cousin, the Duke of Lennox, who had taken Arbella's title and estates. Rather ironically, he was said never to do any man wrong.[11] The most odious of the king's favourites seems to have been his lifelong friend Thomas Erskine, eldest surviving son of Sir Alexander Erskine of Gogar. In 1585 Erskine was made one of the Gentlemen of His Majesty's Bedchamber, and in 1601 he was made a Privy Councillor and given apartments in the royal palace. It was said that the great ladies that visited them came away lousy.[12]

When James travelled south to ascend to the English throne in 1603, Erskine travelled with him and took the title Captain of the Guard, previously held by Sir Walter Raleigh, a position he held until 1617. In 1604 he became Groom of the Stool and was given the title Lord Erskine of Dirletoun. That year he also married for the second time; his bride was Arbella's cousin and childhood friend Elizabeth Pierrepont, daughter of Sir Henry Pierrepoint and Frances Cavendish of Holme Pierrepoint, Nottinghamshire. In 1606, he was created Viscount Fenton (or Fentoun). It was Arbella's misfortune that she should see more of this odious Scots lord, who a contemporary described as 'one who lay sucking at the breasts of the state'.[13]

According to one source at the court, 'there was not one courtier of note that tasted not of Spain's bounty, either in gold or jewels, and amongst them, not any in so large a proportion as the Countess of Suffolk'.[14] It was said that in order for her to live on such a grand scale there was nothing to which she would not stoop. She was intimate with Cecil and on the king's behalf took it upon herself to 'look out choice young men whom she daily curled and perfumed their heads'.[15]

After her long isolation at Hardwick, Arbella reluctantly entered the melee of the royal court where the Howards, Herberts, Scots Lords and Cecil's relatives were to be her constant companions. They did not welcome her arrival. Far from it, they resented the fact that by virtue of her birth she should be given precedence, and this made her very unpopular. They saw her as a rival for the royal favour, a competitor for the farms and fees for which they all competed, and no one had any inclination to share. Her popularity with the king and queen aroused the jealousy of the bickering court ladies, and she was not qualified to compete. Their underhand and undercover activities were child's play to them; jockeying for position was their chief preoccupation.

The Earl of Worcester informed Gilbert that amongst the queen's entourage 'we have ladies of different degrees of favour – some for the private chamber, some for the bed-chamber, some for the drawing chamber and some for neither certain'. Having described these leeches, he concluded, 'The plotting and malice amongst them is such that I think envy hath tied an invisible snake about most of their necks to sting one another to death.'[16]

There was nothing in Arbella's former lifestyle that could have prepared her for this type of conduct. She was a novice amongst this cut-throat, unpleasant, selfish crew, who were old hands at a game that required scheming and skill. Arbella had no experience to help her survive. She was unversed in personal relationships and inept at intrigue. The years spent at Hardwick in the company of Bess and her family had a profound influence on Arbella, who supported sound principles of religion, honesty and justice. She found little honesty or justice at the court of James I – the standards of propriety were quite different from those to which she was accustomed. She must have often thought how different things would have been if she had been selected to be queen and in a position to dictate the conduct of her courtiers.

Although these people were Arbella's contemporaries and with them she must entertain the queen and share the many diversions, she did not enjoy their company or the frivolous aspects of court life, the expensive clothes, face painting and incessant bickering of the court ladies. She was not comfortable and deplored the crude behaviour of the courtiers. She found the playful antics of the queen and her ladies rather childish and often in bad taste.

Sir William Fowler, son of Thomas Fowler who had been Lady Lennox's secretary, was one of the few people at court who saw Arbella's discomfort. One-time spy for Walsingham, he was now knighted and had been appointed secretary to Queen Anne. He was a great admirer of Arbella and wrote to Gilbert from Woodstock on 17 September 1603: 'I cannot forebear from giving you advertisement in my great and good fortune in obtaining the acquaintance of my Lady Arbella who may be to the first seven, justly the eighth wonder of the world.'[17] Feeling great affection for her, he enclosed two sonnets she had inspired him to compose, blinded by love but knowing a great lady would never consider him:

> Whilst organs of vain sense transport the mind,
> Embracing objects both of sight and ear
> Touch, smell and taste to which frail flesh inclines
> Prefers such trash to things that are more dear
> Thou, godly nymph, possessed with heavenly fear
> Divine in soul devout in life and grave
> Rapt from thy sense and sex they spirits steer
> Toyes to avoid which reason doth bereave
> O graces rare! What time from shame shall save
> Wherein thou breath's (as in the sea does fish
> In salt not saltish) exempt from the grave
> Of sad remorse, the lot of worldling's wish
> Ornament both of thyself and sex
> And mirror bright where virtues doth reflect![18]

The favourite exercise of the new monarch and therefore that of the court was hunting, so during the day the party hunted or the lords rode at the rings. Other daytime entertainments were the tilts and tourneys, with their medieval trappings like the mock forts that were set up (the tilt was a contest between horsemen armed with spears). Swords were used for the tourney on horseback; in the foot tourney, the contest was thrashed out with pike and sword across a wooden barrier. Because James was not *habile* (that is, having no general skill) with the spear or sword, he preferred running at the ring, which required greater horsemanship, while Prince Henry was an enthusiastic tilter.

Only men were allowed to compete. The ladies watched and presented the prizes. Pageants were presented, troops of musicians entertained and knights dressed in the trappings of medieval warfare with shields and emblems paraded around. The days were concluded by massive banquets, as both James and Anne preferred quantity rather than quality in their food. There followed dancing, plays by the king's men and masques that continued for as long as anyone had energy. Arbella watched plays by Shakespeare and even saw the playwright act, but was not impressed; the classical emphasis of her education gave her no high opinion of his work. She had toothache over Christmas, which didn't help her mood when she complained about 'the never-intermitted attendance on the queen who daily extendeth her favours more and more towards me'.[19]

Perhaps Arbella was feeling nostalgic for the simple life at Hardwick. Whenever she could she would escape to her books and insisted upon spending several hours a day studying. She wrote to her Aunt Mary: 'I must continue to study. I must return at an appointed time to go to my books.'[20] She also spent time with Prince Henry and his tutors Sir David Murray and Adam Newton. Prince Henry was interested in the visual arts and he was stimulated by the discussions that took place with his older companions. In the seven years that Arbella spent at the court, there is evidence that she had an affectionate relationship with young Henry.[21]

Being separated from her family resulted in a number of candid and revealing letters from Arbella, who describes court life with wit and scandalous, penetrating observation. Aunt Mary was worried and cautioned Arbella on the subject of discretion as the interception of letters was a serious concern. Letters were known to go astray and it was suggested that Arbella should number hers for security. The king's post was primarily a government convenience and anything it carried might be subject to scrutiny. In response, Arbella replied, 'If I had thought they would have been sent by post, I would have written more reservedly.'

Her letters also reveal her sense of isolation and her misgivings of what the future at court held; but she felt she had no options. She wrote to Gilbert:

> I dare not write unto you how I do, for if I would say well, I were greatly to blame; if ill, I trust you will not believe me, I am so merry. It is enough to change Heraclitus (the weeping philosopher) into Democritus (the laughing philosopher) to live in this most ridiculous world, and enough to change Democritus into Heraclitus to live in this most wicked world.[22]

Her powerful position at court made her a useful mediator in the perpetual family rows, and she was constantly being called upon to help. Arbella showed great wisdom and kindness when dealing with family troubles and often acted as mediator. Gilbert and Mary Talbot were not speaking to Henry Cavendish after his part in trying to help Arbella escape from Hardwick. Both Gilbert Talbot and Charles Cavendish were deeply in debt and lawsuits were pending between Charles and Bess, and Gilbert and Bess. In return, because Arbella was finding her life at court rather too demanding and not to her taste, she asked Gilbert if she could have a room at his home in Broad Street on occasions.

The court spent Christmas at Hampton Court. The infant Prince Charles was brought down from Scotland for the Twelfth Night celebrations, upon which he was made Duke of Albany and knighted with several other little boys; just five years old, he was too frail to walk and was carried throughout the ceremony by the Lord Admiral. When Arbella wrote to give Gilbert news of what was planned for the season, she couldn't hide her disgust that 'the queen intendeth to make a masque this Christmas to which end my Lady of Suffolk and my Lady Walsingham have warrants to take of the late queen's apparel out of the tower at their discretion ... It is said there shall be thirty plays.'[23]

There was an unusual number of foreign ambassadors in the country to pay respects to the new king, including an ambassador from Poland sent to ask for Arbella to become the wife of Sigismund III Vasa, King of Poland, but the offer was rejected. During this time, there were several suitors for Arbella's hand: Queen Anne's brother, Duke Ulric of Holstein, Count Maurice, who pretended to be the Duke of Guelders, and the Prince of Anhault.

Although in September Arbella's pension had been fixed at £800, in December her allowance was increased by the king from £800 a year to £1,000. She still could not meet all the demands made on her purse, but was also becoming wary of having to constantly demand money. At New Year, gifts were exchanged, and although as a member of the royal family Arbella could expect to receive more than she gave, she could not appear to stint. She gave the queen silk stockings and gloves; to the king she gave a purse of new gold sovereigns, as he preferred cash to kind. 'This time will manifest my poverty more than all the rest of the year,' Arbella moaned. 'But why should I be ashamed of it when it is other's fault, and not mine?'[24]

But she did feel ashamed of her poverty, and she became increasingly resentful towards the king whom she held responsible. He had left a poverty-stricken Scotland and arrived in a country of milk and honey. The coffers of the English court must have seemed bottomless to James, and he spent money with a crude and wilful abandon; his expenditure quickly doubled that of the old queen. In 1603, the year Queen Elizabeth died, gifts to his favourites amounted to £12,000 in cash. By 1612 that figure had multiplied by six.

16

THE BYE PLOT AND
THE MAIN PLOT

James was never a popular king, either in Scotland or England, and no sooner was he on the throne of England than the counter-reformation began plots to remove him. Although charges were not made public, during the first fortnight in July 1603, eight people were arrested. They included two Catholic priests, Father William Watson and Father William Clarke; Lord Grey of Wilton; Antony Copley; Arbella's cousin, Henry Brooke, 11th Lord Cobham; his brother George Brooke, Bess's godson; Sir Griffin Markham of Ollerton; and Sir Walter Raleigh, married to Bess Throckmorton, granddaughter of Adrian Stokes, second husband of Frances Grey, mother of the Grey girls.

With the exception of Raleigh, who was confined to his house, they were sent to the Tower. Soon it was established that there was conspiracy afoot but details were not made public until 14 August. The interlinked conspiracies became known as the 'Bye Plot' and the 'Main Plot' ('main' here meaning principal and 'bye' meaning secondary).

The Bye Plot was the work of the Protestant George Brooke and Catholics Sir Griffin Markham, Lord Grey of Wilton, Anthony Copley, Father William Watson and Father William Clarke.

The plan was to kidnap James and force him to ease the political persecution of English Catholics. They assumed it would work in a similar manner to that attempted by the Protestant lords in Scotland in 1582, when James had been forced to send Esmé Stuart out of the country. They wanted a promise of greater religious tolerance and assurance that instead of James giving the main positions in court to his Scottish favourites, he would be forced to give them to his English lords who were entitled; Brooke was to be Lord Treasurer, Markham to be Secretary, Grey to be Lord Marshal.

George Brooke's sister Elizabeth had been married to Cecil and, thinking he would help their cause, Cecil was told of the Bye Plot. But Cecil was at the height of his power and intended to stay there by impressing the new king. By using his cunning, he was able to learn that a second plot was afoot. This became known as the Main Plot and it was apparently far more ambitious. Cecil persuaded Brooke to feed him information about the Main Plot until he had virtually single-handedly accomplished what he wanted. The French Ambassador, de Beaumont said, 'Cecil undertakes and conducts it with so much enthusiasm that it is said he acts more from interest and passion than for the good of the state.'[1]

It may be that Cecil was also in the background manoeuvring things to his own ends. With promises of financial rewards and advancement, Cecil could have easily encouraged his brother-in-law to contrive the plots.

The Main Plot was intended to raise a regiment of soldiers and force a coup d'etat to overthrow James and install Arbella as queen with the financial assistance of Spain. One of the main conspirators was George Brooke's brother Henry Brooke, 11th Lord Cobham and another of Cecil's brothers-in-law. On 27 October 1603, Cecil wrote to Gilbert Talbot warning him that his brother-in-law Henry Cavendish should go to London. It was probably to see if there was any connection with Arbella's rescue attempt from Hardwick earlier in the year with Stapleton. He wrote, 'Doubt not that the matter can hurt any you respect; yet he must be spoken with, and I dare warrant he shall have no harm, for any weight the matter is of.'[2]

There was no further mention of Henry Cavendish's possible involvement and he was not asked to give any evidence at the trial. Lord Cobham at some stage wrote to Arbella, suggesting that she should enter into correspondence with Philip III of Spain. Cobham said that in return for his assistance in making her queen, she should promise tolerance, peace with Spain, and pledge not to marry without his consent. Rather surprisingly, Arbella sent Cobham's unopened letter to Cecil immediately. It was said that this was an act of loyalty that saved her life, or imprisonment at the very least.[3] We will never know why she sent an unopened letter to James without knowing the contents. Was it an act of divine insight?

Lord Cobham was a long-time acquaintance of the Count d'Arenberg, Minister of Phillip III in Flanders, and on several occasions he had visited the Spanish court. As recently as April, Cobham had spoken to James about terms of peace that could be arranged between Spain and England through the Count's agent in London. Cobham was not a man of great intellectual ability or statesmanship; one of his contemporaries described him as 'a most silly lord, but one degree from a fool'.[4] Cobham was an intimate friend of Sir Walter Raleigh, and Cecil was aware that King James had a strange hatred for Raleigh. Perhaps it was because the king desired peace with Spain, and Spain would not open peace negotiations until Raleigh, Spain's most inveterate enemy, was either disgraced, dead, or imprisoned for life. If Cecil could get Raleigh implicated in the plot, through putting a degree of pressure on George Brook, it would be easy to get Raleigh put out of the way. Thinking to save his own neck, George Brooke agreed.

When Raleigh was first arrested he was questioned about Cobham's dealing with the Count d'Arenburg; he denied all knowledge of them. Later however he wrote to Cecil saying that Cobham had, he believed, sometimes visited the Count's agent in London after leaving his (Raleigh's) house. Cecil probably already knew this through his network of spies. The purpose of the visits was not necessarily sinister, but Cecil deviously made use of this letter. Until then, Cobham had denied Raleigh's complicity, yet on being shown this letter, he thought Raleigh intended to betray him and cried, 'Oh traitor! Oh villain! I will now tell all the truth.'[5]

He poured out to Cecil such an account of Raleigh's activities that would have sent a saint to the block. When Raleigh heard of this, he sent an associate to Cobham to assure him that he was in no such danger of betrayal. Cobham immediately tried to retract his confessions, but the damage had been done. The lack of evidence against Raleigh made little difference – there is no doubt that the enterprising Cecil busied himself procuring faked evidence against Raleigh in order to please the king. The details of the investigation were very murky, but it was obvious that Cecil was determined that the great Elizabethan courtier should not escape the brand of treason.

In July 1603, the main conspirators, Sir Griffin Markham, George Brooke, Henry Brooke, Sir Walter Raleigh, Lord Grey of Wilton and the two Catholic priests William Watson and William Clark, were apprehended on a charge of conspiring to raise Arbella Stuart to the throne in place of James. More, such a motley assemblage had engaged to secure Catholic toleration. (One reason why the Catholics had accepted James as king was because he had offered to grant this, but he had rescinded with the words, 'Na, na, we'll not need the Papist noo.')

It is certain that not all the so-named conspirators in the Bye Plot knew what was happening but were led by Brooke quite unawares. What was not obvious was the person in the background who was manoeuvring things to his own ends – and that person was Cecil. With promises of financial reward and advancement, Cecil could have easily encouraged his brother-in-law to contrive the plots.

With the exception of Grey, who as a peer received a separate trial, the conspirators in the Bye Plot were tried on 15 November at Winchester. Grey had allegedly been deceived as to the intentions of the Bye plotters, who only needed his name and reputation to support their deeds, but this was not enough to free him and he was found guilty along with the others.

The discovery of the plot was extremely convenient for Cecil, who within a few months was able to order seminary priests to leave the kingdom and to enforce the system of Recusancy Laws and fines.

The trial of the conspirators in the Main Plot took place at the Bishop's Palace in Winchester on 17 November 1603. In the version of the Main Plot presented at trial, Lord Cobham was negotiating with the Count d'Arenberg to contact the Spanish court to obtain approximately £160,000. Cobham was to travel to Brussels, then to Spain, collect the money, and go back to England via Jersey, where Sir Walter Raleigh was governor. Raleigh and Cobham were then to divide up the money and decide how best to spend it in furtherance of sedition.

The prosecution was conducted by Sir Edward Coke, protégé and nephew-in-law of Cecil and of a similarly devious cast of mind. But Raleigh had the better intellect, and soon it was obvious that Raleigh could only be charged on the grounds of Cobham's confession. When asked about his dealings with the Count d'Arenburg, Raleigh denied all knowledge. When asked about his involvement in the allegedly conspiracy to make Arbella Stuart queen, he replied,

I protest before God that I never heard one word of it. If that be proved, let me be guilty of 10,000 treasons ... I never heard so much as the name of Arbella Stuart, but only the name Arbella. I had been a slave, a villain a fool if I had endeavoured to set up Arbella and refused so gracious a lord and sovereign [as James].

At this stage, it seemed likely that Coke would have been better questioning Arbella – a much weaker target than the forceful Raleigh. Instead, Sergeant Hele, Coke's right-hand man, in opening the case for the prosecution said, 'The Lady Arbella, upon my conscience hath no more title to the crown than I have, which before God I utterly renounce.'[6]

Cecil thought it fitting to address the court:

Here hath been a touch of the Lady Arbella Stuart, a near kinsman of the king's. Let us not scandal the innocent by confusion of speech; she is as innocent of these things as I or any man here; only she received a letter from my Lord Cobham to prepare her which she immediately sent to the king. So far was she from discontentment that she laughed him to scorn.

Arbella sat in a withdrawn gallery beside the Lord Admiral, Charles Howard, Earl of Nottingham, who stood up and addressed the court at this stage: 'This lady here doth protest upon her salvation that she never dealt in any of these things, and so she willed me to tell the court.'

The letter to Arbella was undoubtedly from Cobham, but after hours of bitter verbal exchange Coke realised that he had no hope of embroiling Raleigh in the scandal. However, the jury was swayed by the letter that Cobham had written implicating Raleigh, despite the later retractions. Then, when they were told that Raleigh had persuaded Cobham to procure for him a pension of £1,500 from Spain, it took just fifteen minutes for the jury to bring the verdict of guilty. Clearer thinking would have questioned such an unlikely arrangement: Raleigh and Phillip III of Spain were bitter enemies, so why would they engage on any common project? Why would Spain voluntarily give money to Raleigh after the great destruction he had inflicted on the principal Spanish port of Cadiz only a few years earlier? The trial was an unscrupulous manipulation and a total farce. Despite the fact that two witnesses were legally required for a treason trial, only Cobham was cited despite Raleigh continually pressing for a second witness to be called. He and Cecil knew that no one else could be produced, and at length the judge instructed the court that precedent existed for the calling of a single witness.

Although it must have been obvious at the time, hindsight makes even more of a nonsense of the Main Plot and leaves us with a number of anomalies. A document, allegedly only found in the 1990s, cast a new light on Arbella's complicity in the plot. It looks at the evidence gained from the interrogations and finds that Brooke confessed Cobham wrote to Arbella to persuade her to write not just to Phillip III but also to the infanta and the Duke of Savoy. In court there is only mention of the one, rather mysterious letter that Cobham sent to Arbella, who sent it immediately to the king unopened. According to Cobham, he wrote and received letters from Arbella but burnt the documents. If she did in fact write to these people and received answers, they would have been damning evidence, as would any correspondence between her and Cobham.[7]

The question presents itself: why was this line of enquiry not investigated further? Again the answer lies with Cecil. When the plot was discovered, did Arbella agree to save her neck by providing documentary evidence for Cecil? It would explain why she was treated so lightly when later offenses were treated so gravely. Even if Arbella was totally innocent, it is worth remembering that so too was Lady Jane Grey, who had gone to the block for presuming to take the throne.

But why was Cecil so motivated? The death of his old enemy Essex had left him with no competitor in the kingdom for James's favour except Raleigh, a man of long-thwarted ambitions and great ability. Raleigh and his friends Cobham and the Earl of Northumberland had been nicknamed the 'diabolical triplicity'.[8]

The so-called triplicity had attempted to win the friendship of the Scottish king early in his reign, which, polished courtiers as they were, may have beguiled James. Cobham, with his attractive personality and lively talk, had quickly become a favourite of Queen Anne, so there was a possibility that James might follow suit. Cecil saw his absolute power threatened by the trio and early in the king's reign had concentrated on degrading Raleigh, who had been evicted from his mansion. He had also lost his post as Captain of the Guard, but Cecil wanted more; Cecil wanted self-preservation. His position as the king's adviser was not yet secure. At any moment he might have been supplanted by a favourite, one of the upstanding young men who enchanted the king. There was stiff competition from the Scottish lords who had come down from Scotland with the king, so Cecil had to demonstrate that he was indispensable. There was no surer way to do that than to alarm an unusually susceptible king with talk of plots against the royal person. In this regard, Cecil's discovery of the Main Plot and the Bye Plot was most convenient. A state trial in the seventeenth century was less an assessment of innocence than a public demonstration of guilt; the accused were allowed no lawyers and given only the most restricted opportunities to plead their own defence.

The thinness of the available evidence, coupled with alarm raised by the Bye Plot and the general disarray amongst the plotters, were all too easily disguised from a jury when directed by a prejudiced judge. Though the men who were involved in the Bye Plot were less eminent, theirs was plainly the main plot. Because of the lack of substance, it's doubtful whether there would have been a Main Plot; the core evidence against Cobham and Raleigh was Cobham's own word and his silly correspondence. An informed contemporary suggested that George Brooke was a venal agent through whom Cecil could operate, but who had intended all along to reveal the plots as fakes when the time was right. If that was so, it was a dangerous game for him to play. Brooke was described as a man of 'great wit, small means and vast expenses'. We assume the wit was comedic, not intellectual. He might have thought to outwit Cecil by taking the money, inventing and promoting the plots then admitting they were false.

Arbella sat through the most dramatic trial of the time but wisely refrained from committing her opinion to paper. She must have been acutely aware that her position as cousin of the king was rather precarious. If she did realise how tenuous the evidence was against Raleigh, she must have surmised that if it was considered necessary, a similar case could be fabricated against her. Raleigh's trial must have demonstrated to her just how little evidence was needed to secure a conviction. She had witnessed this, not just in the Bye and Main plots, but in the evidence against Mary, Queen of Scots in the Babington Plot, and the trial of her cousin Lady Jane Grey. They had paid with their lives.

Brooke and the two priests were executed with all the brutality accorded by the state on 5 December. Cobham, Grey and Markham were to be executed on 10 December, but James decided to reprieve them in a cruel cat-and-mouse game. The men were individually led to the scaffold where the instruments were set out and allowed to prepare themselves for death. The sheriff intimated to each in turn that the proceeding would be delayed and the men were led away and locked up again. An hour later, they were led back to the place of execution and, having again prepared to die, were then told of the king's clemency. Raleigh was similarly reprieved and left Winchester on 16 December to begin his long incarceration in the tower; he was released after thirteen years, but was eventually executed in 1618. The sick Cobham was released in the same year, dying some months later.[9]

THE COSTLY COURT OF
KING JAMES

By 28 March 1605 the king and court were at Greenwich waiting for the queen's lying-in. Queen Anne gave birth to a baby girl on 6 April 1605, who was named Mary after James's mother, Mary, Queen of Scots. Arbella was asked to be her godmother and sponsor. The christening was arranged for early May and was to be the first christening of a royal Stuart princess on English soil. It was also the first royal christening in England since that of Edward VI in 1537, which had been clouded by the death of his mother, Queen Jane Seymour.

New peers were to be created to mark the occasion, and the king gave Arbella a blank patent for a peerage, 'to be created either then or herafter to be named and created at her pleasure'.[1] Her first choice would be her Uncle Henry, who had helped her escape from Hardwick, but his disorderly attempts and the whisper of his name amongst the Bye and Main plotters prohibited his elevation to the peerage.

Her second choice was her Uncle Gilbert Talbot, but because both were hard pressed for money, neither could afford the sizeable douceur James would require. Gilbert had not recovered from the extravagance of entertaining the king at Worksop on his royal progress south, and his estates were uncertain. Gilbert had already approached Arbella for money, probably in repayment of the loans he had made her in the past, even though she had insufficient funds for her own expenses. Both Gilbert and Henry were out of favour with Bess, whose vast resources only her beloved son William could rely on.

When William heard about the peerage, he started to put pressure on Arbella to give it to him, but she had never liked him and was loath to give him the baronetcy. He was a mean, grasping man who Bronker had described as 'of little love or respect'. He even went to the court in London to plead with Arbella to promote him.[2]

But before anything was decided, Bess fell very ill and Arbella felt duty bound to return to Hardwick. Before she left court, she confided in James that she was unsure what kind of reception she would receive, and as a favour to her, James wrote to Bess telling her to receive Arbella with her former bounty and love. The letter annoyed Bess, who wrote a waspish letter of complaint to her confidant, Dr James Montague, Dean of the Royal Chapel, to be read to the king; he merely laughed, which did not improve Bess's temper. She was suspicious of her granddaughter's motive for returning to Hardwick. She was not prepared to forgive her and decided that Arbella was only after her money.

In a way, she was – but not for herself. Arbella saw no reason why her grandmother's vast resources could not be raided to secure for William the honour Arbella would have preferred he should not have. Much as he wanted it, he was loath to hand out to the king the usual large sums of money for such an honour, but when Arbella inserted William's name on the blank patent for the peerage, the cost of £2,000 was no doubt paid by Bess. By the end of April, William had been granted the baronetcy of Hardwick and Arbella had been forgiven. She left Hardwick with £300 and a cup of gold worth £100.[3]

Among the other three barons created to honour the christening of the infant Princess Mary was Sir John Stanhope, old neighbour and enemy of the Cavendishes, and Cecil, who was created Earl of Salisbury.

The royal coffers were ransacked to observe the christening ceremony at Greenwich. James must have surveyed the glittering scene of pageantry with satisfaction; the christening marked more comfortably than any other ceremony the security with which the family of James I held the throne of England. Princess Mary's christening was a grand affair in contrast to her funeral two years later. Like her grandmother, she was buried in Henry VII's chapel in Westminster Abbey. Queen Anne gave birth to another daughter, Sophia, in April 1606, but she died the same day and the queen became very ill afterwards. When Queen Anne's brother the King of Denmark visited a few months later, in July, Anne spent very little time entertaining her brother, but the visit was noted because the court indulged in some of the worst excesses of disgraceful behaviour on record. They held numerous tilts and other diversions and James delighted in watching animals being baited.

The Tower held a menagerie that housed lions, the symbol of Scotland and the king of beasts. Lions were of great interest to James, described as 'the most grotesque of kings'.[4] He provided the lions with a fine exercise yard in the moat of the Tower, as well as a nursery to encourage them to breed and successfully rear their young in captivity.

On 3 June the court visited the Tower for the lion baiting that took place in the Lion Tower, now demolished, at the south-west corner of the Tower. On this occasion the lions were fed with sides of mutton, a live cock, and a live lamb lowered into their pit, then baited with three dogs. One might have thought the feasting would have slowed them, but James watched with mounting excitement as the beasts showed their mettle by savaging the assailants.[5]

The court spent the month of June 1604 at Whitehall. On the morning of 1 July, it was discovered that Sir Robert Dudley had eloped during the night with Elizabeth Southwell, one of the queen's maids of honour. Elizabeth had disguised herself as a boy and passed as his page. Elopement with one of the queen's maids was a reprehensible liberty, and officials were warned to arrest them. It was assumed that they were heading for the Continent, and Sir William Monson, Admiral of the Narrow Seas, was instructed to intercept them. Monson had enough to do, acting as a high-class ferryman for such diplomats as Hertford; the previous month he had been responsible for preventing the Dutch and Spanish ships attacking each other in English territorial waters. On 8 July Elizabeth Southwell was stopped by the Governor at Calais, but he let her go because she declared that she had left England not for love but to enter a nunnery, a pretext made more plausible since her uncle had been Robert Southwell, the martyred Jesuit.

Salisbury set his spies to search for further news. The greatest of his agents was now William Wadd, apprentice of Walsingham, who had trusted him to search the papers of Mary, Queen of Scots, in 1586. Since then he had been the secretary of the council, assisting Cecil to gather evidence for the Main Plot. He had proved himself to be a man of great cruelty towards Catholics – one of the meanest men of a time noted for being exceptionally rich in examples. He was known to the court as 'Salisbury's great creature'.[6]

Wadd wrote to Cecil on 3 August, informing him that Elizabeth Southwell was entering the order of St Claire in Brussels.[7] But August passed and Elizabeth had not arrived in the Low Countries. It was not until October that Cecil learnt that she and Dudley were in Lyon, associating openly and waiting for a papal dispensation so that they could marry. When this approval eventually arrived, the couple were united. They had successfully defied James.

Despite giving the wrong information about Elizabeth Southwell and Robert Dudley, Wadd was appointed Lieutenant of the Tower of London. Cobham and Raleigh were jailed in the Tower for their part in the Main Plot, and Wadd was determined to make sure that whatever limited freedoms they had enjoyed under his predecessor would now stop. Cobham had been spending his time translating from Latin and Spanish; Raleigh had converted a hen house in the lieutenant's garden into a laboratory and study, where he entertained his numerous visitors. The queen, Prince Henry and the queen's brother the Duke of Holstein had all visited and put forward a case for his release to the king, but to no avail. The eleven-year-old Prince Henry was willing to be a pupil of such a man and took a great interest in Raleigh's knowledge of ships and the navy. He was so fascinated that he sent his own spy to see how the Royal Navy worked and to note what defects were apparent. Understandably, men like Salisbury did not like this self-assertion on the part of the young prince.

In the summer of 1605, the royal court made a four-day formal visit to Oxford. While the elders lodged at Christ Church, Prince Henry, an attractive, intelligent, well-mannered young man, totally unlike his father, was formally admitted as a member of the university and stayed at Magdalen. On his arrival he was formally escorted to his lodgings in the president's apartments, where he was entertained with disputations in which Mr William Seymour performed the part of respondent. No doubt Arbella joined Prince Henry, William and his companion, and it is said that they 'gave his Highness so much satisfaction in the readiness of their wit that, in testimony to it, he gave them his hand to kiss'.[8]

The autumn of 1605 has gone down in history because of another plot to dispose of James, the infamous Gunpowder Plot. English Catholics had suffered severe persecution since 1570 when the Pope had excommunicated Elizabeth. Catholics were forbidden to hear Mass and were forced instead to attend Anglican services, with steep fines for those recusants who persistently refused. Before James came to the throne, he had made sympathetic gestures indicating that he was warmly disposed to Catholics. His mother, Mary, Queen of Scots, had been a figurehead for Catholics at home and abroad, and his wife, Queen Anne of Denmark, was a Catholic; the early signs were encouraging. On his accession James ended recusancy fines, a relaxation that led to considerable growth in the number of visible Catholics. Then he reneged back on his word. The Main Plot and the Bye Plot tried to draw attention to the problem, but the conspirators were treated like traitors plotting treason. The situation deteriorated further when James expressed open hostility against the Catholics and publicly announced his 'utter detestation' of Catholicism. Within days all priests and Jesuits had been expelled and recusancy fines reintroduced.

Robert Catesby was a devout Catholic and familiar with the price of faith. His father had been imprisoned for harbouring a priest, and many of his friends were Catholic. He organised a meeting on 20 May 1604 at the Duck and Drake in the Strand, where he was joined by Thomas Wintour, Jack Wright, Thomas Percy and Guy Fawkes. Over the next few months their number gradually increased to ten, with the addition of Robert Keyes, Robert Wintour, John Grant and Kit Wright; over the following two months Catesby recruited Ambrose Rookwood, Francis Tresham and Sir Everard Digby.

Their plan was simple: to blow up Parliament House when James and his son Prince Henry were in residence. To do this, they leased a small house in the heart of Westminster and installed Guy Fawkes as caretaker under the alias of 'John Johnson'. They also took out a lease on a ground-floor cellar close by the house that lay directly underneath the House of Lords. Over the following months, thirty-six barrels of gunpowder were moved in. As Guy Fawkes was an explosives expert he was to be responsible for lighting the fuse. The second part of the plan was to coincide with the explosion: Digby would lead a rising in the Midlands and kidnap King James's daughter, Princess Elizabeth, ready to install her as a puppet queen. Hoping for foreign support, Fawkes travelled back to Flanders where he had been serving in the Spanish Army (under the name Guido Fawkes), but Cecil's spies had been alerted and the link between Fawkes and Catesby was made.

On 28 October 1605, Lord Monteagle received a perplexingly phrased letter from his brother-in-law Francis Tresham, who was also Catesby's cousin through marriage. It contained an ominous sentence: 'For though there be no appearance of a stir, yet I say, they shall receive a terrible blow in this parliament and yet shall not know who hurt them – the danger is past as soon as this letter is burnt.' The letter was passed to Salisbury and at midnight on 4/5 November, Sir Thomas Knyvet, a gentleman of the Privy Council and Justice of the Peace for Westminster, searched the cellars and found the gunpowder along with Guy Fawkes, the man responsible for lighting the fuse. At four in the morning the king and all the court were woken with the news.

Six plotters – Catesby, Rookwood, the Wright brothers, Percy and Bates – escaped from London and rode north to Warwickshire where they took refuge at Warwick Castle. By then they were wanted men and, with their stolen horses, they rode to Holbeche House in Staffordshire. On the morning of 8 November Sir Richard Walsh, the High Sheriff of Worcestershire, and 200 men attacked and scuppered the Midlands rebellion. Catesby, the Wrights and Percy died from their wounds; Thomas Wintour, Rookwood and Grant were captured. Five others remained at large.

The identities of the plotters were not originally known but it was widely recognised that Mary Talbot was a Catholic, and this was enough to account for the rumours that her husband Gilbert was involved.[9] Like many of those implicated, Father Garnet, who acted as confessor to some of the conspirators, was well known to them. Gilbert and Mary's son John Talbot refused to get involved when his son-in-law Robert Wintour requested asylum with him. Robert Wintour was still free in December, the last to be captured.

The Privy Council sent instructions to the Derbyshire justices to watch over the safety of Bess:

> In consequence of the horrible treason intended by Thomas Percy and his adherents, we require you to be extra vigilant in suppressing any disorder in your county. And as Lady Shrewsbury, Dowager, dwelling at Hardwick is a widow and solitary, we request you to have a care of her safety and quietness, and if Lord Cavendish shall have occasion to ask your assistance on her behalf, that you will aid and assist him for securing her safety.[10]

If the plot to install the young Princess Elizabeth on the throne as a puppet leader had been successful, they might have used Arbella as a figurehead in a rival Protestant party. Arbella was not directly implicated in the plot but might again have found herself in a strong position to take the throne.

A number of Jesuit priests who were recognised as being involved in the plot were still free at Christmas, but in January the trial of the surviving plotters commenced. The trial of Father Garnet took place at the Guildhall on 28 March. It held special interest to many curious spectators who watched as the proceedings, under Coke's skilful direction, turned into an attack on the Jesuits and their doctrines. Father Garnet lacked the personality, the agile mind and physical strength to defend himself. He admitted he had known of the plot, though under the seal of confession; the verdict was given in less than fifteen minutes. As with the Main and Bye plots, a state trial in the seventeenth century was less an assessment of innocence than a public demonstration of guilt, which had already been decided by the Privy Council.

* * *

In 1607 the Venetians were again watching Arbella. Then nearly thirty-two, she was described as

> ... not very beautiful ... highly accomplished and of most refined manners ... She speaks fluently Latin, Italian, French and Spanish, reads Greek and Hebrew and is always studying. She is not very rich and the poor lady cannot live as magnificently nor reward her attendants as liberally as she would. The king promised when he ascended the throne, that he would restore her property, but he has not done so yet, saying she shall have it all and more on her marriage, but so far the husband has not been found and she remains without mate and without estate.[11]

It was true that Arbella's financial situation was becoming desperate. Living in what was decidedly the most expensive court in Europe was not easy. As a princess of the royal blood, her dresses and jewels could not be less fine than those of a countess with a dowry of £10,000; she could not have fewer servants, entertain less or have poorer living conditions. In December she wrote to thank Gilbert for sending her a haunch of venison to eke out her diet from the royal table. This seems rather strange, knowing that James was so fond of hunting. It would be assumed that the royal tables would have been groaning under the weight of venison.

Her income at this time was £2,160 a year, with which she was expected to support herself and around ten servants. It was a considerable amount that would have sufficed in the ordinary world but it was nothing like enough for her to maintain her position at court. The historian Lawrence Stone estimated that the smallest amount that would support an earl at court was £5,000. Arbella was on less than half that amount.

During the winter of 1607, the court was at Whitehall. Old and uncomfortable, the building dated back to the thirteenth century

A sketch copied from the portrait of Arbella commissioned by her grandmother Margaret Lennox, inscribed 'Arbella, Countess of Lennox, aged 23 months. 1577'. (From Blanche Hardy's *Arbella Stuart: A Biography*, 1913)

Above: Bess commissioned this full-length portrait of her granddaughter Arbella aged thirteen and a half, with her hair hanging loose as a symbol of virginity and eligibility for marriage. By Isaac Oliver, French miniature painter active in England 1565–1617. (Courtesy Lewis Walpole Library, Yale University)

Left: Arbella's coat of arms. (Courtesy Durant)

Above: Margaret Douglas, Countess of Lennox, Arbella's paternal grandmother. (A variant taken from *Britain* magazine)

Right: George Talbot, 6th Earl of Shrewsbury, was Bess's fourth husband. (From John Daniel Leader's *Mary Queen of Scots in captivity*, 1880)

Robert Dudley, 1st Earl of Leicester, Queen Elizabeth's lifelong friend, rumoured to be her lover. Leicester tried to arrange a marriage between Arbella and his son Robert, the 'noble imp', but he died in infancy. Portrait from the workshop of van Ravesteyn (1609–1633). (Courtesy Rijksmuseum)

The courtly Lord Robert Devereux, 2nd Earl of Essex, w a showman and flatterer who flirted with Arbella and incurre the queen's jealousy. (Unknowr artist)

Queen Elizabeth used Arbella as she had once used herself, offering her in marriage along with the throne of England as a sweetener to foreign powers. Print by van de Passe in the manner of Isaac Oliver (1603–1620). (Courtesy Rijksmuseum)

Sir Walter Raleigh met twelve-year-old Arbella at court and told her about his experiences searching for El Dorado. She gave him an outline of the story in Spanish, which so impressed him, he said she had intellect beyond her years. (Courtesy Library of Congress)

After her escape from Scotland, Mary, Queen of Scots, was placed under house arrest in the care of the Earl and Countess of Shrewsbury. She remained in the Cavendish/Shrewsbury household, living alongside Arbella for sixteen years. (Courtesy David Loades)

James VI was Arbella's cousin and her closest rival for the English throne. He was also in Cecil's pocket and his succession was a foregone conclusion. Portrait by van Somer, (c. 1618). (Courtesy Yale Center for British Art)

Right: The Countess of Shrewsbury, better known as Bess of Hardwick, Arbella's maternal grandmother. (From Blanche Hardy's *Arbella Stuart: A Biography*, 1913)

Below: Bess's effigy in Derby Cathedral is quite magnificent but the Latin text was not added until 1677 and they forgot to add her age. (Author's collection)

Banned from court, Arbella was forced to remain at Hardwick Hall where she became a prisoner on instructions from Queen Elizabeth. (From Blanche Hardy's *Arbella Stuart: A Biography*, 1913)

Above: The Old Hall at Hardwick was Bess's birthplace and where she was forced to escape when driven out of Chatsworth House. After the death of her fourth husband, she was wealthy enough to afford to build a New Hall very close by (pictured below). (Courtesy Flickr)

Above: Elizabeth Cavendish and Charles Stuart, Earl of Lennox, met and married at Rufford Abbey, causing the angry Queen Elizabeth to place them under house arrest. (From old postcard)

Below: Worksop Manor, the impressive 500-room mansion built by the 6th Earl of Shrewsbury was where his son Gilbert, Arbella's uncle, played host to James I on his journey south to claim the English crown. (From an original engraving by Samuel and Nathaniel Buck 1745)

Above: Tutbury Castle was a secure prison for Mary, Queen of Scots, but the damp, unhealthy conditions exacerbated her rheumatism. From a seventeenth-century engraving. (Author's collection)

Below: Chatsworth House, built in the 1560s by Bess and her second husband, Sir William Cavendish. The design was incorporated into the modern build by their grandson William Cavendish, 1st Duke of Devonshire, around 1696; on the left is the original western facade. (Author's collection)

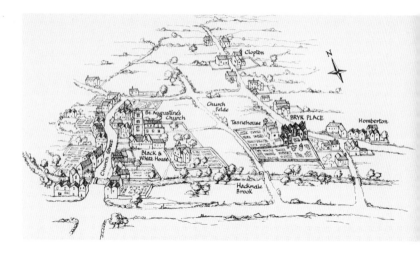

Above: Tudor Hackney was then a leafy suburb of London, where Margaret Lennox lived at King's Place and where the newly-weds were kept under house arrest. (Enhanced sketch taken from an old manuscript)

Below: Richmond Palace, Queen Elizabeth's favourite palace, on the north bank of the River Thames. She died here in 1603 and all that now remains is the gatehouse and fragments of the old building. (Sketch based on engraving by James Basire)

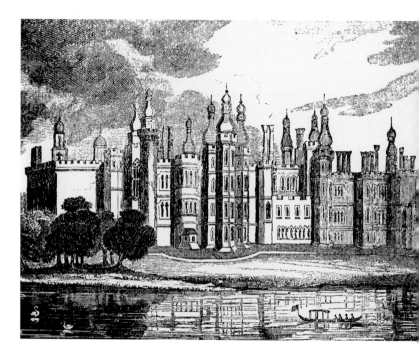

Above and below: South Wingfield Manor was a fortified castle used as a prison for Mary, Queen of Scots. It offered protection for thirteen-year-old Arbella when it was feared she could be taken hostage at the time of the Spanish Armada. (Courtesy Flickr)

Above: Ault Hucknall church on the edge of the Hardwick estate was to be used as a vantage point to watch for Arbella in an abortive attempt to kidnap her. (Author's collection)

Below: Fotheringay Castle was Mary's final prison and where her execution took place on 8 February 1587. (Author's collection)

Above: The interior of the Swan Playhouse, a typical Tudor theatre. Nearby, at the Blackfriars theatre, Ben Jonson's *Epicoene* scandalised the audience with its reference to Arbella's questionable gender. Sketch by Johannes de Witt (1596). (Courtesy Jonathan Reeve)

Below: The Tower of London, where Arbella occupied the rooms of many notable former prisoners and where she died on 25 September 1615, aged forty. (Courtesy Flickr)

Above: Detail from Claes van Visscher's 'Panorama of London' (1616) showing the Tower of London. (Courtesy British Library)

Below: 'The Papists Powder Treason' (1689), contemporary anti-Catholic satire by anonymous artist in the manner of Samuel Ward. Lettered with texts in Latin, English, Dutch and German, the most prominent reads, 'To God, in Memory of His double Deliverance from ye invincible Navie [the Spanish Armada] and ye unmatcheable Powder-Treason'. (Courtesy British Museum)

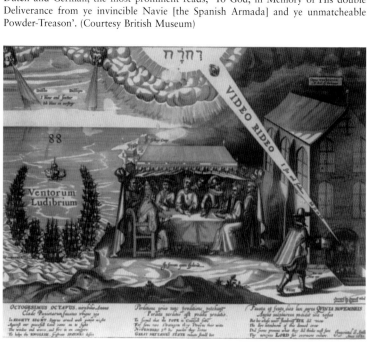

and lingered on until 1698 when a fire ruined it beyond repair. Twelfth Night celebrations only drew attention to how difficult it was for Arbella to support her position in a court where rich materials and jewellery were the height of social display; talent, wit and manners counted for very little.

Early in December, Gilbert and Mary Talbot and Charles Cavendish visited Hardwick Hall and reported that although Countess Bess's mind was clear enough, her main topics of conversation were her age and her money. He described the visit to their brother Henry Cavendish in a letter dated 4 January 1608: 'She did eat very little and was not able to walk the length of her chamber betwixt two, but grew so ill at it as you might plainly discern it.'[12]

William's wife wrote that Bess was worse, and Bess's waiting woman sent a secret message that Bess was so ill that she could not be away from her day or night. Her alchemist had made up nostrums of antimony and liquid of pearl but they had done little to relieve her ailments. She was in her eighty-eighth year – a remarkable age and a rarity amongst the great personages of the sixteenth century. She had outlived four husbands and was dying as one of the wealthiest women in the kingdom, in the tapestried room of one its finest houses.

The first months of 1608 were bitterly cold and the Thames froze over making a highway of ice. In Derbyshire Bess had workmen standing idle because although the frozen water used to mix the plaster was boiled, it froze again in the mix making it impossible to use. The ever resourceful Bess ordered the workmen to boil ale but that was also ineffective. Superstitious people were quick to say how a fortune teller had predicted that Bess would never die while she kept building. Bess had her own astrologer, as did many influential people. Queen Elizabeth had regularly consulted the extraordinary John Dee, as mentioned earlier.

Bess died on 13 February 1608. She had made peace with all her relatives and left Arbella £1,000, but quarrels soon broke out. William took charge of Hardwick, Owlcotes and a London property even before the will was read. He also claimed all the contents of Chatsworth House although the house was entailed on Henry.

Bess of Hardwick had achieved much, yet despite all her efforts, nothing had come of the triumphant marriage of Elizabeth Cavendish and Charles Stuart. She was not grandmother of a sovereign. But she could add the prefix 'Lord' to the name of Cavendish and later her son William was to take the title Earl of Devonshire (and the fourth Earl was to raise this to a dukedom). Bess had seen her daughter Mary become Countess of Shrewsbury, and Mary's daughter Alethea married to Thomas Howard, 2nd Earl of Arundel. Her son Charles fathered the Dukes of Newcastle and her daughter Frances mothered the Earls of Kingston-upon-Hull. The biographer who edited the Talbot papers at the end of the eighteenth century summed up: 'She was a builder, a buyer and seller of estates, a money lender, a farmer and a merchant of lead, coal and timber.'[13]

In her 1601 will, Bess stipulated that 'my funeral be not over sumptuous or otherwise performed with too much vain and idle charge'. She was buried at All Hallows Church, Derby (now Derby Cathedral) on 4 May 1608. Only the West Tower is contemporary with her impressive tomb that dominates the aisle; the standing wall monument had been finished in 1601 on Bess's instructions and just needed installation. She supervised the inscription, describing herself as *inclytissma*; beneath the inscription lies her effigy in alabaster. Up until 1848, over forty of her descendants were buried in a vault below the tomb. Rather unexpectedly, her sons Henry and William are buried at Edensor Church, and Charles at Bolsover.

Her great houses, with the exception of Owlcotes, have survived. Their number and their splendour were never rivalled. In the eighteenth century Horace Walpole wrote the following verse in the margins of his copy of Collins' *Historical Collections of the Noble Family of Cavendish*:

> When Hardwick Towers shall bow their head
> Nor mass be more in Worksop said
> When Bolsover's fair frame shall tend
> Like Oldcotes to its destined end
> When Chatsworth knows no Candish bounties
> Let fame forget this costly countess.[14]

Walpole's epithet was fair although slightly misleading: she was not a 'costly countess'. Bess spent money prudently and in many ways was extremely frugal. The purchase of the Hardwick tapestries is a typical example. Her houses were costly, her expenditure great but their value was even greater. She left an amazing legacy, and none of her descendants were bankrupted by her expenditure.

18

ARBELLA FINDS INDEPENDENCE

Throughout her time at court Arbella was forced to live far beyond her means, which meant accumulating debts she hoped to be able to pay off sometime in the future. The problem was, the future didn't seem to be offering any financial help – that is, until she acquired the services of Hugh Crompton as a gentleman usher or major-domo of her household. He was an able, intelligent young man with a head for figures and helped her to make the most of her poor resources. He kept her accounts, did her pawning and tried to keep her affairs discreet. Arbella must have accumulated many jewels as presents, but as gold, pearls and diamonds were pawned on a regular basis, it is hard to estimate how much jewellery Arbella actually had or its value. It must have riled her that she never possessed the Lennox jewels.

Arbella had every confidence in Hugh Crompton's ability, and it was possibly due to his influence that she began to make more effort to secure her share of the pickings that were available to those in James's favour. Chief of these were the monopolies by which the Tudor and Stuart monarchs replenished the royal Exchequer.

Gilbert assisted her to draw up a petition to the king to allow her the monopoly of oats sold to travellers by innkeepers throughout the kingdom. He pointed out that the advantage to the king would be an increase in revenues of £1,000 per annum without any charge to himself, something that James would expect in any case from a person to whom he granted such a profitable monopoly. Perhaps Gilbert's approach was too tentative and ineffective against ruthless competition because James was hesitant to present the monopoly to his cousin Arbella. During the summer she continued to petition the king but, as the months dragged on, she became desperate, looking for any opportunity.

At thirty-three, without a dowry and no longer in the first bloom of her youth, she orbited alone around the court, a perpetual odd one out. At times she must have felt that this intolerable situation was more than she could put up with. Her melancholy position was almost as unsupportable as her long confinement at Hardwick had been.

It was during the summer of 1608 that Arbella decided to seek a refuge from the court where she could pursue her own interests. To do this, she bought her own house. Arbella had spent a total of four years at court when, at Michaelmas 1608, she bought herself a residence at Blackfriars for £200. Michaelmas occurs on 29 September in the liturgical year; in medieval England, it marked the ending and beginning of the husbandman's year, when harvest was over and the bailiff or reeve of the manor would be making out the annual accounts.

Her townhouse was at Blackfriars, a desirable area just outside the City, a riverside district that had previously belonged to the Dominicans, or 'Blackfriars', and had become a fashionable sanctum within the wall of the former friary. 'For want of a nunnery I have for a while retired myself to the Friars,' she wrote to Gilbert on 8 November from her new address.[1]

About five acres in area, the precinct was bounded on the south and west by the rivers Thames and Fleet and on the north and east by Ludgate Hill. One of its privileges was its exemption from the regulations that forbade the erection of playhouses within the City. Advantage had been taken of this when, in 1577, the former upper *frater,* or recreation room, of the monks was converted into a theatre. It had remained private, reserved for the people of quality rather than the general public, who flocked to the inn-yards and the open-air theatres. The theatre had been disbanded due to debts in 1584. In 1597 the Burbage family, the employers of Shakespeare, bought the major part of the upper *frater*. They built in a stage, auditorium and boxes so that the theatre could be used for winter performances when the open air theatre at Shoreditch became uncomfortable. This did not please the aristocratic inhabitants, who petitioned for its closure.

The Burbage family had just regained the king's permission to put on plays in 1608, around when Arbella moved into Blackfriars, so the place was a riot of colour, noise and excitement. Arbella bought her house from the successors to Sir Thomas Cheney, whose original grant from Henry VIII also included the Blackfriars Theatre. This could indicate that the two properties were formerly one and Arbella's house was adjacent to the theatre. In Cheney's time it was newly built and included a garden backing onto the River Fleet (almost on present-day Blackfriars Lane). After Cheney's death the house had been occupied by Lord Henry Seymour, the old Earl of Seymour's brother.

The precinct was a place of trees and gardens, still reminiscent of a former monastery, but it also stood on the ancient thoroughfare from Ludgate to the water stairs and would have been busy with people all day long. There would be litter in the yards and streets and, to make matters worse, at this time the River Fleet was used as an open sewer. A short distance away was situated St Paul's and the City's other churches where she could hear the most controversial preachers, and, in the cheek by jowl nature of the City, there also were mansions and luxury stores. Arbella must have found the transition to Blackfriars something of a novelty.

At all her previous homes and at court, she had been sheltered from the lives of ordinary people; at Blackfriars, the place was busy with courtiers, preachers and their congregations, actors and their audiences. There were also many artists and artisans as during the 1580s a colony of Huguenot refugees had settled along the Ludgate boundary of the precinct, many of them goldsmiths, printers, booksellers and bookbinders.

With her own house, Arbella spent increasingly less time at court. In December she was struck by smallpox. In that period it was a crippling disease that killed and left many disfigured. When Queen Elizabeth had smallpox in 1562, four years into her reign, it had caused a major succession problem (as touched upon in earlier chapters). Lady Skinner attended to Arbella and she prescribed the 'red light' treatment, which meant hanging red cloth over the windows. Giving smallpox patients red liquid to drink, wrapping them in red cloth and sitting them in rooms decorated with red hangings had been around for centuries, stemming from the idea that like repels like, so red repelled the red rashes of smallpox. In part this treatment can be explained because being wrapped up and sitting by a fire would make the body sweat, which, like bloodletting, was considered a remedy for most ills – that and arsenic, mercury and sheep droppings, all believed to restore the body's natural balance. Whatever treatment Lady Skinner used, it apparently worked and by the second week in February Arbella was convalescing with her aunt and uncle Mary and Gilbert Talbot at their home in Bond Street.[2]

Shortly after, she attended the opening of a new mercantile enterprise that Lord Salisbury had erected next to his house in the Strand, carved from the purlieus of Durham House where Sir Walter Raleigh had once lived. On the site of the former stables, Salisbury had built two galleries that housed a variety of shops licensed under regulations intended to maintain a high standard of goods and service to attract people of quality. In March 1609 it was suggested that the new building should be named 'Armabell' to pay a compliment to a certain gracious lady, but James opened the arcade and preferred the name 'Britain's Burse'.[3] However the new venture was not successful until after the Restoration, when it was renamed the New (later Royal) Exchange.

On 23 June, the court attended what the king considered to be a gripping spectacle at the Tower. A bear that had killed a child was set against one of the lions, but the king of beasts refused to be baited.[4] The fact that Cobham and Raleigh were still imprisoned there for their parts in the Main Plot seems ironic, but they would have been kept well out of the king's sight. Arbella attended this spectacle; within a few years she would also be a prisoner in the Tower.

During 1609, Arbella was active in her petitions for monopolies. She entered a petition for a licence to export 40,000 Irish hides a year into England, and forwarded for consideration another license to nominate the sellers of wines and whiskey in Ireland. It can be assumed that Hugh Compton was involved in this enterprise – he certainly kept accurate records of the amount she spent on her journey north that year.[5]

On 22 August 1609, Arbella left Whitehall for St Albans in a coach accompanied by a retinue of twenty horses for the gentlemen-in-waiting and personal servants. There she was entertained by a peal of the church bells and a performance by a trumpeter and other musicians. The stay cost Arbella £10 15s 0d. The next stop was Lady Cheney's at Toddington near Dunstable, the daughter-in-law of the Sir Thomas Cheney whose house in Blackfriars had been bought by Arbella. She gave gratuities of £7 15s 0d.[6]

On 26 August, a footman of Sir James Crofts conducted her to his master's house at Northampton. She then travelled on to Prestwood near Loughborough, the seat of Sir William Skipworth. She left Prestwood on 28 August and travelled on to her home ground of Mansfield. It was here six years previously where her uncle Henry Cavendish and Henry Stapleton had attempted to carry her off from Hardwick. Now, she was enough of a local celebrity to be welcomed by verses by the schoolmaster, who was paid six shillings for his goodwill.

Her entourage then took the main road between Mansfield and Chesterfield passing near Hardwick Hall, which after Bess's death belonged to William Cavendish. It would have seemed obvious to have broken the journey there, but, rather surprisingly, they didn't. At Glapwell, the gates of Hardwick Hall were only a mile away through the little hamlet of Ault Hucknall, where Henry Cavendish had tried to gain access to the church tower in his bid to help Arbella escape. As they passed through Glapwell, the leaf springs of the coach broke down and had to be repaired. Arbella did not even attempt to obtain help from Hardwick, and after an irritating delay, they set off again on their bone-bruising progress towards Chesterfield. Was her failure to seek William's hospitality intentional? A little further and looking back she would have seen the high castellated walls of Bolsover Castle on the ridge over on her left and the familiar towers of Hardwick above the trees on her left. Passing through Heath, they would have seen Owlcotes in the valley. This was the place where she had been sent in 1603 when she refused to eat or drink at Hardwick. Did she pass these familiar places without emotion as they continued towards Chesterfield?

Her next destination was Walton Hall on the outskirts of Chesterfield, the home of her good friend Lady Isabel Bowes, a great supporter of radical Protestants. Her first husband, Godfrey Foljambe of Aldwarke, Yorkshire, and Walton, Derbyshire died on 14 June 1595. During their marriage she had a suspected demoniac named Katherine Wright brought to their house at Walton, near Chesterfield, while various ministers attempted to cure her of possession. John Darrell, later shown to be a charlatan, was given credit for accomplishing the task. By 1599, Isabel had married

Sir William Bowes of Streatlam and Barnard Castle, Durham who had succeeded his uncle Robert Bowes in the Scottish embassy.

During her stay Arbella spoke to Lady Bowes about looking for a country house for herself away from London. Arbella was determined to reduce her attendance at court, but this was the first sign that she was contemplating a possible marriage and a country estate of her own. The two ladies would have considered all the options and the exciting prospect of being neighbours. It's also possible that Arbella discussed business and certain financial plans with Isabel Bowes' brother-in-law Sir George St Paul, husband of Isabel's sister Frances.

While Arbella was in Chesterfield, the horses were re-shod and a foot of the old coach horse, which had been injured, was dressed. The Mayor and Council of Chesterfield sent a deputation to their remembered lady with a present in honour of her return. The Earl of Rutland's musicians played to her, yet there is no mention of William Cavendish or any of his family, which would suggest some deep rift in the family.

On 2 September, as Arbella passed through the town of Chesterfield on her way to Sheffield she distributed £2 amongst the poor. At Sheffield she enjoyed the hospitality of her Uncle Gilbert and Aunt Mary, hunting a stag at Handsworth on the edge of Sheffield Park.

On 9 September, the journey continued towards Bawtry and Stockwith, where poor roads and the meandering rivers Trent and Idle affected progress. Arbella was ferried across the water and spent the next five days at Melwood Park, South Yorkshire, where her host was Lady Bowes' sister Frances and husband Sir George St Paul. He and Arbella were both involved in one of the Irish monopolies. Here she had to purchase another coach horse for £20 as the dressing put on the hoof of the old horse was ineffective.

Her return journey began on 13 September, where she spent the night at Worksop, entertained again by Gilbert and Mary.

Next day she went ten miles north to Aston Hall near Sheffield, the home of a childhood friend Lord Darcey, at that time a widower with three children. How different things might have been if Arbella had married him, but instead, almost six years after the death of Sir William Bowes, on 7 May 1617, Lord Darcey married Arbella's friend Lady Bowes of Walton Hall, Chesterfield.

After four days, Arbella left Aston and headed for Chatsworth where her uncle Henry Cavendish would receive her. This was a very difficult journey. One of the horses went ill, the saddle and rein of the sumpter horse had to be repaired, and they got lost on the open moors. These were thinly populated, wild areas and needed a guide to negotiate a successful journey.

Arbella and her entourage spent only one night at Chatsworth House then, accompanied by a guide and four coach horses borrowed from Henry Cavendish, she continued towards Buxton. Her stay at the spa lasted until the 20th, during which time she visited the famous St Anne's Well, drank and bathed. On the 19th and 20th, the man who kept the well received the substantial sum of £1 and his man 6s; two women in attendance further received £1 between them. This was a lot of money – Henry Cavendish's coachman and his man were allowed just 6p each for a meal during their stay.

The next halt was Sheffield, but before arriving the coach broke down in the middle of the moors. Gilbert's son-in-law, the Earl of Pembroke, sent his coachman to collect Arbella and guide them across the moors. Arbella was welcomed at Sheffield with a peal of bells. She stayed at Sheffield until 25 September, when she and her aunt Mary set off for Rufford Abbey. This was where Bess had organised the ill-fated marriage of Arbella's mother and father in 1574. It was part of the dowry of George Talbot's daughter by his first wife, the then Lady Savile. Arbella also visited the Ollerton seat of the Markhams; she was hosted by George Markham, brother of Sir Griffin Markham, a conspirator in the Bye Plot.

On 28 September Arbella was at South Wingfield and from there arrived at the county town of Derby. She no doubt stopped to visit the church where Bess was so regally entombed. The journey south continued, calling at Quarndon Manor near Loughborough, the home of the Farnham family. Following this she stayed at Market Harborough then Easton Manduit near Wellingborough, the house of Sir Christopher Yelverton. On 4 October she travelled on to Wrest House, where she remained for six days as the guest of the Greys, then finally on 8/9 October they journeyed back to St Albans and arrived in London by 10 October.[7]

She again pressed James on the subject of her future. He had promised to find her a husband and restore her Lennox estates but had done neither. The situation wasn't helped by the fact that Ludovic Stuart, the owner of the Lennox title that had been her father's and should have been hers, had a prominent position at the court of King James. Not that Arbella wanted the title itself, but she was entitled to the income or compensation for the income. There were also the Lennox jewels that the old Countess of Lennox had willed to Arbella and which had mysteriously disappeared. No wonder Arbella felt resentful. Arbella during this time was again venerated in verse with a sonnet by George Chapman, playwright and poet. He referred to her as 'our English Athenia, chaste arbitress of virtue and learning'.

It was probably due to Hugh Compton that on 2 November 1609 she applied for the lucrative licence, shared with Henry Yelverton and George St Paul, to nominate the sellers of wine and whiskey in Ireland for a period of twenty-one years. It was granted on 22 March 1610.[8] The Venetian ambassador, writing on 1 April, estimated that it should bring her 4,000 ducats a year, worth nearly £2,000.[9]

On 5 December 1609 Arbella heard from her old friend Lady Isabel Bowes at Walton Hall. She had found Arbella a country house.[10] This must have motivated Arbella to consolidate her resources because in December, just a month after applying for the wine and whisky license, she wrote to Salisbury asking him to compound the monopoly in exchange for the payment of her debts.[11]

Arbella also asked for an increase in her allowance so that 'I may be able to live in such honour and countenance hereafter as may stand with his majesty's honour and my own comfort'. She also informed him that as she intended to spend more time away from the court, the dishes to which she was entitled from the king's table would be useless to her. She suggested that his majesty be pleased to let her have £1,000 yearly instead.

It seems unclear what Arbella was planning, but in 1607 a Moldavian prince and claimant to the Moldavian throne visited London seeking to establish trading links with England. Arbella was looking for investments and, with Hugh Compton to advise her, she was tempted to take the opportunity to get involved in commercial transactions with the country of Moldavia (now Romania). The working relationship between Arbella and the prince developed into something deeper and he asked for her hand in marriage. James assured the prince that he would look favourably on the union if he made good his claim to establish trade links. The prince assured James he would. Showing a remarkable lack of judgement on her part, and risking all the money she could lay her hands on to finance an unknown venture, Arbella gave the prince 4,000 ducats. The prince left England bragging that the king had given him a royal pension of £300 and promised him a royal bride. Passing through Venice, he even had the effrontery to take possession of the English ambassador's house as a lodging in the latter's absence, on the pretext that he was engaged to marry Arbella. Then it was disclosed that the so-called prince was a pretender to that distant throne, a mountebank named Stephano Janiculo or alternatively Stephen Bugdania (another name for Moldavia), shortened to 'Bugdan'. All his promises were hollow, and within a short time he had married someone else.[12]

James had been duped. The king was enraged and he wanted the matter kept secret because the commercial and social repercussions were equally unpleasant. However, it was much worse for Arbella: not only had she been jilted at the altar, she could not afford to lose such a large amount of money. She sent Douglas, one of her relatives through her grandmother Lady Lennox, to Constantinople to retrieve the money from a man she had trusted and who had made such reprehensible use of her name.

The Venetians, always keen to report on Arbella's movements despite not knowing the facts, reported: 'His Majesty had a hint last week that she intended to cross the sea with a Scot named Douglas and had some idea of marrying him.' Despite knowing that the Venetians were not averse to telling a few tall tales, James seemed to take this at face value and sent Fenton, his Captain of the Guard, to locate Arbella and invite her to sup with them. Because Fenton was married to Arbella's cousin and childhood friend Elizabeth Pierrepoint, she had no reason to question the invitation, and was led away entirely unsuspecting. No doubt to her surprise, she was then placed under guard for several days and committed to the Lord Knyvett, the Justice of the Peace. He was the man who had exposed the barrels of gunpowder under Parliament House on 5 November, for which he continued to reap the grateful indebted king's rewards.

Hugh Compton and some of Arbella's other servants and waiting maids were also arrested. Douglas and a number of his servants were arrested and appeared before the council. Arbella would neither confirm nor deny that she had intended to leave the country. She merely said that, ill-treated as she was by all, it was only natural that she thought of going.

Were the stories and the arrests a cover-up of the true reason why Douglas had been sent abroad – to protect Arbella's commercial interests and James's reputation – or was there something else that was never revealed?[13]

At the time of her arrest Arbella was at the home of the Seymour family, which provides a possible motive for the arrest. In 1608, with Cecil's help, Edward Seymour, Earl of Hertford, had found the anonymous clergyman who had married him to Katherine Grey forty-eight years earlier. James reluctantly agreed to give their heirs the legitimate right to inherit the title Earl of Hertford, thus restoring to them their rightful place in the English succession. In the small world of Jacobean aristocracy, Arbella would have mixed and mingled with the Hertford family. The Countess of Hertford, the earl's young third wife, was much the same age as Arbella and was with her at the court of Queen Anne, so it would have been quite acceptable for them to be sociable – but was there something more? Was there another plot afoot to forge an alliance between Arbella and Hertford's grandson, and thus provide an acceptable alternative to the unpopular Scottish king?

Edward, who had been proposed as a bride for Arbella back in 1602/3, took the title Lord Beauchamp on the death of his father in 1612, but he was now married to Anne Sackville, daughter of the Earl of Dorset. Edward's younger brother William was unmarried, and although there is no mention of him other than the meeting between William and Arbella at Oxford in the summer of 1605, it is possible that they had become firm friends.

19

THE SECRET WEDDING AND ITS CONSEQUENCES

Like most of the court, Arbella loved to attend plays, and Blackfriars Theatre was right on her doorstep. The group of boy actors who performed there, like other troupes of actors, received royal favour and between 1603 and 1605 became the Children of the Queen's Revels. They performed plays by Ben Jonson, George Chapman, John Marsden, Thomas Middleton and others during the following years, specialising in satirical comedies of manners that appealed to court wits and a more refined audience, in contrast to the more popularly oriented drama of William Shakespeare, Thomas Heywood, Thomas Dekker and similar writers. The Children of the Queen's Revels experienced popularity and success in the first years of the century, yet they also experienced the pitfalls of this brand of drama. The play *Eastwood Hoe* (1605) won official censure and landed two of its authors, Ben Jonson and George Chapman, in jail. The actors also earned a share of the disapproval, lost their Royal Patent, and became simply the Children of the Revels (1605–6).

After another scandal in 1606 they became known as the Children of the Blackfriars, then managed to offend the king a third time in 1608. When Arbella moved into Blackfriars the

Burbage family had just regained the king's permission to put on plays, and the King's Men took over the lease of the Blackfriars Theatre, effectively evicting the previous tenants, and the children's company moved to the new Whitefriars Theatre. They became the Children of the Whitefriars, before in 1610 they returned to royal favour and were once again the Children of the Queen's Revels.

It was at this stage that the playwright Ben Jonson wrote a play entitled *Epicoene, or the Silent Woman*, premiered in January 1610 and performed by the Children of the Queen's Revels. Jonson's play, set in London, was topical. Epicoene is thought to be a silent gentlewoman who marries Morose, a wealthy old man with an obsessive hatred of noise. Morose soon regrets his marriage when his wife is revealed as a loud, vain and scheming woman with intellectual pretensions. He looks for a means of obtaining a divorce and reveals that Epicoene is, in fact, a man.

Up until this point there is nothing to link Arbella with the silent gentlewoman-cum-gentleman Epicoene, although the intellectual pretensions might be a clue. The identification rests on one line about the Prince of Moldavia and his mistress, the Lady Epicoene, with a crack about whether the boastful bachelor has 'found out her latitude'. The mention of the Prince of Moldavia was more than a coincidence and could not be missed; the theatre-going set knew Arbella had recently been involved with the Prince of Moldavia when he visited London. Their names had been romantically linked, so it wasn't hard to join it all together. This was just the kind of thing that would appeal to and shock the sophisticated audience, thirsty for scandal.

It was the ridicule of these people that Arbella would have felt most deeply. She complained and the play was suppressed, but the damage had been done. Jonson was no stranger to controversy. He had a reputation for scurrility and slander and was also in trouble with Lady Bedford over a slanderous epigram. The Venetian Correr reported that Arbella was very ill-pleased and showed a determination to secure the punishment of certain persons. It was Correr who had bestowed on Arbella that pithily accurate epithet, 'without mate and without estate'.

To squash the persistent rumours, Arbella decided to launch herself towards wedlock on a tide of desperation. On 8 January 1610, the Venetian ambassador wrote, 'She is living far from court in deep melancholy, both on account of the little esteem in which she is held and because her income is insufficient.'[1] Although confined to her own apartments, Arbella was restored to favour and her former place at court, but kept herself very much to herself and was visited only by a few intimates. It was reported that she was seldom seen outside her room and lived in greater dejection than ever.[2] At the end of February he added that there remained much suspicion about this lady of high spirit and ability who lived in seclusion. Was it likely such a person would indefinitely tolerate the situation he had already described so accurately?[3]

Arbella took the opportunity to voice her grievances about her marital state, her patrimony, the estate she should have inherited from her father, and her income. If James would not arrange for her to be wed, she asked that she might be allowed to choose for herself. This time, her forceful pleading at least got some results: James agreed to increase her pension and bequeathed to her 'a cupboard of plate better than £200 for a New Year's gift and 1,000 marks to pay her debts'.[4]

The Venetians reported on 25 February that James had given her 10,000 crowns to pay her debts (ten times the amount reported by Chamberlain), and increased her diet from eight dishes a day to thirteen. If this is true, James had evidently disregarded her request to commute the diet for cash.

He'd also ignored Arbella's request to find her a husband, despite her making it known that if James would not, she would. James was still smarting about the Moldavian affair and made Arbella promise that she would not consider another foreign bridegroom.

In return for her assurance that she would not marry a foreigner, she received James's permission that she could take as her husband any man she pleased so long as he was a loyal subject of the realm.

Arbella said nothing about a deep and meaningful relationship that had been blossoming between herself and William Seymour. William had graduated from Magdalen College, Oxford in 1605 at the age of seventeen and arrived at court in a minor capacity to expand his education and acquaintances. Arbella and William probably formed a bond as neither enjoyed the frivolity, extravagance and horseplay at court; both enjoyed studying and spending time at their books. He was described as a man of great honour, interest and estate and, like Arbella, he was fluent in both Latin and Greek. They enjoyed each other's company, and inevitably rumours of their association began to leak out as Arbella and William became more open about their relationship. But no one seemed to take it seriously – even the Venetians, always anxious to spread gossip, could not believe that a man of twenty-two could be in a romantic relationship with a lady of thirty-three.

On 2 February 1610 William went to Arbella's rooms and asked her to marry him. She agreed and they went through some form of betrothal ceremony. They had two more meetings within the next few days at the houses of friends, Mr Bugg's of Fleet Street and Mr Baynton's in Lambeth, making little or no attempt to keep the betrothal secret. The news soon reached James. When the king discovered the true object of his cousin's affection, he was furious and had them brought before the council for questioning.[5]

On 15 February, James Beaulieu, secretary to the diplomat Sir Thomas Edmondes, wrote:

> The Lady Arbella who, as you know was not long ago censured for having without the king's privity, entertained a motion of marriage, was again within these few days apprehended in

the like treaty with Lord Beauchamp's second son, and both were called and examined yesterday at the Court about it. What the matter will prove I know not, but these affections of marriage do give some advantage to the world of impairing the reputation of her constant and virtuous disposition.[6]

On 20 February, two days after their last meeting, William was summoned before the court again. He wrote a formal submission about the affair, addressed deferentially to the 'Right Honourable my most singular good Lords, the Lords of His Majesty's Most Honourable Privy Council'. It is extremely cautious and explains that no offence was intended. He believed that Arbella had been given leave by King James after her examination in January to 'make her choice of any subject within this kingdom'. This had given him hope that he could honestly endeavour to gain Arbella's hand in marriage. He gave assurance that neither he nor Arbella would contemplate marriage without the king's permission. He detailed when and where they had met. He was obviously doing his best to placate the king: 'I do plainly and honestly endeavour lawfully to gain her in marriage, which is God's ordinance common to all, assuming myself if I could affect the same with his Majesty's most gracious favour and liking without which I resolve never to proceed.'[7]

There is a rough draft of an unsigned letter in the Longleat papers, discovered by Canon Jackson, librarian to the 4th Marquis of Bath in the mid-nineteenth century, which would appear to be addressed to Arbella. It has all the signs of being dictated by William's grandfather, the old Earl of Hertford, who instructed a servant to write:

He hath seriously considered of the proceedings between your Ladyship and himself, and does well perceive, if he should go on therein, it would prove exceedingly prejudicial to your contentment but extremely dangerous to him, first in regard of the inequality of degrees between your ladyship and him, next the Kings Majesty's pleasure and commandment to the contrary, which neither your ladyship nor himself did ever intend to neglect. He doth therefore humbly desire your Ladyship, since the proceedings that is past does not tie him nor your Ladyship to any necessity, but that you may freely commit each other to your best fortunes, that you would be pleased to desist from your intended resolution concerning him, who likewise resolveth not to trouble you any more in this kind, not doubting that your Ladyship may have one more fitting for your degree (he having already presumed too high) and himself a meaner match, with more security.[8]

This cruel letter may have reflected the way William felt, but it was a very adolescent act to hide behind a letter written by someone else. The writer was not only trying to placate the king, he wanted to ensure Arbella felt in no way bound to continue their relationship. He suggests that for Arbella's sake the engagement should be broken off, and she should find someone who could take care of her in the manner she deserved. Was this what William wanted? He was twenty-two, the penniless younger son at the start of his career. They had similar tastes but there was never any insinuation of love. Also, William would be only too aware of the consequences of the marriage made by his grandfather to Katherine Grey. Having been reared in a family that was out of favour with the court, he was obviously trying to make sure that history was not going to repeat itself. The inference is that the choice was Arbella's more than his. The question is, why did she choose a young, timid youth, and a Seymour, after all her previous dealing with the family?

If he had been older he would have been a wiser choice, but the big disparity in age was a major problem. He was a nice man, unlike the scheming, self-centred, selfish courtiers that usually surrounded her; and such men were rare. The court of James I was an unhealthy social environment with its intrigues and cabals, its greedy self-assertion and its ruthless ambition. James and Anne could not control the corruption they unwittingly encouraged, the extravagance and pursuits of pleasure, the licentious atmosphere, and the decadent banquets that became orgies.

Was Arbella revenging herself on James for his treatment of her, or was she making a point to stop the gossip caused by Ben Jonson's shocking 'revelation' that she was a man? Such an insinuation was obviously not going to enhance her reputation and could be positively disastrous for her, as it seemed rather neatly to account for why, aged thirty-five, she had never married. The easiest way to categorically repudiate this was to take a husband. No one could say this was a sensible idea – but what other means could she use to squash the rumour's allegation? The gossips had nothing but fabrications to feed their rumour mill and such falsehoods had always been associated with her name. Denying them was no use, and if she did nothing they would continue, equally damning. She had been forced into a humiliating position, and by trying to rectify it she was being accused of an act she quite rightly considered not to be a crime.

James had once again shown himself to be without heart where Arbella's happiness was concerned. He seemed to have been satisfied that this was all a big misunderstanding that was now sorted out, and both William and Arbella were welcomed back at court at the end of March. Arbella was meditating on how best to proceed, but things were put on hold until after the investiture of sixteen-year-old Prince Henry as Prince of Wales on 4 June. This was a title that had not been held since the days of the Plantagenets and so was an occasion for a week of celebrations. Throughout this time, Arbella and William managed to be fairly discreet if they met, but court gossip abounded.

William's conscience was troubling him and he admitted to his close friend Edward Rodney that 'he found himself bound in conscience, by reason of a former pledging of his faith' to marry Arbella. This confession showed him in a poor light. When later questioned, Rodney had little more to add and had no knowledge of any letter, token, message or aught else that had passed between them.[9] This may mean nothing or it may mean that Arbella was making all the plans. William was weak and easily led, but Arbella was determined that she was not going to be deprived of the company of a rare man who shared many interests with her and whose company she enjoyed. There was never any mention of love, or appreciation; they were not necessary to bond them together as husband and wife. (That does not mean they were wholly absent.)

On the evening of Thursday 21 June, William called on Edward Rodney at the lodgings he shared with William's younger brother Francis in Lambeth and asked him to go with him to act as witness at the marriage of himself and Arbella. They went down the river to Greenwich Palace where they arrived about midnight. They were admitted to Arbella's chambers, where four of her servants, Kirton, Edward Reeves, Mrs Biron and Mrs Bradshaw, were assembled, plus her gentleman usher and steward Hugh Crompton. The ceremony was performed at four in the morning by a Mr Blague, probably a contemporary of William's at Oxford. Performing a marriage ceremony at this hour may have been intended to suit astrological conditions, just as Bess of Hardwick's marriage had been. Hugh Crompton wrote on the flyleaf of his account book: 'One Blaque son of the Dean of Rochester was the minister that married them.' Hugh Crompton left the only written evidence of the marriage, a document that came to light in the 1850s when Canon Jackson accidentally came across it in the previously mentioned Longleat papers.[10]

What seems so surprising is their decision to marry in secret without the king's consent. Both had family experiences of the risk they were taking. Arbella's parents had married in secret at Rufford Abbey and been placed under house arrest, while her grandmother the Countess of Lennox was sent to the Tower for arranging it. William's grandparents had also secretly married without royal consent and been sent to the Tower. Did they really think their situation was any different? Could they see no alternative? They both knew what the consequences would be, and for two extremely intelligent people they seemed to lack common sense.

On 8 July, two weeks after the wedding ceremony had taken place, the news reached James. Unsurprisingly, he immediately had Arbella and William arrested, along with all concerned. William was sent to the Tower and Arbella was placed under house arrest with Sir Thomas Parry at Copt Hall, Lambeth. Arbella's two servants, Hugh Crompton and Edward Reeves, were thrown in the Marshalsea Prison in Southwark, and the parson Blague was taken to the gatehouse at Westminster.[11]

Sir Thomas Parry was Comptroller of the Royal Household and recently retired from the post of ambassador to France. He was then appointed Chancellor of the Duchy of Lancaster and a Privy Councillor. The warrant that he received read:

> It is thought fit that the Lady Arbella should be restrained of her liberty, and choice is made of you to receive her and lodge her in your house ... these are therefore to give you notice thereof, and to require you to provide convenient lodging for her to remain under your charge and custody, with one or two of her women to attend her, without access to any other person until His Majesty's pleasure be further known. And this shall be unto you a sufficient warrant. From the court at Whitehall, this 9th July 1610. Your very loving friends R. Cant; T. Ellesmere, Nottingham; J Suffolk; R Salisbury; E Worcester.[12]

After the marriage was discovered, Edward Rodney gave his account in a forced declaration, saying,

About Whitsuntide meeting with Mr Seymour at Lambeth, it pleased him to acquaint me with his resolution concerning his marriage ... he never spoke of the means ... only that since it pleased her to entertain the matter, having the king's consent to make her own choice without exception, and since he found himself bound in conscience by reason of a former pledging of his faith unto her, that he resolutely intended it, engaging me by oath unto him that I should not reveal it, until he absolved me, and seeming to me to fear no other let or obstacle than his grandfather, my Lord of Hertford. From that time until the marriage day, he used no more words to me concerning it, at what time he requested me to accompany him to her chamber at Greenwich, to be a witness to his marriage there to be solemnised, to which I consented, all this while nothing doubting of the King's consent.[13]

NO PARDON FOR ARBELLA

Arbella would have been quite comfortable at Copt Hall, described in a survey of the manor of Kennington made in 1625 as a handsome tenement built of brick, opposite the capital tenement, called Vaux Hall, to the south. Lying between the River Thames and the way leading to Kingston, it had a garden and orchard on three sides and was enclosed with a brick wall. There Arbella had her own set of apartments, women to wait on her, any books and amusements she required, freedom to correspond, and a large garden to walk in. It's also been suggested that she had the freedom to leave Copt Hall from time to time.[1]

William was first lodged with the Lieutenant of the Tower, Sir William Wadd, then he was allowed an apartment in St Thomas's Tower above Traitor's Gate. On one side it overlooked the wharf and the river, though the moat divided the two. On the other side was Raleigh's Walk. Despite the official State rooms in the White Tower being still royally furnished, the lions, the jewels, the collection of naval instruments and other interesting features, the Tower was also a prison, a place of torture and execution.

For the long-established prisoners, the conditions were not too hard. They were allowed their own servants who prepared or brought in their food, their own hangings and furniture. They could take exercise and entertain visitors, although the routine was uncertain; privileges could be withdrawn without reason and too much depended upon the whim and corruptibility of the gaoler. All prisoners invariably suffered in health from the nearness of the river with its cold and damp, the ancient stones and poor ventilation. Outbreaks of distemper were regular. William was able to furnish the apartment to his own liking and had tapestries, furnishings, plate and linen brought in. His grandfather gave him an allowance and, with the king's consent, £50 for his maintenance.

Arbella wrote to her Uncle Gilbert on 16 July from Copt Hall, Lambeth, asking if he would take care of matters while she was unable to do so. She was particularly concerned about

> … my servants with whom I thought never to be parted whilst I lived and none that I am willing to part with. Since I am taken and know not how to maintain either myself or them, being utterly ignorant how it will please his majesty to deal with me, I were better to put them away now …

She signed the letter, 'the poor prisoner your niece, Arbella Seymaure', and added a postscript, 'The bay gelding and the rest are at your lord's commandment.'[2]

She wrote to the Privy Council saying how sad she was to be in His Majesty's displeasure, assuring him that 'if I may re-obtain [his pleasure] all the course of my life hereafter shall testify my dutiful and humble thankfulness. Arbella Seymaure.'[3] She also sent a letter to Queen Anne enclosing a small gift and assuring Her Majesty that she was her humble and most dutiful servant.[4] She wrote again to the queen in October enclosing a petition for the king, saying she was sorry to have offended, and believed she was acting as the king would wish. As she reminded him,

The love of this gentleman that is my husband, and my fortune drove me to a contract before I acquainted your majesty … It was impossible for me to imagine it was offensive to your majesty having a few days before given me leave to bestow myself on any subject of his Majesty.[5]

Through her cousin Jane Drummond, a favourite of the queen, Arbella was told that Her Majesty had read her letter and given the petition to the king. Although the queen assured her of her continuing favour, she did not see an easy end to Arbella's troubles. Arbella wrote back saying the continuance of Her Majesty's favour had cheered her, and enclosed a pair of gloves that she had embroidered for the queen.[6] On 10 August, she also wrote to the Privy Council regarding the plight of her faithful servants, Compton and Reeves, who were not so comfortably housed in the Marshalsea Prison. The highly contagious prison fever was rife and Arbella feared that they might die. She pleaded for them, 'that if it will please His Majesty they may be removed to some other healthful air'.[7]

William Wadd, the gaoler, had at first rigorously enforced William's imprisonment, but since his health was suffering the council granted him more freedom. They wrote regularly to each other, and although only one of Arbella's letters has survived, it shows her deep and loving concern for him. That winter, both Arbella and William were ill. 'Let not your grief of mind work on your body,' Arbella wrote in a letter to William, then ended it with 'be well, and I shall account myself happy in being your faithful, loving wife Arb. S.'[8]

Although the newly-weds had friends who supported them and William's brother Francis was a staunch ally, the old Earl of Hertford was too frightened of the royal displeasure to plead for his grandson's release. William wrote to Francis thanking him, while grumbling about the attitude of their grandfather.[9]

William did not petition the king and Arbella's many letters went unanswered, but things changed in January 1611 when the king heard that Sir Thomas Parry was being far too lenient with Arbella and that she was allowed to leave Copt Hall for her own purpose and pleasure. There were even rumours that Arbella had enjoyed secret assignations with her husband in the Tower. Arbella immediately wrote to the Lord Chief Justice of England and the Lord Chief Justice of the Common Pleas stating that she had been long restrained from her liberty and wanted a trial where she could be examined, tried and then condemned or cleared. She asked 'by a Habeas Corpus or other usual form of law, what is my fault? Justly convicted, let me endure such punishment as is due ... and judge charitably until I be proved to have committed any offence, either against God or his majesty, deserving so long restraint or separation from my lawful husband.'[10]

On 4 January 1611, the Earl of Rutland learnt that Arbella was to be sent to Durham and there committed and confined to the care of the bishop. This was kept a closely guarded secret. It was not until 4 March that the earl learnt that 'on Thursday last in the afternoon, the Viscount Fenton was sent to Lambeth to the Lady Arbella with directions to will her to prepare for her journey to Durham.'[11]

Arbella could not have been pleased to see the Captain of the Guard at Copt Hall. He had tricked her the previous November when he invited her to sup with him and his wife, her cousin Bessie Pierrepont, then placed her under house arrest. Arbella had every reason to be wary. This time he had instructions that she was to prepare for a journey to Durham, where she would be placed under the custody of William James, Bishop of Durham. Banishing Arbella to Durham was not a good idea, although it was probably intended to make sure the distance prevented Arbella and William ever meeting again. The frail, fifty-nine-year-old bishop found his task a formidable one, and Arbella was so distressed she became ill.

On 13 March 1611, the king issued a warrant to the Bishop, stating that:

Our cousin Lady Arbella hath highly offended us in seeking to marry herself without our knowledge ... We have therefore thought good to remit her to your care and custody there to remain in such sort as shall be set down to you by direction from the council. This being as you see, the difference between us and her – that whereas she hath abounded towards us in disobedience and ingratitude, we are, on the contrary still apt to temper the severity of our justice with grace and favour towards her.[12]

A warrant was also issued two days later to Sir Thomas Parry ordering him to deliver Arbella to the Bishop of Durham and stating that his service was discharged. Amongst the ten Lords of the Council at Whitehall who on 15 March put their signatures on both the documents was that of Arbella's uncle Gilbert, the Earl of Shrewsbury.[13]

They set off immediately on the first leg of the journey to Barnet. Arbella maintained that she was too ill to travel but she was forced into a litter. After several hours of travel, stopping many times because of her sickness, the party arrived at Highgate at about ten o'clock at night. It was obvious to Dr Moundford, Arbella's physician, that she was quite unfit to travel. A warrant was immediately issued to Sir William Bond to provide her with accommodation for the night at his fine house on Highgate Hill. Gilbert signed this warrant, also:

For as much as here is some occasion to make provision for one night's lodging for Lady Arbella, in respect that she cannot conveniently recover Barnet contrary to our expectations, we have thought good to entreat you not to refuse such a courtesy as the lending of a couple of chambers for her ladyship.[14]

The house on Highgate Hill was built in 1582 as a private home for three-times Lord Mayor of London, Sir Richard Martin. Now named Lauderdale House, it is set in the beautiful Waterlow Park, which along with the house was presented to London County Council in 1889 by the then owner Sir Sidney Waterlow. It now functions primarily as an arts and education centre, welcoming over 65,000 visitors each year.[15]

Arbella's stay was supposed to be overnight but instead she stayed a week. It is strongly suspected that William managed to see Arbella at Highgate and that they signed a document, an original discharge of the financial accounts they gave to Hugh Crompton. It is dated 21 March, and Rodney and Kirton are the signed witnesses. It seems a rather strange thing to do at this stage.[16]

On 21 March, the same day that they signed the document regarding the discharge of their financial accounts, Arbella was forced to move six miles north to Barnet. She was still ill, and the ailing bishop was so worried about her condition and his task of attending to her that he handed over her supervision to Sir James Croft, a friend of Arbella's she had visited on her progress. He blamed his own ill health and excused himself for not attending Arbella on her arduous journey on the fact that he had to prepare his palace for her in Durham.

They were heading to Church Hill House, East Barnet, the home of Mr Thomas Conyers. But Conyers had only recently acquired the property and it was not ready for occupation, so temporary accommodation was found at an inn.

Gilbert Shrewsbury was not well himself but wrote to Dr Moundford at Barnet thanking him for taking care of Arbella on such a taxing journey. Gilbert also informed the king, who was totally unsympathetic; he was of the opinion that his cousin was not physically ill but putting on a show. To confirm his suspicions, on 26 March he sent the highly esteemed Dr Hammond to the inn at Barnet where Arbella was temporarily housed. The physician spent three days with her, and reported back to the king that she was in poor health. She was free from any fever or any actual sickness but she was very weak and her pulse dull; amongst her symptoms was the abnormal state of her urine, which was dark red. She was in no state to travel until restored to some better strength, both of body and mind. He concluded, 'Her own melancholy thoughts have gotten the upper hand of her.'

Shrewsbury had received a letter from Dr Moundford expressing doubt about the efficiency of the cordials Dr Hammond had prescribed for Arbella's depression. Shrewsbury was of the opinion that her melancholy was due to her imprisonment and his majesty's disfavour to her. For her part, Arbella wrote to the council protesting that in her weak state she was likely to die if forced to move, her last journey having almost ended her days. She asked for time to recover her strength and hoped his majesty would show compassion.

Sir James Croft, who had now taken responsibility for Arbella, wrote to Shrewsbury on 31 March that Arbella had tried to dress herself and become so frustrated, it had provoked a violent attack of hysteria and weeping. The following day, they finally moved to Church Hill House but Arbella was ill during the journey. It must have been a relief to hear that the king had granted her a month's respite from the continuation of her journey. The bishop, now on his way to Durham, had only reached Cambridge when he wrote to Dr Moundford and Sir James Croft on 17 April informing them that he had been sick and suffered several fits. He had seen the king at Royston and told him of the grief Arbella was suffering at being in the king's displeasure and whose only wish was restitution into his majesty's favour: 'My poor opinion is that if she wrong not herself, God in time will move His Majesty's heart to have compassion upon her.'[17]

On 17 April Sir James Croft also wrote to the Privy Council, informing them that Arbella was somewhat better, although she rarely left her bed and had not yet walked the length of her bedchamber. 'The remoteness of the place whereunto she must go, driveth her to utter despair,' he wrote. In their conversations, Arbella had described Durham as being 'clean out of the world'. It probably did seem remote when the furthest she had previously travelled was Derbyshire. Being banished to Durham did seem rather extreme, especially as the bishop was obviously unwell, but Sir James's plea did not move the king.[18]

The month's sojourn at Barnet was almost at an end, but Croft was still worried about Arbella's health and knew she was unfit to travel. On 27 April, he sent Sergeant Minors to London to plead for an extension to her stay. He told of Arbella's weak state, but was only granted a few days respite: she was to leave the following Monday. Arbella still protested that she was quite unable to face the journey. Dr Moundford and Sir James Croft agreed with her and they made a further plea to the king for an extension of her stay.

Arbella also wrote to the king asking for a further three weeks to recuperate: 'I account myself the most miserable creature living, yet none is so grievous to me as the loss of your Majesty's favour ...'[19] Attached to Arbella's letter is another written in a different hand and signed 'J'. In this letter, Arbella offers her obedience to undergo the journey after the three-week convalescence without any resistance or refusal; she was confident that if she promised to obey the king now, his hurt pride and honour would be satisfied. He granted her a further extension until 5 June, which gave her an extra month to recuperate. From the accounts of her expenses at the time, a coach and horses were hired for her. Evidently she was granted the freedom to ride around the area so was not always under house arrest.

Her Aunt Mary made another attempt to obtain a pardon for her niece through the king's latest favourite Robert Carr, Lord Rochester, but he refused to do anything to help. Undeterred, she began to take drastic steps to help her niece get away, mirroring the escape of Elizabeth Southwell and Robert Dudley in 1606, in which Elizabeth had disguised herself as a boy and passed as Robert's page. As we have seen, they had reached Calais where she was stopped by the governor, but he had let her go because she declared that she had left England not for love but to enter a nunnery, the order of St Claire in Brussels. August passed and Elizabeth did not arrive in the Low Countries, then in October she and Dudley were in Lyon, associating openly and waiting for a papal dispensation so that they could marry. When this eventually arrived, the couple were united. They had successfully defied James: could Arbella and William do likewise?

That was the basic plan. But Elizabeth had been nineteen and fit; Arbella was almost thirty-six and ill. Would dogged determination and desperation compensate for Arbella's poor mental and physical state? Mary was a clever, strong-minded woman who possessed the sterling qualities of her mother, Bess of Hardwick. She must have been in constant touch with both Arbella and William, who, having spent a year in the Tower with no sign of any reprieve, was willing to accept the opportunity. They used the respite in Barnet to plan an escape to France, and Mary worked unceasingly to raise money. Not only was there the fare to France, transport and accommodation, but a large amount would be needed for bribes. Mary gave Arbella £1,400 of her own money, saying that it was to purchase a unique piece of needlework in Arbella's possession that had been worked by Mary, Queen of Scots. An independent valuation placed this at £850 but, undeterred, Mary insisted that the remaining £550 was so that Arbella could clear her debts before departing for Durham. She didn't mention that she had managed to raise a further £1,400 from friends, family and well-wishers.

Historians have since blamed the failure of the plot on the fact that too many people knew about it. Obviously Arbella's steward Hugh Compton was in on the plan, as was William's friend Edward Rodney, Arbella's maid Anne Bradshaw, and William Markham, uncle of George Markham whom Arbella had visited at Ollerton in 1609. They were the main players. Hugh Crompton was to take men's clothing for Arbella to wear, and he was also to take horses to an inn about a mile away. William Markham was to accompany Arbella to the inn, then she and Crompton would ride fourteen miles to London and rendezvous with William at an inn at Blackwall at around six o'clock.

The previous day Rodney was to collect the baggage and deposit it in a hired room overnight and then take it to the inn at Blackwell. Once the two parties had met up, a boat would row them down to Leigh, where a French vessel was to meet them to take them across the Channel.

On Monday 3 June 1611, Arbella was ready to put the first part into operation. She had lulled Croft and her attendants into believing that she was ready to leave for Durham, which was scheduled for 5 June. She had pretended that she was stealing out to pay a last visit to her husband but would be returning in the morning. Having set the scene, Anne Bradshaw then helped Arbella to disguise herself by 'drawing a pair of great French fashioned hose over her petticoats, pulling on a man's doublet, a man-like peruke with long locks over her hair, a black hat, a black cloak, russet boots with red tops, and a rapier by her side'.

Thus Arbella, in a disguise similar to that worn by Elizabeth Southwell, was ready to escape. Accompanied by William Markham, they left Mr Conyer's house in East Barnet between two and three in the afternoon:

> After they had gone a mile and a half to a sorry inn where Crompton attended with horses, she grew very sick and faint,

so as the hostler who held the stirrups said that gentleman would hardly hold out to London; yet being set on a good gelding astride, in an unwonted fashion, the stirring of the horse brought blood enough to her face; and so they rode on towards Blackwall where arriving about six of the clock, finding there in readiness two men, a gentlewoman and a chambermaid, with one boat full of Mr Seymour's and her trunks, and another boat for their persons, they hastened from thence towards Woolwich.[20]

This would suggest that the first part of the plan was working well. The devoted Anne Bradshaw and a maid were waiting for Arbella, but the 'two men' mentioned were Edward Kyrton and Edward Reeves. William and Rodney were not at Blackwell as arranged. They could not linger if they wanted to catch the tide and the light, so leaving Edward Kyrton and the maid at Blackwall, the rest of the group set off with the entire luggage in two boats. They passed Woolwich and, under the cover of darkness, went on to Tilbury where the watermen insisted on a rest and went ashore for refreshment. On their return, they were reluctant to continue towards the mouth of the river in the night, but the little group were anxious to move on. The stakes were high and the risks great – it must have taken a lot of persuasion and a hefty bribe for the watermen to continue.

Chilly mists swirled over the water as they set off again from Tilbury. They needed to keep constant watch for obstructions as they continued mile after lonely mile past flat saltings bordering the river on either side. Desolate and dismal in daylight, at the dead of night the creepy haunt of birds and hardy smugglers was positively menacing. The boats were loaded and heavy, the tide was against them for several hours and the rowers were tired. They were not a cheerful party. This was Arbella's first experience of going to sea and it was anything but pleasant. Squashed in a rowing boat, cold, weary, sick at heart and full of trepidation, the night must have seemed endless. Their only consolation was the fact that as they reached the little fishing port of Leigh at dawn, they were free and, so far, undiscovered.

The estuary at that point is five miles wide, and they could not find the French ship on which they were supposed to sail. Crompton hailed a likely craft but found it was sailing to Berwick not Calais, and despite being offered a substantial bribe, the master John Bright would not change his destination. He did however point out the French ship they sought. Seeing the anxiety of the small group, he took note of them – a muffled figure, a fair-haired man with a beard about forty (Reeves), a younger man with a small black beard (Crompton) and a black-hatted woman (Anne Bradshaw). He watched as they rowed towards the French ship and climbed aboard. Crompton was aware of the master's interest and felt it was wise to set sail immediately. Arbella wanted to wait for William but Crompton overrode her wishes and they set out to sea, but the tide was against them and they had to wait two hours before they could set sail. Even then the wind was in the wrong direction, which caused yet more delay.[21]

Despite all the delays, the French ship carrying Arbella eventually reached Calais free of detection by the authorities. Arbella could have gone ashore; she could have thrown herself on the mercy and accepted the hospitality of the King of France as Elizabeth Southwell had done. Defiantly she insisted upon staying on board the ship, waiting for William – uninformed and oblivious of where he was or what he was doing.

21

THE ESCAPE PLANS FAIL

Meanwhile, William had arranged his escape from the Tower. His accommodation was in St Thomas's Tower over Traitor's Gate, but this grim entry was too secure for an unauthorised exit and his windows too narrow for a descent to the moat. However, he was not far from the west entrance to the Tower, and William's plan of escape was simple. Firewood was delivered by a carter regularly to his rooms in the Tower, and William, disguised as a carter, intended to walk out through the West Gate behind the cart when it left (he had probably used a similar ruse before and knew that it worked).

Instructing his barber Thomas Batten to tell any visitors that he had gone to bed for the night with toothache, he explained to Batten that he was going to spend the night with his wife before she went to Durham. He then disguised himself as a carter's labourer with a black beard and wig and waited, but the carter was late doing his delivery and William was not able to leave the Tower until eight o'clock. He passed through the West Gate unchallenged by the guards, left the cart and slipped along Tower Wharf, past Traitor's Gate and the warders at the South Gate. At the irongate wharf, the river landing, he found his friend Rodney waiting for him with a boat.[1]

Anxious to make up for lost time, they did not stop at Blackwall, where Kyrton was waiting to give them news, but went straight on to Leigh. They were too late. The French ship had set sail. A rising storm threatened to delay their departure, but they made a quick decision: they paid twenty shillings to a waterman to row them out to a ship that was just hoisting sail, a collier named *Charles*. It was bound for Newcastle upon Tyne, but giving the master a £40 bribe, he was persuaded to take them across the Channel to Calais. Rodney did the negotiating, telling the master that they were leaving England because of a quarrel and had missed the ship on which they had planned to travel to France.

When examined by the Bailiff of Ipswich later, the master of the *Charles*, who gave evidence to the Earl of Suffolk, described the party as one gentleman wearing a suit of red satin with silver and gold lace (Rodney), another young man in a suit of 'murray-coloured stuff' (William still disguised as a carter), a Frenchman and a servant.

The main problem was, no contingency plan was drawn up in case those involved failed to make the prearranged rendezvous. However, around noon, as the *Charles* proceeded downriver, they spotted a French ship at anchor. It was highly possible that it was the French ship they should have travelled on; it could have been that the wind was against them and halted their progress, or they may have been deliberately waiting for them to catch up. Anxious to find out, Rodney persuaded the master to anchor at a buoy and row over to enquire, but instead of William, still in disguise, rowing over with the Frenchman interpreter they had with them, the master went instead.

The whole thing then really does become a French farce. The master of the *Charles* only knew half the story. As far as he was concerned his passengers were a gentleman, a carter, a Frenchman and a servant on their way to France, and no doubt false names had been used to conceal their identities. The party from the

Charles boarded the French ship and made enquiries. It is quite likely that they saw Anne Bradshaw and even Arbella still wearing her disguise, but they would not have recognised them. Travelling in disguise, they would also have been using false names – there was nothing to link them with the passengers on the *Charles*. The master of the *Charles* saw no reason to lose a lucrative fare, so on his return he reported that it was the wrong ship.

Although the destination for the wealthy passenger and his three companions was Calais, the wind remained against them and they decided to make for Harwich, where they stayed the night. The French ship remained anchored in the same place, waiting.

The wind was still against them the following day and they decided to abandon their attempt to get to Calais and make for Ostend, where they arrived at eight o'clock on the Friday morning. William immediately sent enquiries down the coast to 'hearken after the arrival of his lady'. Thinking it unsafe to remain on the coast, he and Rodney went inland to Bruges, where William sent messengers to Gravelines to find out what had happened to Arbella and if she had landed there. He soon learnt that she had been captured and returned to England.

At eight o'clock on the Tuesday morning, by which time Rodney assumed they would all be safely in France, William's younger brother Francis Seymour received a note from Rodney. The two shared lodgings and the note was intended to inform him in vague terms of what was happening so that he would not be concerned about his absence. Francis however was so perturbed that he rushed off to the Tower and, thrusting Batten aside, entered his brother's bedchamber. He found it empty: the prisoner was missing.

No alarm that Arbella was missing had been given from Church Hill House. A few bribes and a lot of loyalty and affection from Sir James Croft and the household had kept them silent. Arbella had probably been absent from the house before, and they expected her back at any time to prepare for her journey to Durham.

It was the discovery of William's escape from the Tower that alerted the king and set the wheels in motion. The king and council worked themselves up into a frenzy, as messengers hurled themselves between Greenwich and London bearing dispatches marked 'haste' and 'post haste'. While James seethed with rage, Salisbury issued a proclamation warning of the terrible punishment that would befall anyone assisting Arbella or William, who by the assistance of Markham, Crompton, Rodney and others had found means to break prison and escape to foreign parts. If they had escaped to the Continent, the Catholic powers might have used their claims as an excuse for interfering in English affairs, so dispatches were sent to the European courts requesting that the fugitives be sent back without delay:

> Whereas we are given to understand that the Lady Arbella and William Seymour, second son of the Lord Beauchamp, being for divers great and heinous offences committed, the one to the Tower of London, and the other to a special guard, have found the means by the wicked practices of divers lewd persons, as namely Markham, Crompton, Rodney and others, to break prison and make escape, on Monday the third day of June with an intent to transport themselves to foreign parts. We do hereby straitly charge and command all persons whatsoever, upon their allegiance and duty, not only to forebear to receive harbour or assist them in their passage in any way, as they will answer it at their perils; but upon the like charge and pain to use the best means they can for their apprehension and keeping them in safe custody, which we will take as an acceptable service. Given at Greenwich the 4th day of June 1611 (per Ipsum Regem).[2]

The fugitives had left ample traces. The ostler at Highgate, the watermen and the masters of ships off Leigh all came forward with their suspicions. Everyone connected with the pair was questioned.

The route was traced without difficulty and, as they were making for Calais, Sir William Monson sent his fastest pinnace, *Adventure,* to scour the Channel. It was either late on 6 June or early in the morning of 7 June when the French ship was found. Griffin Cockett, the *Adventurer*'s captain, ordered them to stand to, but the master was willing to put up some resistance and he had to fire thirteen shots over the bows before the command was obeyed.

On 5 June, Monson wrote to Lord Nottingham, the Lord High Admiral:

Right Honourable. After I had received direction from my Admiral for the interception of the Lady Arbella and Mr William Seymour, we stood off and under the South Sandhead we saw a small sail which we chased, and proving little wind, we sent our boat with shot and pikes, and half the channel over our boat did overtake them, and making some few shot, they yielded, where we found divers passengers, amongst the rest, my Lady Arbella, her three men and one gentlewoman. We cannot find yet that Mr Seymour is here. My Lady sayeth that she saw him not, but hopeth that he got over. My Lady came into the French barque at Quinborough and is now aboard the Adventure safe until we shall receive further directions from your lordship. We do keep the barque with all those passengers in her until such time as we shall hear further from your lordship. I humbly rest your Lordships humbly to command, Griffin Crockett. From aboard the Adventure off His Majesty's Downs.[3]

At ten o'clock on 7 June he wrote to Salisbury, 'For more conveniency we do embark in the French barque wherein they were taken, and goeth with her to the North Foreland where we shall have choice of ketches to put my Lady and her servants in.' He added a postscript that he had no news of the *Charles* or of

William Seymour.[4] Monson searched the Channel for two days but could find no trace of William, so abandoned the search.

Arbella was taken to Sheppey where William Monson boarded the *Adventure*. He wrote immediately to Lord Salisbury asking what he should do with the fugitive: 'I am unwilling that she should go ashore until I have authority, but in the meantime she shall not want anything the shore can afford, or any other honourable usage ...'[5] By James's express command Monson was ordered to bring Arbella upriver to be delivered into the Tower. She was never to be free again. Neither was she to see nor hear from William Seymour for the next few years.

In perpetual fear of arousing the king's anger, Francis Seymour wrote to his grandfather the old Earl of Hertford. His letter outlines the facts, and ends, 'He [Batten] confessed the truth, which he had no sooner done, but at the very same instance comes the Lieutenant, to whom I showed this letter of Edmund Rodney, which I had intended presently to show to the Lord Treasurer. The Lieutenant being acquainted herewith went straight to Greenwich.'[6]

Ridiculous rumours circulated, one of which stated that Lord Hertford, William's grandfather, had died of shock. In fact he had only been sent for to see if he had a hand in his grandson's escape. The poor old man was in a state of abject terror. He made a written statement protesting that he knew nothing of it. His hand trembled so much while reading Rodney's note to Francis that he burnt part of it with the candle he used (he added a postscript to his own letter apologising for his carelessness; the bit burnt away was the word 'Tower').[7]

With Arbella safely in the Tower, Tassin Corve, captain of the French boat, was taken prisoner. Everyone who had been involved in the escape was arrested. Within twenty-four hours, Mary, Countess of Shrewsbury was arrested and sent to the lieutenant's lodgings in the Tower; William Markham and Crompton were committed to

Fleet Prison. They were tortured under interrogation for no reason as their part in the escape was well known. Sir James Croft and Dr Moundford, who had taken no part in the escape, were released soon after Arbella had appeared before the council. Mrs Adams, the minister's wife from East Barnet, and Edward Kirton were sent to the Gatehouse; Batten the barber and William's butler were put in a dungeon in the Tower; Tassin Corve, the French skipper, and John Baisley, a waterman, were imprisoned in Newgate.[8]

The general public, moved by the romance of Arbella's escape, abhorred the king's harsh treatment of her. The kindly Bishop Goodman later taxed James with his treatment of Arbella, against which James defended himself. He claimed that as Arbella was his nearest kinswoman, both 'in duty and respect unto him, he should not have been neglected in a business of that high nature' (i.e. her marriage). As she was his ward, in the course of common law she 'ought not to have disposed of herself' (this is not correct as James was not Arbella's ward); and that he 'in tender care and love unto her did he often proffer marriage, and she ever said she did no way incline into marriage' (she did indeed say this when Prince Maurice was proffered in 1604, but later made it clear that the statement was not a remark about marriage in general). James really was grasping at straws. James concluded:

> Had she of herself proposed any one to the King, whom she did like and affect, the King did promise his best endeavour to further it. That she did not match with one of the blood royal who was descendent from Henry VII, so that by this match there was a combination of titles, which princes have ever been jealous of; and considering what issue the King had, and that his only daughter was matched to a foreign prince, what the multitude might do in such a case and upon such an occasion he thought in honesty and policy he might prevent.[9]

These statements were not tenable. In 1611, James could not claim the defence of his issue because his eldest son, Prince Henry, did not die until 6 November 1612, and his daughter Elizabeth did not marry the Elector Palatine until 14 February 1613. Arbella did not prejudice the peaceful succession of his children. James just wanted Arbella to pay the penalty for her disobedience. After the death of Prince Henry, he may have had reason to be careful; his other son Charles was sickly, weak and, in James's eyes, deficient in the manly accomplishments desirable in an heir to the throne.

Arbella had offended James by disobeying his wish that she should not marry William. Perhaps if she had gone peacefully to Durham, he might have forgiven her in time.

The council did not view the situation in the same light as James. Their main concern was the threat she represented to the security of England. Abroad she would have been a possible danger to the state – a potential cause of war. She was fourth in line to the throne, but if she had become a Catholic, she would then become a candidate for the throne to be set against James and his Protestant issue. That is why it was imperative that she was deprived of her freedom and returned to England.

In reality Arbella had no wish to act against James or aid the Catholics: all she wanted was to live a private life with her husband. She wanted her freedom. She had spent too much of her life in one or other form of confinement. A fluent linguist and woman of culture, life on the Continent would not have been disagreeable to her.

ARBELLA IN THE TOWER OF LONDON

On her arrival at the Tower, Arbella was probably lodged in the Bell Tower. In the turret of this two-storey octagonal structure in the inner ward hung the bell that gives the place its name; the bell is rung when the gates are closed at sunset, then as now. This isolated apartment on the south-west corner of the inner fortress was in the oldest, gloomiest part of the Tower. It was reserved for top security prisoners, as the only exit was through a narrow passage into the governor's house, but the rooms were considered to be some of the best. As with all special prisoners, Arbella was allowed her own furnishings and wall hangings, but it must have still had a chilly feel due to the stone floor and walls covered in graffiti, scratched into the soft sandstone by earlier inmates. The small window was glazed, unlike the chamber below, lit only by arrow slits through which the draughts whistled. From the window she would have been able to see the traffic on the wharf and the river, and the people strolling by on the opposite side of the moat, anxious to get a glimpse of the unfortunate prisoners. To the north she would have seen Tower Hill and the way to the place of execution. To the east lay the Lion Tower where the royal beasts roamed.

Despite it being one of his favourite pastimes, James did not attend a baiting while his cousin was in the Tower.

The difficulties of escape from the upper room were almost insuperable. No staircase connected it with the Tower. It was reached either through the lieutenant's lodgings or along the battlements from the adjoining Beauchamp Tower. When well enough, Arbella was taken for exercise along these battlements, where her cousin Elizabeth had once walked when held there a prisoner after the Thomas Wyatt rebellion. Lord Leicester, the queen's favourite, was kept in the Beauchamp Tower, which is only a walkway from the Bell Tower, and they supposedly met frequently; the young Leicester and his brothers carved a verse and the ornate Dudley crest in the soft sandstone of the walls. Guildford Dudley, husband of the short-lived queen Jane Grey, scratched out her forename. Many other notable prisoners had occupied these rooms – several related to Arbella either through blood or circumstances. There was Raleigh, a prisoner for thirteen years in all, and Cobham, who had allegedly plotted to place Arbella on the throne.

The Tower was permeated with Arbella's family history. Half a century before it had housed William's grandmother Katherine Grey, for marrying the Earl of Hertford without the queen's permission. It was there that Beauchamp, Arbella's father-in-law, had been born. Arbella's grandmother Meg was imprisoned there three times; each time it was for love. The first time was for her association with Thomas Howard, uncle of the ill-fated Anne Boleyn. When Anne fell from grace both Meg and Thomas were put in the Tower for their presumption and never met again. Thomas Howard died of gaol fever shortly afterwards. The second time Meg Lennox was imprisoned was for her involvement in the ill-fated plot to marry her son to Mary, Queen of Scots. It was there in the Tower that her husband Matthew Lennox, the grandfather Arbella never knew, had been housed while Meg was placed in the custody of Sir Richard and Lady Sackville at Sheen. Fearing that he too would die of gaol fever, Meg appealed to William Cecil, Lord Burghley, for her husband to be allowed to join her at Sheen. The request was granted, but when they continued to promote the marriage, the furious queen stripped the earl of his properties and imprisoned the countess in the lieutenant's lodgings at the Tower. Meg and her ladies scratched into the wall the time and date and place of their imprisonment when Darnley married Mary, Queen of Scots. Meg Lennox was captive again when Arbella's parents married.

Mary Talbot, Countess of Shrewsbury, was also no stranger to the Tower, and for her part in planning Arbella's escape she also was placed in the lieutenant's lodgings. Although her husband Gilbert Talbot was not implicated, he was put under strict guard at his home. He believed the inconvenience was temporary, but he was mistaken. The council were not concerned about Gilbert: 'The good earl is found untainted with her faults, but forbears the Council table for her sake.'[1]

On 30 June 1612, Mary and Arbella had a semblance of a trial before the Privy Council in the Star Chamber. Mary was furious at not having a public hearing and refused to answer anything in private, saying that if she had offended the law, she would only answer in public. She was accused of contempt of court. This inconvenience and the prosecution case put by the formidable Sir Frances Bacon did not bode well. The principal charge against Mary was the discovery that she had amassed £20,000 to provide for the fugitives. That was a considerable amount of money, and she'd also made provisions for more bills of exchange for her niece's use. The counts against Arbella were twofold. She had offended James by marrying without his consent, but the council's main concern was the threat she represented to the security of England.

On the Continent in the company of her Aunt Mary, there was a strong likelihood that she would be swayed by the persuasive tongue of the Jesuit priests and convert to Catholicism, which would make her a possible danger to the state and a potential cause of war. Arbella individually might have hoped for forgiveness, but because Aunt Mary had meddled in the affair, the offence was considered by Salisbury to be against Protestant England. Arbella was therefore a danger to the realm, and for that there was no forgiveness. Although it was found impossible to make the prisoners' offence one of high treason, it was enough for the obsequious lords that Arbella Stuart and Mary Talbot, Countess of Shrewsbury, were an ill-defined threat.

Mary was fined £20,000 and confined during the king's pleasure, which meant immediate imprisonment for an indefinite period of time. Arbella was also committed to the Tower for an indefinite period. Sir John More described the scene to Ralph Winwood:

On Saturday last, the Countess of Shrewsbury was lodged in the Tower where she is likely long to rest as well as the Lady Arbella. The last named Lady answered the Lords at her examination with good judgement and discretion; but the other is said to be utterly without reason, crying out that all is but tricks and gigs, that she will answer nothing in private, and if she has offended the law will answer in public. She is said to have amassed a great sum of money to some ill use, £20,000 are known to be in her cash; and that she had made provision for more Bills of Exchange to her niece's use than she had knowledge of. And though the Lady Arbella hath not yet been found to incline to popery, yet her aunt made account belike that beyond the seas in the hands of Jesuits and Priests, either the stroke of their arguments or the pinch of poverty might force her to the other side.[2]

Mary had some of the best accommodation in the Tower but she complained bitterly. What was never in doubt was her love for and loyalty to Arbella, for whom she had to endure a long imprisonment. Mary was to remain in the Tower for two years, with one short break to nurse her husband Gilbert.[3]

Arbella was ill during her first days at the Tower. She asked for medication and her own servants, but the request was refused. When she had been captured she had £868, a parcel of gold and her jewels, but these were taken from her and given to Sir William Bowyer, who was instructed to sell her jewels to pay for her capture.[4] Neither the lieutenant nor his staff received salaries so they recouped their expenses and made their livelihoods from prisoners – a source of funds so lucrative that posts at the Tower were bought and sold.

She wrote to Viscount Fenton, appealing for his help to allay her discomfort and distress on the grounds of their long acquaintance and kinship. She wanted people around her whom she could trust:

Be assured that neither physician nor other but whom I think good shall come about me while I live till I have his Majesty's favour without which I desire not to live. I can neither get clothes nor posset ale, for example or anything but ordinary diet, nor compliment fit for a sick body in my case when I call for it, not so much as a glister.[5]

Arbella did not give up hope that James would relax the severity with which he was treating her, but he didn't. When he returned a small present she had embroidered for him, she was convinced that he had been encouraged to do so by Fenton who, despite being kin, was doing her no favours. Her constitution was sapped by the damp, draughty rooms, and no solicitude from her women could restore her health.

William and Rodney loitered in Holland, then made their way to Belgium and the court of the Archduke Albert in Bruges (he was titled archduke because he governed the Netherlands in right of his wife Isabella). Salisbury told William Trumbull, the English ambassador there, to keep a close eye on William and report how he was treated, who his associates were and what course he proposed to take either for his stay or his removal. William sent a messenger to James to request that Arbella be allowed to join him on the Continent, where they could live quietly together. James's only reply to this was a message from Salisbury telling William Seymour that he would never find favour with the king as long as he remained in the territories of the archdukes of Spain or Rome. Taking note of this warning, William and Rodney moved to Paris on 3 September 1611.

With Arbella under lock and key, William Seymour's whereabouts seemed of little concern, and although he was at liberty, he was roaming the Continent without money. Arbella sent him support drawn from her skimpy funds: £62 in January 1614 and £40 in March the same year.[6] In December 1611, William requested the Lieutenant of the Tower to send him the clothes and furnishings he had left behind when he made his escape. These were considered a jailor's perk and Wadd was not pleased.

Arbella wrote to Queen Anne:

May it please your most excellent majesty to consider how long I have lived a spectacle of His Majesty's displeasure, to my unspeakable grief, and out of that gracious disposition that moved your royal mind to compassion of the distressed, may it please your majesty to move His Majesty on my behalf. I have presumed to present your majesty herewith the copy of my humble petition to His Majesty against this time, when the rather I am sure His Majesty forgiveth greater offences as freely as he desires to be forgiven by him whose sacrament he is to receive, though your majesty's intercession at any time I know, were sufficient. Thus hath my long experience of your majesty's gracious favour to me and all good causes encouraged me to address myself to your majesty, and increased the obligation of my duty in praying continually unto the Almighty for your majesty's felicity in all things.

That's eleven 'majesties'. It is very doubtful that this rambling petition had any effect at all on James.

On 24 May 1612, forty-nine-year-old Robert Cecil, the most powerful privy councillor of the Tudor reign, died of stomach cancer. Although he was the one most likely to keep the king from political excesses, he had been out of tune with the James's court as the king gave more and more power into the hands of his male favourites.

Cecil's death made no difference to Arbella except that shortly after his death her allowance from the Exchequer was halved. The entry in the receipt book of the Exchequer shows her pension as being £1,600 per year during her life, but this is crossed through and noted 'obit' thereafter; from July, she was paid only £800 annually in half-yearly instalments.[7]

William was sorely pressed for money throughout his exile, and wrote to his brother Francis to get their grandfather to pay his debts and increase his allowance of £400 a year. The old man wrote to William stating that provided he remained peacefully abroad he would not be molested, so William Seymour remained in Paris an impoverished exile without making any effort to help or communicate with Arbella. This was a huge blow to Arbella's hopes of ever seeing him again. Perhaps there was not much he could have done, but his support would have been appreciated.

He was twenty-three years old and content to live on an allowance from his grandfather and to let Arbella languish in the Tower.

That summer Prince Henry became ill. By the beginning of October his health was deteriorating rapidly, and he died on 6 November. The death of the king's eldest son and heir had a devastating effect on the country. Two months before Henry's death James had had the body of his mother, Mary, Queen of Scots, removed from its simple grave in Peterborough Cathedral to a splendid tomb in the Henry VII Chapel in Westminster Abbey. The body of Prince Henry was placed here beside the grandmother he had never met in life.

Markham was released from prison by 13 November 1612 and Hugh Crompton on 25 July 1613. He tried once again to organise Arbella's affairs and raise money on jewellery.[8]

On 14 February 1613, Princess Elizabeth married the Prince Palatine, the Elector Frederick. Arbella hoped James would use the occasion for one of his famous displays of mercy and release her from the Tower to attend the wedding; she ordered four new gowns 'wherof one cost £1,500'. It was richly embroidered with pearls that cost £400, but as the bill was never paid, the dress was set aside to be returned to the seller. Elizabeth tried to reason with her father, hoping he would relent and allow Arbella out of the Tower to attend the wedding, but to no avail. In March 1613, Arbella was ill again.[9]

On 6 May 1613, the Lieutenant of the Tower, Sir William Wadd, a vicious man whom Arbella had met previously, was removed from his post. Many people had complained about him, and he had been embezzling gold belonging to Arbella. His wife and daughter were also implicated; the daughter was committed to the Tower on 19 May.[10]

Though Wadd had been an efficient gaoler, his replacement, Sir Gervase Elwes, was a much gentler man, too mild for such a position. He held wise and honest opinions and was a religious man; few in the court equalled him.[11] Elwes was also lax enough for Arbella's friends to consider the possibility of an escape from the Tower, and all that winter, Arbella was optimistic of escaping her confinement. The details are vague, but on 23 November Mary Talbot was allowed to leave the Tower to nurse her sick husband, but two days later she was recalled as it was suggested this could be part of a plan to help Arbella escape. Nothing more is mentioned until eight months later, when Chamberlain wrote to his friend Carlton: 'Dr Palmer – a devine and Crompton a gentleman usher were committed to the tower last week for some business concerning the Lady Arbella who is far out of frame this mid-summer moon.'[12]

Arbella's accounts show a payment of £20 to a Dr Palmer; the service that Palmer performed for Arbella was unrecorded. Later in July, Edward Reeves was charged with being involved in a plan for Arbella's escape from the Tower, so despite the lack of detail, it is obvious that there was an escape planned but it failed.[13]

Arbella sank into bouts of black despair. She lost her bright spirit and suffered hysterical outbursts that grew more frequent. Her last known letter written at this time was to the king in a desperate attempt to move him to pity:

In all humility, in most humble wise, the most wretched and unfortunate creature that ever lived, prostrates herself at the feet of the most merciful king that there ever was, desiring nothing but mercy and favour not being more afflicted for anything than for the loss of that which hath been this long time the only comfort it had in the world, and which if it were to do again, I would not venture the loss of any for any other worldly comfort. Mercy it is that I desire and that for God's sake ...

The unfinished letter was found in her room after her death so was obviously never sent, unless a copy was made.

Arbella had given William Seymour many gifts and tokens during their time together.[14] The last one was the Book of Hours given to her by Mary, Queen of Scots. She inscribed it: 'Your most unfortunate Arbella Seymour'. After this she took to her bed in despair, refusing all remedies. She was determined to die to save her dearest William. Was he worth it? He took no further action after his first request to be united with Arbella was rejected. It may have been because he was not prepared to get involved in the 1614 plot to help Arbella escape that she gave up on life. For a year she would not let doctors feel her pulse or inspect her urine, and she refused all food during the last weeks of her life.

Her devoted and loyal lady-in-waiting Ann Bradshaw left, perhaps through ill health. She returned to her native Derbyshire, where at Duffield she rejoined her husband, another faithful servant of Bess's household, Samuel Smith, who had become Arbella's servant on her marriage to William and had been the messenger between the couple when she was at Copt Hall. He had also taken letters from her to the king and Privy Council while she was in Barnet, and for his part in her escape he had been incarcerated in the Tower. Upon his release in the spring of 1614, he had returned to serve Arbella;[15] it was Samuel Smith who dealt with visitors and kept away creditors. He was with Arbella when she turned her face to the wall and died on 25 September 1615.

Only two days prior, her Aunt Mary, also imprisoned in the Tower, had been told that Arbella was much better, although it must have been obvious that she was much worse and only a short step from death. She was distraught that she was not with her niece when she died.[16] Francis Seymour wrote a note to his brother William, still hiding away on the Continent: 'The Lady Arbella died on Tuesday night being 25th September 1615.'

Arbella was just forty years old. To eliminate any doubts as to the circumstances of her death, Sir Ralph Winwood directed Dr Mountford, as President of the College of Physicians, and five members of the college to examine her body. The following day, six physicians went to the Tower at eight in the morning and carried out the post-mortem. The cause of death was determined:

A chronic and long sickness; the species of the disease was 'illam jamdiu producem in cachemiam' which increasing as well by her negligence as by refusal of remedies, by long lying in bed she got bed sores and a confirmed unhealthiness of the liver, and extreme leanness and so died.[17]

Arbella's body was embalmed for the sum of £6 13s 4d and placed in a plain coffin. She was carried out at night and taken up the river to Westminster Abbey with no ceremony except a hurried burial service, and on 27 September 1615 she was laid in the vault of Mary, Queen of Scots, alongside her aunt and cousin Prince Henry. The meagre funeral, without a stone to mark her burial place, was deplorable for the cousin of James, King of England and Scotland. Years later a plain stone was laid on the floor by the tomb. It states simply: 'Arbella Stuart 1575–1615'.

No epitaph was inscribed on her stone but Richard Corbet, Bishop of Norwich, composed these lines:

How do I thank thee death and bless thy power
That I have passed the guard and escaped the Tower!
And now my pardon is my epitaph
And a small coffin my poor carcase hath
For at they charge both soul and body were
Enlarged at last, secured from hope and fear
That among Saints, this amongst Kings is laid
And what my birth did claim, my death has paid

The people were stirred by Arbella's story and for a short time it was a popular subject amongst the balladeers and rhymesters:

> Where London's Tower its turrets show
> So stately by the Thames side
> Fair Arbella, child of woe
> For many a day had sat and sighed
> And as she heard the waves arise
> And as she heard the bleak winds roar
> As fast did heave her heartfelt sighs
> And still so fast her tears did pour.

The sad life of the beautiful, much-injured and ill-fated Lady Arbella Stuart, whose only crime was having royal blood coursing through her veins, forms one of the most touching stories in English history. The things she wanted were the things she was most strenuously denied by the jealous Queen Elizabeth – a husband and children, and ultimately the English crown.

APPENDICES

1 After Arbella's Death

Four months after Arbella's death, a warrant from the Privy
Council ordered any of her fellow prisoners who possessed any
of her goods to give them up to the Crown. Raleigh, who was
known for his love of precious stones, was in possession of some
of her jewels (he had been imprisoned since 1612 and probably
purchased some of the stones from his servants).

Mary Talbot petitioned the council for her release from the
Tower and was given her freedom on Christmas Day 1615 to go
home and nurse her husband Gilbert. Long plagued by ill health,
he died the following year. In 1618, Mary was recalled to face
questioning about the rumours that Arbella had borne a child.
She refused to answer the questions and the previously unenforced
fine of £20,000 was reimposed.[1]

Worksop Manor, that magnificent show palace where they
had entertained the king on his royal progress south to claim the
English crown, was confiscated in lieu of payment.[2]

1. The rumours of Arbella's child are mentioned in Acts of the Privy
   Council, 1615–6, published by the Public Record Office, pp. 183–4.
2. Arundel Castle MSS, w, f. 151.

Mary was condemned to life imprisonment in the Tower, but she was finally released in 1623. She was almost seventy, and died nine years later in 1632.[3]

A few months after Arbella's death, William Seymour. still lurking in exile, wrote a penitent letter to James asking to be allowed to return to England. Now that James had made his point, William's request was granted and he returned in February 1616. In James's eyes William Seymour had never been the culprit, and ten months later he was restored to favour and created a Knight of the Bath. In 1621, William Seymour became Earl of Hertford on the death of his eighty-two-year-old grandfather. By this time he had married the daughter of Milord Essex; they called their eldest daughter Arbella. During the Civil War, William served the king with distinction, and at the Restoration Charles II rewarded him by making Seymour the Duke of Somerset, a title dormant since the execution of his great-grandfather, the Lord Protector of Edward VI. William Seymour died only a few weeks after receiving the title.

Hugh Crompton was transferred to the Fleet Jail and, nine weeks before Arbella's death, was released on the grounds of good behaviour. He and Edward Kirkton joined the household of William Seymour and were Members of Parliament for Great Bedwyn in the 1620s. Crompton died in 1645 and Kirton in 1654.

Henry Cavendish, who Arbella had once relied upon, died in debt in October 1616 and was buried at Edensor. As the Cavendish heir, he inherited Chatsworth House but sold it to his brother William. His illegitimate son Henry became the Lord Waterpark. His descendants are the Cavendishes of Doveridge. The family seat of Doveridge Hall was demolished in about 1938.

William Cavendish added the prefix Lord to the name of Cavendish. He chose to spend his vast fortunes to gain a further title, the Earl of Devonshire.

3. State Papers (Domestic), vol. cliv, no. 17.

Later her son William, the 4th Earl, was to raise this to a dukedom in 1694. The title has passed down the family. Chatsworth House and Hardwick Hall remained the principal seats of the Cavendish family until Hardwick was taken in lieu of death duties.

Charles Cavendish, Bess's third son, died in 1617 almost as wealthy as his older brother William. In 1607, he took Bolsover Castle and the Welbeck lands from his stepbrother Gilbert Talbot, and rebuilt Bolsover Castle in the medieval style with battlements, turrets and vaulted rooms. His descendants were the dukes of Portland and the dukes of Newcastle.

Of Bess's three daughters, the dukes of Kingston-upon-Hull and eventually the Earl Manvers came from the line of her eldest daughter, Frances Cavendish, who married Sir Henry Pierrepont.

Bess's youngest daughter, Mary, married Gilbert Talbot and become Countess of Shrewsbury. Mary's oldest daughter, also Mary, married William Herbert, 3rd Earl of Pembroke. Her middle daughter, Elizabeth, married Henry Grey, 8th Earl of Kent, and her youngest daughter, Alethea, married Thomas Howard, 2nd Earl of Arundel, whose descendants took the title dukes of Norfolk.

Despite all Bess's efforts, nothing came of the triumphant marriage of Elizabeth Cavendish and Charles Stuart, Earl of Lennox, in line to inherit the thrones of both England and Scotland. Arbella Stuart, their only child, was deprived of her title, not permitted to marry and died aged forty, a captive in the Tower of London.

Bess, Countess of Shrewsbury, is buried in Derby Cathedral, where up until 1848 over forty of her descendants were buried beneath her in the family vault, Rather unexpectedly, her sons Henry and William are buried at Edensor Church, and Charles at Bolsover.

2 Line of Succession

Arbella Stuart's life was affected by two major obstacles. She and her cousin James of Scotland were considered equal in succession to the Tudor/Stuart crown, but Queen Elizabeth refused to name her successor. Secondly, any noble in the royal lineage needed the queen's or king's permission to marry – and this was Arbella's downfall. Things have changed: the heir to the throne is acknowledged and the line of succession established, though the first six in line still need the queen's permission or approval to marry.

After the current monarch comes her eldest son, Charles, Prince of Wales, followed by his son Prince William of Wales, Duke of Cambridge, followed by his son, George of Cambridge. Shortly after George's birth, in July 2013, the Succession to the Crown Bill 2013 changed the succession laws so that the right of male primogeniture no longer applies; males born after 20 October 2011 no longer precede their elder sisters in the line of succession. The birth of Princess Charlotte in May 2015 thus made her fourth in line to the throne, and she will remain in that position even if she has a younger brother. The Bill removed the disqualification of those who marry Roman Catholics and also repealed the Royal Marriages Act 1772, so that only the first six people in line to the throne require the Sovereign's permission to marry. This means that Princess Beatrice and Princess Eugenie, the queen's granddaughters who are seventh and eighth in line after their father and cousin Harry, no longer require the queen's permission to marry.

3 Porphyria

Arbella complained of a continual pain in her side and head that sometimes persisted for weeks. As well as the acute pain, she had periods of vomiting, mental instability, uncontrollable weeping and discoloured, purplish urine. She was easily moved to tears of frustration, hysteria and anger. One minute she could be kind and generous, the next cruel and callous. She showed a certain amount of eccentricity and behaved in a self-destructive manner that no one could explain until recently, when modern medical research has revealed that she was suffering from the hereditary disease of porphyria. Arbella was just one of the many members of the royal family who suffer from this condition, which is believed to have run through the generations.

There is a striking similarity between Arbella's symptoms and those of her aunt Mary, Queen of Scots. Both were considered unstable and both had the accompanying symptoms of acute pain and muscular weakness. For many years Queen Elizabeth suffered from some form of mental instability, although at this distance in time it is impossible to diagnose what her condition was. She could be charming, witty and graceful, but she could also be rather paranoid and, increasingly, bitter.

Porphyria is more common in women and often lies latent in men who can pass it on to the next generation, but James also suffered from the same wide range of symptoms as his mother and cousins. James's son Henry, Charles I's youngest daughter Henrietta and her daughter Marie Louise died of this fatal disease. More than a century later, the strange and tragic illness of George III is well documented but was not diagnosed as porphyria until the 1960s; it is believed that most of his children suffered from the symptoms of porphyria too. Queen Victoria is suspect. In her lifetime it was referred to as 'the hereditary malady'. She passed the dread gene on to her daughter Vicky, granddaughter Charlotte and great-granddaughter Feodora. More recently, Prince William of Gloucester was diagnosed and Princess Margaret may also have been a sufferer.

The physical suffering they endured as well as the bouts of mental derangement made them gravely ill, but one of the remarkable features of the illness is how quickly the patient can recover. Looking for a common ancestor, the finger points to

James and Arbella's great-grandmother Margaret Tudor, eldest daughter of Henry VII, and 13x great-grandmother to Queen Elizabeth II.

4 *History Hot 100 (2015)*

After six weeks of voting, the result of the *BBC History Magazine's* 2015 nomination for the historical figures readers and historians are most interested in was announced (http://www.historyextra.com/hot100-2015-2 accessed November 2016). The only criterion was that the individuals nominated had to be dead before 1 January 1985. Arbella Stuart ranked 47th. Rather surprisingly, this placed her ahead of Queen Victoria, William the Conqueror, Empress Matilda and other famous faces. She died on 25 September 1615, so 2015 marked the 400th anniversary of her death.

5 *Places*
The Tower of London

A grand palace early in its history, the Tower of London served not only as a royal residence but also as a prison from 1100 until 1952, and is where Arbella spent the last years of her life. Despite its name, the Tower is officially a castle and one of several royal palaces located on the north bank of the River Thames in central London. It was founded towards the end of 1066 as part of the Norman Conquest of England, and built for William the Conqueror in 1078 as a symbol of oppression. As well as a castle and prison, it has also served as an armoury, a treasury, a menagerie and zoo, the home of the Royal Mint, a public records office, and the home of the Crown Jewels of England. The general layout established by the late thirteenth century remains despite later phases of expansion, but during the eighteenth century the royal lodgings in the Bell Tower were dismantled; a lawn now covers the spot. The Tower of London has played a prominent role in English history and is still a very popular tourist attraction.

Palace of Westminster

When William II built the Palace of Westminster between 1097 and 1099 it was the largest, most impressive hall in England, sitting proudly on the banks of the Thames in central London. It was remodelled and extended by various royal residents until its role as a royal residence ended abruptly in 1512 when fire gutted the privy chamber. Henry VIII decided to move to a nearby building in Whitehall, and in the late fifteenth century the Palace of Westminster became the home of the main Courts of Law. It hosted many high-profile trials such as that of Guy Fawkes and his co-conspirators in the Gunpowder Plot, tried and executed in 1606.

The Courts of Law only vacated the building in the 1800s after a fire in 1834 destroyed most of the old structure. Inside today's Perpendicular Gothic building is the Great Hall, otherwise known as Westminster Hall – all that remains of the medieval Old Palace and the place where Parliament has convened regularly since the reign of Henry III.

The Palace of Whitehall

In the fourteenth century, the archbishops of York built a house, known as York House, conveniently close to the king's palace at Westminster. When the Palace of Westminster was destroyed by fire in 1512, Henry took over the house, renaming it Whitehall and extending the whole to twenty-three acres. The Palace of Whitehall became the main residence of the English monarchs in London from 1530 until 1698. In 1581, Queen Elizabeth built the Banqueting House, which James I replaced in 1609 as an appropriate setting for a new and elaborate form of court entertainment, the masque. The building burnt down in 1619, but James immediately rebuilt it; a major fire in 1698 finally ended its days of grandeur.

Hampton Court Palace

Hampton Court Palace, along with St James's Palace, is one of only two surviving London palaces out of the many owned by King Henry VIII. Hampton Court is 11.7 miles (18.8 kilometres) south-west and upstream of central London on the River Thames at East Molesey, Surrey. In 1515, Cardinal Thomas Wolsey undertook the redevelopment of a former manor house, adopting new Renaissance architectural styles. Wolsey had always been a favourite of Henry VIII, who coveted this grand new building and on Wolsey's fall from grace confiscated it; he forced Wolsey to accept Richmond Palace in exchange. Wolsey died two years later.

Henry enlarged Hampton Court Palace, but in the following century William III rebuilt and extended it further. Work ceased in 1694, leaving the palace in two distinct contrasting architectural styles, domestic Tudor and Baroque. Although classed as a royal palace, it has not been inhabited by the British royal family since the eighteenth century, George II being the last monarch to reside there. Today, the great palace by the river is open to the public and is a major tourist attraction.

Shrewsbury House

Shrewsbury House, Chelsea, the London house of the Shrewsbury family, lay beside the river, west of the present day Oakley Street on Cheyne Walk, and adjoining the palatial residence set up by Sir Thomas More. Shrewsbury also possessed Coldharbour in the City below London Bridge, but neither house remains.

King's Place, Hackney

King's Place, Hackney, where the Countess of Lennox lived and where Arbella's parents were placed under house arrest, and where Arbella was born and spent her formative years, became Brooke House in 1621. Samuel Pepys wrote in his diary about the exotic gardens of King's Place/Brooke House, where he saw oranges growing on trees for the first time and sampled the fruit. From 1759 to 1940 the house was used as a private mental asylum. Bombing during October 1940 damaged the house, and Hackney Borough Council acquired it in 1944. It was demolished in 1954/5 and a college built in its place. The location is the corner of Lower Clapton Road and Kenninghall Road, beside what is now the Lea Bridge Roundabout. The Roman Ermine Street is still one of Hackney borough's main thoroughfares. Now the A10 Kingsland Road, it is one of the straightest roads in London. The church of St Augustine in the centre of the ancient village of Hackney, where Arbella may have been christened was demolished in 1798, but the tower of St Augustine's church, now Grade 1 listed, survived intact. It is Hackney's oldest building and a familiar landmark, which appears on the borough's coat of arms.

Richmond Palace

Richmond Green was originally a common where villagers pastured their sheep, but around 1501 Henry VII built a palace to replace the former Sheen Palace, built on the site of a manor house. The town of Sheen, or Sceon to use its Saxon spelling, had grown up around the royal manor, but by command of King Henry VII the name was changed to Richmond. The palace was given the name Richmond Palace after Henry's earldom and ancestral home at Richmond Castle in North Yorkshire. Richmond is a Norman name, *Riche Mont* meaning strong hill – a rather strange name for a town that is virtually flat on the bank of the River Thames. Richmond Green became a medieval jousting ground alongside the palace. The district we now call Sheen developed in the nineteenth and twentieth centuries and was never in ancient times within the manor of Sheen.

In 1502, the new palace witnessed a betrothal between Henry VII's daughter Margaret and James IV of Scotland, Arbella's great-grandparents. In 1509 Henry VII died there. and in the 1520s Cardinal Wolsey took up residence after being forced out of Hampton Court by Henry VIII. In 1540 Henry gave Richmond palace to his fourth wife, Anne of Cleeves, as part of her divorce settlement.

In 1554, the future Queen Elizabeth was held prisoner at Richmond by her sister Mary, but once she became queen Richmond Palace became Elizabeth's favourite home. She enjoyed hunting stags in the 'Newe Parke of Richmonde' (now the Old Deer Park), and died there on 24 March 1603. James preferred the Palace of Westminster to Richmond, but it remained a residence of the kings and queens of England until the death of Charles I in 1649. Within months of his execution, the palace was surveyed by order of Parliament and was sold for £13,000. Over the following ten years it was largely demolished, the stones and timbers being reused as building materials elsewhere.

By the eighteenth century all that remained of the palace was the gatehouse and local street names, including Old Palace Lane, Old Palace Yard and The Wardrobe, in the area between Richmond Green and the River Thames. The gateway with Henry VII's arms above still faces Richmond Green. To the left of the gateway, fragments of the old palace remain, including two half-towers. Old Palace Yard, inside the gateway, was originally the courtyard of the palace. The largely reconstructed Wardrobe, once a store for furniture and hangings, still incorporates some of the Tudor brickwork. Both it and what remains of the Old Palace are leased as private residences.

The Cavendish/Shrewsbury Properties in Derbyshire/Nottinghamshire

The palaces and vast estates against the backdrop of Sherwood Forest have for four hundred years, from 1550 to 1950, been owned by some of the highest and most powerful families in the land. All can trace their roots back to the dynasty formed by the Cavendish/Shrewsbury union. Many were acquired at the time of the Dissolution of the Monasteries and the outlawing of the Catholic faith in 1536. These stretched throughout Nottinghamshire, Staffordshire, Shropshire, Leicestershire, Lincolnshire, Derbyshire and Yorkshire.

Rufford Abbey

It was at Rufford Abbey where Arbella's mother and father met and married. The original abbey, from which Rufford takes its name, was built around 1170 on behalf of the Archbishop of Lincoln, Gilbert de Gaunt, as a Cistercian monastery. It was part of the great Yorkshire Abbey of Rievaulx founded in 1146. It was converted to a country house in the sixteenth century; part of the house was demolished in the twentieth century, but the remains, standing in 150 acres of park and woodland. is open to the public as Rufford Country Park.

Worksop Manor

Despite Shrewsbury's concerns over money, between 1580 and 1585 he went to enormous expense building a new house at Worksop. The new Worksop Manor was a magnificent mansion, designed by Robert Smythson. It was very tall, with a narrow tower in the centre of each façade capped by a domed lantern, and on the ends of the long facades were projecting square bays. The long gallery, 224 feet long and 38 feet wide, was famous throughout England, and ran along the top floor giving magnificent views over the earl's parkland; it was described by Robert Cecil in 1590 as 'the fairest gallery in England'. The master mason was Giles Greves who had also worked on Chatsworth.

Until the early part of the seventeenth century, when it passed through an heiress to the dukes of Norfolk, Worksop Manor formed part of the ancient estates of the Talbots. In the autumn of 1761 the original manor house, which contained about 500 rooms, was destroyed by fire. Although a new manor was commissioned to replace the previous building, only one wing was completed and work stopped in 1767. The wing was demolished in the 1840s, and after a number of years the surviving parts of the house – the stable, the service wing and part of the eastern end of the main range – were reformed into a new mansion. It is now in private ownership.

Chatsworth House

The original Tudor mansion, built in the 1560s by Bess, was in a quadrangle layout approximately 170 feet (50 metres) from north to south and 190 feet (60 metres) from east to west with a large central courtyard. The front entrance was on the west front, which was embellished with four towers or turrets. The south and east fronts were rebuilt around 1696 for William Cavendish, 1st Duke of Devonshire, and is a key building in the development of English Baroque architecture. The 1st and 6th dukes both inherited an old house and tried to adapt to the lifestyle of their time, which resulted in the interior reflecting a collection of different styles. Although it's not obvious, the Tudor building is incorporated into the main building; the Great Hall, which in the medieval tradition was on the east side of the courtyard, was where the Painted Hall is today.

The Elizabethan garden was much smaller than the modern garden. Its main visual remnant is the belvedere, known as 'Queen Mary's Bower', where Mary, Queen of Scots, was allowed to take the air. Chatsworth House has remained the principal seat of the Cavendish family, but the house and grounds are open to the public. It is one of Derbyshire's premier tourist attractions.

Hardwick Hall

A magnificent statement of the wealth and power of Bess of Hardwick, Hardwick Hall has been described as a huge glass lantern because of its many windows. It dominates the surrounding area and is remarkable as being almost unchanged since Bess lived there with her granddaughter Arbella. This perfectly preserved house and estate is now owned by the National Trust and is a showpiece.

Hardwick Old Hall

The old hall, now managed by English Heritage, stands in the grounds of Hardwick Hall. This roofless medieval manor house was the birthplace of Bess of Hardwick, which she later transformed into an impressive Tudor mansion. Visitors can still ascend four floors to examine surviving decorative plasterwork, as well as the kitchens and service rooms.

South Wingfield Manor

Another Shrewsbury property where Arbella spent many years, South Wingfield Manor has become more synonymous with Mary, Queen of Scots, who was a prisoner there. Now a vast, impressive ruin arranged around a pair of courtyards, South Wingfield Manor has an impressive undercroft, Great Hall and 72-feet-high

(22 metre) tower. Managed by English Heritage, visits must be pre-booked.

Tutbury Castle and Priory

The small and picturesque town of Tutbury lies on the banks of the River Dove on the border of Derbyshire and Staffordshire. Tutbury Castle was a fortress, large enough to be more like a fortified town and was the most hated prison of Mary, Queen of Scots. Largely in ruins, what used to be a south tower with a winding staircase, two chambers and the high tower are all that remains. It is a Scheduled Ancient Monument in the ownership of the Duchy of Lancaster and is open to visitors.

Tutbury Priory was the home of Henry Cavendish. The original priory occupied an area of 4 acres on the hillside below the castle, with the monastic buildings lying on the north side of the church. The foundations of the cloister, dormitory and apartments were still visible circa 1832 in the field adjoining the church to the north. Now only the parish church of St Mary remains standing, and that has been much reduced in size.

6 *The Gregorian Calendar*

Julius Caesar introduced the Julian calendar in 45 BC with each new year beginning on Lady's Day, 25 March. Queen Elizabeth died in the early hours of Thursday 24 March 1603. (see page 154) As the Elizabethans still used the Julian calendar with the New Year beginning on 25 March, the queen died on the last day of the year 1602. However, in February 1582, the calendar that we recognise was established by Pope Gregory XIII and the new year was to begin on 1 January. To rectify the ten-day time difference that had occurred, the day following 4 October 1582 was to be 15 October, with the intervening days being dropped. Disregarding papal authority, England ignored the new calendar and until 1751, English time continued ten days behind that of the Catholic states of Europe. This may cause slight confusion when dating events throughout the period covered by this book.

7 *The Portraiture of Arbella*

The number of portraits and miniatures spuriously identified as Arbella Stuart is a measure of the reputation she once enjoyed, and can be judged on a sliding scale of probability. Arbella was a leading candidate for the name on the frame of a lesser known sitter. Of the many dubiously identified portraits, two have never left Hardwick Hall. There is a painting of Arbella Stuart clearly titled 'Arbella Comitessa Levinox. Aetae Sue 23 Menses. AD 1577', which translates as 'Arbella Countess of Lennox, aged 23 months, 1577'. The other painting, similarly titled, is Arbella at the age of thirteen and a half. Both are on display at Hardwick Hall.

A copy of the latter hangs at Welbeck Abbey and is a later reproduction, painted on canvas not wood. Longleat also claim to have two portraits, one full length, one half. The full-length portrait now at the British Embassy at The Hague is a variant, closely resembling the full-length portrait at Longleat, and from the studio of P. van Somer (*c.* 1610). Several versions of these portraits exist.

A number of woodcut prints of Arbella survive. The original woodcut seems to have been the work of J. Whittakers and was probably based on a contemporary portrait, not necessarily one that has survived. It was printed and published, possibly in 1619 by George Humble, printseller of Pope's Head Alley, four years after Arbella's death.

Successive versions of the engraving were made for publications such as John Thane's British Autography 1793. The engraving with the letter attached is used in this book.

NOTES

Chapter One

1. For a detailed discussion on this Act of Parliament see Eric Ives' *Tudor Dynastic Problems Revisited*.
2. Doleman, *A Conference about the Next Succession to the Crown of England 1594*, pp. 126.
3. State Papers (Domestic), Elizabeth vol. xxxvi, p. 25.

Chapter Two

1. Public Record Office, State Papers (Domestic), Addenda, 1566–79, p. 39.
2. 'Countess of Lennox to Leicester, petitioned the queen to be allowed to go north 3 December 1574', State Papers (Domestic), Eliz I 1547–80, 489; vol. xcix, no. 13; Handover, P. M., *Arbella Stuart, Royal Lady of Hardwick*, p. 49.
3. Durant, D. N., *Arbella Stuart: A Rival To The Queen* (Weidenfeld and Nicolson, 1978), p. 5.
4. Walsingham's interrogations, July 1575. State Papers (Scottish), vol. 30; Public Record Office, State Papers (Domestic), 12/99, no. 13; Durant, D. N., *Arbella Stuart. A Rival To The Queen*, p. 6.
5. *A Calendar of Shrewsbury and Talbot Papers in the College of Arms*, ed. G. R. Batho, vol. G, f. 170 (Historical Manuscript Commission publication, jointly with the Derbyshire Archaeological Society); Durant. D. N., *Arbella Stuar:. A Rival To The Queen*, p. 7.

6. Shrewsbury to the Queen, 4 December 1574, State Papers (Scottish), vol. lxviii; Handover, pp. 49–51.

7. E. Wingfield to Bess, 21 October 1568; Hunter, p. 63.

8. The details of Meg's debt to Bess that necessitated an annual payment of £500 over four years is in State Papers (Domestic), 64/30, no. 333.

9. *A Calendar of Shrewsbury and Talbot Papers in the College of Arms*, ed. G. R. Batho, vol. f, p. 103 (Historical Manuscript Commission publication, jointly with the Derbyshire Archaeological Society).

10. Cooper, E., *The Life and Letters of Lady Arbella Stuart*, vol. 1 (of 2), p. 31 (1866); Durant. D. N., *Arbella Stuart: A Rival To The Queen*, p. 3.

Chapter Three

1. 'Hackney', www.bsix.ac.uk/PDF/News/2013/History; www.eastlondon history.co.uk.

2. Walsingham's interrogatories, July 1575, Scottish State Papers, v. 30 Dom., 1547–8, 489; Handover, p. 52.

3. Walsingham's interrogatories, July 1575, Scottish State Papers, v. 30.

4. Cooper, E., *The Life and Letters of Lady Arbella Stuart*, vol. 1 (of 2), p. 33 (1866); Durant, D. N., *Arbella Stuart: A Rival To The Queen*, p. 2.

5. Bess obtaining a dowry for Elizabeth is described in Landsdowne, 40–41.

6. Calendar of Scottish Papers, vol. v, no. 202; Durant, D. N., *Arbella Stuart: A Rival To The Queen*, p. 10.

7. Letter from Countess of Lennox to Mary, Queen of Scots, 10 November 1575, thanking her for her 'good remembrances and bounty to her little granddaughter'. State Papers, Mary, Queen of Scots, vol. x, p. 71; State Papers (Scottish), ii, 923 and State Papers (Scottish), v, 202; Handover, *Arbella Stuart, Royal Lady of Hardwick*, p. 52; Durant, D. N., *Arbella Stuart: A Rival To The Queen*, pp. 11, 212.

8. There are two references to Arbella's birth in the Harleian Manuscripts: '*Arbella nata 1575 apud Chatsworth in Anglia*'; Chatsworth is written in different ink from the rest of the document and was obviously added at a later date. Harleian MSS. vol. 588 fols 13, 23.

9. E. T. Bradley, *Arbella Stuart* (1889), vol.1. p. 34.

Chapter Four

1. Letters of Queen Elizabeth, State Papers (Scottish); 2 May 1572 MS.
2. Harleian MSS, vol. 289 fols 196, 200, 202.
3. Handover. *Arbella Stuart*, p. 55; Elizabeth to James, 30 July 1578; State Papers (Scottish), v, 314.
4. Mary, Queen of Scots, wrote to James about the 'LENNOX JEWELS'; Warrant by Mary to Thomas Fowler, 19 Sept. 1579; State Papers (Scottish), v. 350; Handover, *Arbella Stuart*, p. 56.
5. Reference to the allowances are found in State Papers (Domestic); Eliz. I, vol. clii, pp. 42, 43, 53; Also Calendar of Scots Papers, vol. vi, nos 95, 96.6. Historical Manuscript Commission Reports; Salisbury (Cecil), vol. ii (of 24 volumes), no. 675.

Chapter Five

1. Elizabeth to James letter dated March 1581, State Papers (Scottish), v, 658; Handover, *Arbella Stuart*, p. 61.
2. The interview between the queen and Esmé Stuart is found in State Papers (Spain), 1580–6, pp. 241–3, 244.
3. Mary to Fonteney, 28 September 1584, State Papers (Scottish), Ser. iii, 341.
4. The will of Elizabeth Stuart, dated 16 January 1581/2, from Hardwick drawer 279 (4).
5. Countess of Shrewsbury to Walsingham, 28 January 1582. State Papers (Domestic), 1581–90, 43; Countess to Burghley, 28 January 1582, Lansdowne MSS., xxxiv. 2.
6. Countess of Shrewsbury to Walsingham, 6 May 1582, State Papers (Domestic), 1581–90, 53; Countess to Burghley, 6 May 1582, Lansdowne Manuscript 34 (xxxiv), p. 143. 2; Handover, *Arbella Stuart*, p. 57.
7. For full details of Shrewsbury's quarrel with Bess and the 1572 deed of gift, see Durant, D. N., *Bess of Hardwick*, ch 8; cf. fn. 18.
8. Beale's letter, dated 23 May 1584, in is HMC Rutland, vol 1, p. 166; Durant, *Arbella Stuart*, p. 35.
9. Mary to Elizabeth, November 1584; Labanoff, Prince Alexander, *Recueil des lettres de Marie Stuart*, 7 vols, vi. p. 37.

10. Walsingham to Wotton, 28 May 1585, State Papers (Scottish), Ser. i., 496.

11. Walsingham to Wotton to Walsingham, 5 June 1585, State Papers (Scottish), Ser. i., 496–497.

Chapter Six

1. For details of the Shrewsbury's quarrel see Durant, D. N., *Bess of Hardwick,* ch. 8; Refer to Note 13, above.

2. Eisenberg Elizabeth, *The Captive Queen in Derbyshire* (Derbyshire Heritage Series, 1984), p. 31.

3. Lord Paget's letter dated 4 March 1584 (the letter is calendared as 1583), State Papers (Domestic), 1581–90, vol. clix, p. 8. Leicester's letter dated 26 June 1584 is from Miss Lloyd's manuscript at Althorp House, pp.6, 7.

4. Mary's letter to Mauvissiere dated 21 March 1584 is printed in Leader, J. D., *Mary Queen of Scots in Captivity* (1880), p. 551; Handover, *Arbella Stuart*, pp. 63, 64, 65.

5. For full details of the letters of the scandal, see Durant, D. N., *Bess of Hardwick*, pp. 129–131.

6. Pierre de Bourdeille, seigneur de Brantome, as quoted by Walter de la Mare, *Love* (1943), p. 220; Handover, *Arbella Stuart,* p. 60.

7. Letter from Henry Cavendish to Bess, undated, Hunter, Joseph. *Hallamshire* (1819), p. 90; Handover, *Arbella Stuart,* p. 58.

8. Henry Killigrew to William Davison, 12 April 1578, State Papers (Domestic), Addenda 1566–1569, p. 540.

9. Eisenberg Elizabeth, *The Captive Queen in Derbyshire* (Derbyshire Heritage series, 1984), p. 37.

10. For the details of Walsingham's involvement in the Babington Plot, see Johnson, P., *Elizabeth I* (1974), pp.283–6.

11. D. N. Durant, *Arbella Stuart*, p. 40.

12. Read, Conyers, *Mr Secretary Walsingham and the Policy of Queen Elizabeth,* 3 vols, (Oxford, 1925). Conyers suggests several reasons for supporting the idea that Walsingham had more than a little to do with this plot, and that Moody may have been his agent; Cf. Handover, p. 96.

13. James's instructions for Richard Douglas to give to Archibald Douglas, 8 July 1587, Hatfield, iii, pp. 267–268. These were put to the queen on 14 November; Handover, *Arbella Stuart*, p. 75.

Chapter Seven

1. Harrington, *Succession*, p. 44; Handover, *Arbella Stuart*, p. 77.
2. De Chateauneuf to Henry III of France, 27 August 1587. Quoted by Strickland, p. 215; Handover, *Arbella Stuart*, p. 77.
3. Venetian Secretary, 28 May 1603, State Papers (Venetian), x, 39; Handover, p. 79.
4. Stow, *Survey*, i, p. 284; Handover, *Arbella Stuart*, p. 82.

Chapter Eight

1. Handover, p. 82/3; N. Kinnersley to Bess, November 1588, Hunter, p. 90.
2. 21 Phelippes' draft to Paget for Barnes, 31 October 1591, State Papers (Domestic), 1591–1594, 117. Arbella was soon eager to return to South Wingfield Manor and the prospect of a new tutor named Morley. It was formerly believed that he was the musician Thomas Morley, composer, theorist, singer, organist and foremost member of the Madrigal Society. More recently it's been suggested that 'Morley' was actually Christopher Marlowe, poet, translator and rebel. Morley/Marlow had been attracted by the promise of an annuity of £40 a year, but, finding himself unpaid, he looked for an alternative means of making money and took to spying for the Catholics at a time when religion and politics were inextricably linked. After three and a half years as Arbella's tutor, Morley/Marlow asked for an annuity or land equivalent to £40 in value because he had been financially penalised for leaving the university to become a private tutor. Names were often changed through a scribe's mistake so it's not impossible for Morley to be Marlow. Thomas Morley left Oxford with a degree in 1588; Christopher Marlow left Cambridge with a degree in 1587 but there is scant evidence of where either of these men were for long periods after that.
3. 23 May 1590, State Papers (Scottish), x, 360; Handover, p. 87.

4. 12 June 1590, State Papers (Scottish), ii, 1543–1603, 577; Handover, p. 87.
5. *Newes from Scotland,* 14 and 17.
6. Rowse. A. L., *The England of Elizabeth* (1950), p. 5; Handover, p. 89.
7. *The building of Hardwick Hall,* edited by D. N. Durant and Philip Riden (Derbyshire Record Society, 1980), vol. iv, p. xxvi.

Chapter Nine

1. John Ricroft to Cecil, August 1591, State Papers (Domestic), 1591–94, p. 99; Handover, p. 95.
2. Handover, p. 95; Thomas Phelippes' draft to Paget for Barnes, 31 October 1591, State Papers (Domestic), 1591–1594, p. 117.
3. Handover, p. 96; Burghley to Heneage, 12 October 1591, Hatfield, iv, 147.
4. Reinold Bosely to Cecil, 7 April 1592, State Papers (Domestic), 1591–94. p. 209; Handover, p. 96.
5. Confessions dated 27 August 1592, State Papers (Domestic). 1591–64, p. 259; Handover, p. 92.
6. Semple's deposition, 13 August 1591, State Papers (Domestic), 1591–94, p. 87; Handover, p. 93.
7. CPS Dom 1601–1603.
8. 'The marriage treaty', CSP Dom 1598–1601, 327–8.
9. Maximilien de Béthune, Duke de Sully, i, 464. Arbella is written as '*la Princesse Reibelle*'.
10. Harington, *Tract on the Succession,* 43.

Chapter Ten

1. Fugger News-Letters, 2nd series, 324–5.
2. CPS Dom 1601–3, p. 37; Durant, *Arbella Stuart,* p. 88; the rumour of Arbella's marriage to Cecil is mentioned in State Papers (Domestic), vol. 289, no. 72; the argument on the succession is printed in Handover, *Arbella Stuart,* pp. 309–13.
3. Motley, *United Netherlands,* iv, 34, quoted from N. Molin, *Relazione.*
4. For the trial and execution, see State Papers (Domestic), 1598–1601, 545–9.
5. For John Byron's report, see Guy, John, *The Reign of Elizabeth I* (Cambridge, 1995), p. 59.

6. Arbella's comment on Essex is contained in a long letter to Brinker printed in Bradley, *Arbella Stuart*, vol. ii, p. 158.

Chapter Eleven

1. Bess's will is printed in part in Collins, A., *Historical Collections of Noble Families*, pp. 15–19. The copy in the Public Record Office is filed under Prob 11/111C1123 and there is another copy at Chatsworth.
2. Riden, P., *The Building Accounts of Hardwick Hall* (Derbyshire Record Society), taken from the original manuscripts; Durant and Riden, *The Building of Hardwick Hall* (1980).
3. Starkey's confession, undated, Hatfield Papers, xiv, 252.

Chapter Twelve

1. Ives, E. *Lady Jane Grey: A Tudor Mystery* (2009), pp. 47–49.
2. English Ambassador at Madrid to Cecil, October 1559, State Papers (Foreign), 1559–60, 2; Handover, p. 32.
3. BL Add MSS. 37749, f. 75.
4. BL Add MSS. 33749, ff. 47, 66.
5. BL Add MSS. 37749, ff. 58, 49.

Chapter Thirteen

1. Starkey's confession, Hatfield, xiv, 258.
2. Calendar of the Salisbury (Cecil) MSS., Hatfield House, vol. xii, pp. 583–587.
3. David Owen Tudor's letter, Hatfield, xii, 605.
4. Details of Arbella's proposal to Seymour and the subsequent repercussions are from HMC Sal. vol. xii, pp. 681–696; Also in Bradley's *The Life of the Lady Arbella Stuart*, vol. ii; Handover, *Arbella Stuart*.
5. Katherine's deposition, 11 February 1562, Harleian MSS., no. 6286, 37; Handover, *Arbella Stuart,* p. 37.
6. Cecil and Stanhope to Bess, January 1603, Hatfield, xii, 626; Handover, *Arbella Stuart,* p. 143.
7. Chamberlain to Carleton, 11 February 1603, State Papers (Domestic), 1601–3, p. 290; Handover, *Arbella Stuart,* p. 145.
8. Venetian secretary, 6 March 1603, State Papers (Venetian), ix, p. 549; Handover, *Arbella Stuart,* p. 145–6.

9. Cecil Papers, vol. 135, fols 159, 160.
10. Cecil Papers, vol. 135, fol. 164.
11. Venetian Secretary, 13 March 1603, State Papers (Venetian), ix, 552.
12. Earl of Kent, 9 July 1603, Lodge E., *Portraits of Illustrious Personages of Great Britain* (1868), vol. iii, p. 94.

Chapter Fourteen

1. MS. notes, Sloane MSS. 718, p. 39.
2. Gilbert to John Harper, 30 March 1603, Hunter J., *Hallamshire* (1819), p. 93; Hunter transcribed letters from the Talbot Papers that supplemented those printed by Lodge.
3. Stow, J., *Annals* (1615), p. 821.
4. Hatfield Papers, undated, vol. xv, fol. 65.
5. Venetian Secretary, 12 April 1603, State Papers (Venetian), vol. x, 3.
6. State Papers (Venetian), vol. x, fol. 17. It is doubtful that Arbella could raise such a number even if she had been so inclined.

Chapter Fifteen

1. Hatfield Papers, vol. xv, f. 82.
2. Cecil Papers, vol. 100, f. 134.
3. State Papers (Venetian), vol. x, f. 39.
4. BL Add MSS. 22, 563, 41.
5. Ashmolean MSS. 1729 81; printed in Bradley, ii, 178.
6. Nichols, i, 426; Bradley, ii, 179.
7. Arbella's letter to Mary, 16 September 1603, Sloane MSS. 4164.178; Handover, *Arbella Stuart*, p. 200.
8. Goodman, 199; Handover, *Arbella Stuart*, p. 192
9. Chamberlain to Carleton, 5 October 1611, Birch Court of James I, vol. i, 141; Handover, *Arbella Stuart*, p. 193.
10. Weldon, ii, 1; Handover, *Arbella Stuart*, p. 195.
11. Goodman, 71; Handover, *Arbella Stuart*, p. 195.
12. Clifford, 6; Handover, *Arbella Stuart*, p. 195.
13. Osbourne, i, 240; Handover, *Arbella Stuart*, p. 195.
14. Weldon, 338; Handover, *Arbella Stuart*, p. 196.
15. Weldon, i, 376; Handover, *Arbella Stuart*, p. 196.

16. Worcester's letter to Gilbert, 2 February 1604, Lodge, iii, 227; Handover, *Arbella Stuart,* p. 198.
17. Lodge, iii, 168.
18. Lodge's *Illustrations,* vol. iii, p. 182.
19. Arbella's letter to Gilbert, 2 January 1604, Sloane MSS. 4164 186; Handover, *Arbella Stuart,* p. 201.
20. Arbella's letter to Mary, 6 October 1603, Add MSS. 22, 563, 42.
21. Hardy, B. C., *Arbella Stuart: A Biography* (Constable, 1913), p. 193.
22. Arbella's letter to Gilbert, 18 December 1603, Add MSS. 22, 653, 47; Handover, *Arbella Stuart,* p. 199.
23. Arbella's letter to Gilbert, 18 December 1603, Add MSS. 22, 653, 48; Handover, *Arbella Stuart.* p. 200.
24. Arbella's letter to Mary, 8 December 1603, Add MSS. 22, 653, 45; Handover, *Arbella Stuart,* p. 201.

Chapter Sixteen

1. De Beaumont to Henry IV, 13 August 1603, Edwards, i, 377; Handover, *Arbella Stuart,* p. 184.
2. Cecil to Gilbert, 27 October 1603; Lodge, iii, 205; Handover, *Arbella Stuart,* p. 181.
3. Venetian Ambassador, December 1603, State Papers (Venetian), x, 117; Handover, *Arbella Stuart,* p. 184.
4. Weldon, i, 342; Handover, *Arbella Stuart,* p. 180.
5. Texts of Raleigh's trial, Harleian MSS. xxxix; Jardine and Stephen; Handover, *Arbella Stuart,* p. 184.
6. Jardine, i, 402; Handover, *Arbella Stuart,* p. 189.
7. The most comprehensive study of its kind relating to the Main Plot is the one found in Nicholls, M., 'Sir Walter Raleigh's Treason', *English Historical Review,* 110 (Sept 1995), p. 910.
8. Henry Howard to Edward Bruce, 6 December 1601; Handover, *Arbella Stuart,* p. 188.
9. Sloane MSS, vol. 4164, fol. 183.

Chapter Seventeen

1. Edward Lascelles to Gilbert, 30 April 1605, Lodge, iii, 285; Handover, *Arbella Stuart,* p. 213.

2. William Cavendish to Bess, 23 April 1604, Hunter, p. 94; Handover, *Arbella Stuart,* p. 213.

3. Bess to De Montague, Dean of the Chapel Royal, undated 1605, Rawson, 343; Handover, *Arbella Stuart,* p. 213.

4. Williams, 'Preface'; Handover, *Arbella Stuart,* p. 215.

5. Stow, *Annals,* 865; Handover, *Arbella Stuart,* p. 216.

6. The accusations came from Father Tesimond, Morris, 180; Handover, *Arbella Stuart,* p. 216.

7. Wadd to Cecil, 3 August 1605; Handover, *Arbella Stuart,* p. 217.

8. Lefuse, M., *The Life and Times of Arbella Stuart* (Mills and Boon, 1913), p. 184. This is the first mention of William Seymour, younger brother of Edward Seymour, whose name had been linked with Arbella's two years previously, and which had resulted in Arbella being expelled from Hardwick.

9. Slanderous speech by John Clay, gent of Derbyshire (November 1605), Lodge, iii, 120; Handover, *Arbella Stuart,* p. 220.

10. 'Proclamation, 7 November 1605', Historical Manuscript Commission. Found in Rutland MSS at Belvoir Castle, vol.i, p. 399; Handover, *Arbella Stuart,* p. 220.

11. State Papers (Venetian), x, 514.

12. Rawson, 346.

13. Lodge. *Introduction to his Illustrations.*

14. *Letters of Horace Walpole,* ed. Toynbee, P., iv, 425.

Chapter Eighteen

1. Talbot, ii, f. 254.

2. Harrington reported Arbella being ill with smallpox in a letter dated 21 December 1608. Bradley, vol. ii, p. 281.

3. State Papers (Domestic), 1603–10, 501.

4. Stowe, abridged *Chronicles,* 490.

5. The reported value of the Irish liquor license is given in HMC (Hastings), vol iv, p. 9.

6. The details of Arbella's finances and journey are taken from Hugh Crompton's accounts. Longleat, Seymour papers, vol. xxii, partly published by Canon Jackson in *Wiltshire Archaeological Magazine,* vol. ixx, pp. 217–226; Durant, D. N., *Arbella Stuart,* p. 166.

7. Details of the journey and expenses come from Hugh Crompton's accounts, Longleat MSS. Canon Jackson published a paper on the account book in *Wiltshire Architecture Magazine*, xix, 217.

8. State Papers (Domestic), 1603–1610, 555; License, State Papers (Domestic), 1603–10, 594.

9. State Papers (Venetian), xi, 452.

10. Harleian MSS. 7003, 55.

11. Arbella's request is printed in Cooper, *Life of Arbella Stuart,* vol. ii, pp. 96–97.

12. Arbella's involvement is unclear but is printed in Handover, *Arbella Stuart,* pp. 253/4; Venetian ambassador, 28 January 1610, State Papers (Venetian), xi, 414.

13. State Papers (Domestic), 1603–1610, p. 576.

Chapter Nineteen

1. State Papers (Venetian), xi, 405.

2. Venetian ambassador, 18 February 1610, State Papers (Venetian), xi, 427.

3. Venetian ambassador, 18 February 1610, State Papers (Venetian), xi, 433–4.

4. Chamberlain to Winwood, 13 February 1610, Winwood, iii, 117.

5. Ibid.

6. Winwood, Sir R., *Memorials of the Affairs of State,* vol. iii, p. 119.

7. Harleian MSS. vol. 7003, fol. 59.

8. Longleat MSS. Canon Jackson, *Wiltshire Archaeological Magazine,* vol. xix, p. 201.

9. Rodney's confession, undated. Harleian MSS. 7003, 62.

10. Canon Jackson, *Wiltshire Archaeological Magazine,* vol. xv, p. 201.

11. William's confession of marriage is in the Bodleian, Tanner MMM, vol. lxxv, f. 353. The payment to Blague, the minister, the names of the witnesses, dates and times are noted in Crompton's accounts, Longleat, Seymour papers, vol. xxii.

12. Harleian MSS., vol. 7003, fol. iii.

13. Harleian MSS., vol. 7003, fol. 62.

Chapter Twenty

1. Thomas, A., *The History and Antiquities of Lambeth*, p. 368–9. Copt Hall remained standing until the beginning of the nineteenth century. The site is to the north of Vauxhall Stairs, approximately where Vauxhall Walk now joins the Embankment.
2. Harleian MSS., vol. 7003, fol. 71.
3. State Papers (Domestic), James I, vol. lvi, p. 56.
4. Lansdown MSS, vol. 1236, fol. 58.
5. Harleian MSS, vol. 7003, fol. 82.
6. Harleian MSS, vol. 7003, fol. 64.
7. Harleian MSS, vol. 7003, fol. 92.
8. Harleian MSS, vol. 7003, fol. 150.
9. Harleian MSS, vol. 7003, fol. 152; Sloane MSS, vol. 4161, fol. 46.
10. Ibid.
11. HMC Belvoir Papers, i, 428.
12. Harleian MSS, vol. 7003, fols 94, 96, 97.
13. State Papers (Domestic), James I, vol. lxi, p. 30.
14. Harleian MSS, vol. 7003, fol. 92.
15. Lovell, P., *The Village of Highgate: Part I* (London: London County Council. 1936)
16. Document in the Talbot MSS at Longleat.
17. State Papers (Domestic), James I, vol. lxvii, p. 30.
18. State Papers (Domestic), James I, vol. lxvii, p. 38.
19. Harleian MSS, vol. 7003, fol. 118.
20. Taken from Sir John More's letter describing to his master Sir Ralph Winwood, former ambassador in Paris, what happened. Winwood, R., *Memorials of the Affairs of State*, vol. iii, p. 280.
21. John Bright's examination, State Papers (Domestic), James I, vol. lxiv.

Chapter Twenty-One

1. Handover, *Arbella Stuart*, p. 277.
2. Rymer, T., *Foedera*, vol. xvi, p. 710; HMC Belvoir Papers, iv, 211.
3. Harleian MSS, vol. 7003, fol. 128.
4. HMC Bath Papers, ii, 59.
5. Harleian MSS, vol. 7003, fol. 130.
6. Harleian MSS, vol. 7003, fol. 22.

7. The letter is still to be seen in the Harleian Manuscripts.
8. Arrests 4–5 June 1611, Harleian MSS, vol. 7003, ff. 140, 143.
9. Goodman, G., Bishop of Gloucester, *The Court of King James*, p. 209.

Chapter Twenty-Two

1. 28 June 1611, HMC Downshire Papers, iii, p. 99.
2. More to Winwood, 28 June 1611; Winwood, R., *Memorials of the Affairs of State*, vol. iii, p. 281.
3. Mary's lodgings are referred to in *Col of Arms*, vol. M, f. 588.
4. Arbella's jewels are valued in Harleian 7003, f. 138, and the warrant dated 30 June 1611, authorising the use of her money to pay for the capture, in State Papers (Domestic), vol. lxiv, p. 67.
5. Durant, D. N., *Arbella Stuart: Rival to the Queen*, p. 202; Sloane MSS, vol. 4161, fol. 63.
6. Arbella's payments to Seymour are accounted for in Longleat, Seymour papers, vol. xxii.
7. Durant, D. N., *Arbella Stuart: A Rival to the Queen*, p. 203/4; The details of Arbella's allowance or pension are in PRO, E403/2367; The payments she made to William Seymour are in Longleat, Seymour papers, vol. xxii.
8. Arbella's jewels are valued in Harleian MSS, 7003, f. 138; The warrant dated 30 June 1611 authorising the use of her money to pay for her capture are in State Papers (Domestic), vol. xxiv, p. 67.
9. Arbella's gown is mentioned in Acts of the Privy Council, 1615–16, published by the Public Record Office, pp. 263 & 3012, and State Papers (Domestic), vol. lxxii, no. 28.
10. Handover, *Arbella Stuart*, p 289; Chamberlain letter to ?, 23 May 1613; Stratham, 99; Sir Thomas Lake to Carleton, 19 May 1613, State Papers (Domestic), 1611–18, 185.
11. Handover, p. 290; Weldon, i, 382.
12. Chamberlain to Carlton, 7 July 1614, State Papers (Domestic), 1611–1618. p. 242.
13. Rev Thomas Lorkin to Sir T Puckering, 21 July 1614, Birch, T., *Court and Times of James I (1848)*, i, p. 338.
14. Durant, D. N., *Arbella Stuart: Rival to the Queen*, p. 201.

15. Smith returns to Arbella's service by an order dated 29 April 1614, *The Court and Times of James the First,* pp. 422–3.
16. Durant, D. N., p. 207; Mary's reaction to Arbella's death, HMC 2nd Report, Appendix vii, p. 83.
17. The report of the post-mortem, HMC 8th Report and Appendix i, p. 228b.

BIBLIOGRAPHY

Bingham, C., *Darnley: A Life of Henry Stuart, Lord Darnley, Consort of Mary Queen of Scots* (Constable, 1995)

Birch, T., *The Court and Times of James I.*, 2 vols (London: H. Colburn, 1848)

Boynton, L., and Thornton, P., *The Hardwick Hall Inventory of 1601* (1970)

Bradley, E. T., *Arabella Stuart*, 2 vols (London: Richard Bentley & Son, 1889)

Childs, J., *Tudor Derbyshire* (The Derbyshire Heritage series, 1985)

Cooper, E., *The Life and Letters of Lady Arbella Stuart*, 2 vols (Hurst & Blackett, 1866)

Doleman, R., *A Conference about the next succession to the throne of England* (1594)

Dunbar J., *A Prospect of Richmond*, revised edition (White Lion Publishers, 1973)

Durant, D. N., *Arbella Stuart: A Rival to The Queen* (Weidenfeld and Nicolson, 1978)

Durant, D. N., *Bess of Hardwick* (Weidenfeld and Nicolson, 1977)

Durant & Riden, *The building of Hardwick Hall* (Derbyshire record Society Vol. IV, 1980)

Edmunds, W. H., *Wingfield Manor: It's history and Associates* (Self-published, 1975)

Eisenberg, E., *The Captive Queen in Derbyshire* (The Derbyshire Heritage Series, 1984)

Eisenberg, E., *This Costly Countess: Bess of Hardwick* (The Derbyshire Heritage Series, 1985)

Fraser, A., *Mary Queen of Scots: the most tragic and romantic figure of British history* (Mandarin, 1969)

Girouard, M. *Hardwick Hall* (National Trust, 1989)

Gregory, P., *The Other Queen* (Harper Collins, 2008)

Gristwood, S., *Arbella: England's Lost Queen* (Bantam Edition, 2004)

Handover, P. M., *Arbella Stuart* (Eyre & Spottiswood Publishers, 1957)

Hardy, B. C., *Arbella Stuart* (1913)

Hardy, B. C., *Arbella Stuart: A Biography.* (USA: Nabu Press)

Harington, Sir J., *Tract on the succession to the crown* (1602)

Harington, Sir J., *Nugae Antique*, 3 vols (1792)

Harington, Sir J., trans. *Orlando Furioso* (1591)

de Lisle, L., *The Sisters who would be Queen: The Tragedy of Mary, Katherine & Lady Jane Grey* (Harper Press, 2008)

de Lisle, L., *After Elizabeth: The struggles behind the accession of James of Scotland* (Ballantine Books, 1814)

Lodge, E., *Illustrations of British History*, 4 vols 1791–1833 (Kessinger Publishing, 2010)

Lovell, Mary S., *Bess of Hardwick: First Lady of Chatsworth* (Abacus, 2006)

McInnes, Ian, *The Life and Time of Lady Arbella Seymour* (W. H Allen, 1968)

McGrigor, Mary, *The Other Tudor Princess: Margaret Douglas, Henry VIII's Niece* (The History Press, 2015)

Norrington, Ruth, *In the Shadow of the Throne: The Lady Arbella Stuart* (Peter Owen, 2002)

Rowse, A. L., *The England of Elizabeth: The Structure of Society* (London: Palgrave Macmillan, 1950)

Schutte, Kim, *A biography of Margaret Douglas, Countess of Lennox (1515–1578)* (Edwin Mellen, 2002)

Strickland, Agnes, *Lives of the Tudor & Stuart Princesses* (Rarebooksclub, 1888)

Weir, Alison, *Mary, Queen of Scots and the Murder of Lord Darnley* (London: Vintage, 2008)

Weir, Alison, *The Lost Tudor Princess. The life of Lady Margaret Douglas* (London: Jonathan Cape, 2016)

Wood, C. H, *Hardwick Halls* (Derbyshire Countryside Ltd)

ABOUT THE AUTHOR

A lifelong resident of Derbyshire, Jill is passionate about local history and heritage. She is author of many Derbyshire books, including *Derbyshire Women*, *The Headliners of the Day*, and biographies *Dorothy, The Elopement of Dorothy Vernon from Haddon Hall* and *Olave Lady Baden-Powell and Her Derbyshire Roots*.

INDEX